KILL IT TO SAVE IT

An Autopsy of Capitalism's Triumph Over Democracy

By Corey Dolgon

First published in Great Britain in 2017 by

Policy Press
University of Bristol
1-9 Old Park Hill
Bristol BS2 8BB
UK
t: +44 (0)117 954 5940
e: pp-info@bristol.ac.uk
www.policypress.co.uk

North American office:
Policy Press
c/o The University of Chicago Press
1427 East 60th Street
Chicago, IL 60637, USA
t: +1 773 702 7700
f: +1 773-702-9756
e:sales@press.uchicago.edu
www.press.uchicago.edu

British Library Cataloguing in Publication Data
A catalogue record for this book is available from the British Library.

Library of Congress Cataloging-in-Publication Data
A catalog record for this book has been requested.

ISBN 978-14473-1712-8 hardback
ISBN 978-1-4473-1713-5 paperback
ISBN 978-1-4473-1715-9 ePub
ISBN 978-1-4473-1716-6 Mobi
ISBN 978-1-4473-1714-2 ePdf

Cover design by Soapbox Design, London
Printed and bound in the United States of America

Table of Contents

List of Figures

Preface

Books don't write themselves. But sometimes the world moves in ways that authors simply channel more than they create. Kill it to save it has ruminated within me over many years as a paradigm for understanding the absurdities of contemporary social and political life in the United States. The election of Donald Trump as president has only confirmed my analysis and caused me to wonder if the book had come out earlier, could it have made a difference. Probably not, as the analysis itself suggests.

Still a book that debunks the mythologies of America's rugged individualism and the public benefits of private wealth accumulation could not have predicted Trump's rise any better. He seems the epitome of a false icon, whose inane, blustering assertions without evidence, and portrayals without facts, find fertile ground among a population desperate for a new, heroic mythmaker. Newt Gingrich (one of Trump's key mouthpieces) reminded us all a few months ago that liberals may have their statistics and facts, but as a political candidate Trump will take feelings over facts any day. As Trump himself implores after almost every incorrect assertion of fact, "Believe me!"

As I suggest in this book, America's political and cultural consciousness has been rewired since Reagan. Now this consciousness instinctively embraces public policies hellbent on destroying the public good because such policies are packaged within the language of individual freedom and economic prosperity (even if the financial gains are limited to a smaller and smaller few). If Reagan could bottle up old myths about burley go-getters and unrestrained entrepreneurs to sell policies that gutted public education, public health, and public resources, we shouldn't be surprised that "art of the deal" Trump could persuade Americans to double down on neoliberalism and racism as an elixir for all that neoliberalism and racism wrought. As Marx suggested in *The Eighteenth Brumaire of Louis Napoleon* historical forces often arrive repeatedly, "the first time as tragedy, the second time as farce."

Yet, no matter how much the universe may gift the willing vessel a story for the ages, authors require significant support from many places to complete a book of this kind. I want to take this opportunity to acknowledge my community of scholars and critics, comrades and friends, who took so much time out of their own work and lives to make this effort the highest quality possible. Whatever compelling moments this book offers are owed to them.

And while there are so many supporters that the publisher could never afford for me to name them all, let me use this opportunity to thank those who went above and beyond the call. Kathleen Korgen, Debbie Billings, Tom Abowd, Hephzibah Strmic-Pawl, Reuben Roth, Chris Wetzel, Mark Buchan, Laura Orlando, Jeff Muir, Demetrius Bady and David Embrick read many drafts of this book and managed to point out significant flaws and specious arguments without ever diminishing their enthusiasm or my resolve. In fact, they proved that a critical boosterism is possible. A special thanks to Jerry Lembcke, this book's critic-in-chief, who assures me that Trump's victory will make this a bestseller. Even he can find a silver lining in the darkest of clouds.

And I would be remiss if I didn't mention that, one of my best work buddies ever, Steve Corey, was primarily responsible for coining "kill it to save it" as a narrative framework for making sense of contemporary politics and culture. For years, our highway banter helped make the trip from Boston suburbs to Worcester, where we taught, seem inspiring and surprisingly brief. As the 21st century arrived, his iconoclastic wit and intellectual acumen gave me a constant source of analytical tools and endless joy. His humanistic irreverence haunts every page and breathes life into their best stories.

Much appreciation to Policy Press and the many folks there who have supported this work from the outset and stayed patient and committed to its possibilities throughout the process. Their editing, marketing and passion for publishing politically engaged, social justice work remains a beacon for the industry. And similar gratitude to staff at the University of Chicago Press for their confidence in the project and their efforts to sell and distribute the book in the U.S. And, while presses are crucial to getting ideas from page to publication, I want to send a shout out to the hundreds of waitresses, bartenders, and baristas who allowed me to linger over food and drinks while searching for the right words. Luckily for them, I tip based on time spent, not purchases made.

We know it takes a village to raise children; it also takes a neighborhood to raise an author. I am blessed to have people around me who help plow snow in winter and blow leaves in Fall. Our neighbors watch my children, chat with my wife, and make sure our home is safe from intruders and the impact of global warming. It's an honor to be in a community in which people treat each other with basic human decency, regardless of political ideology or religious affiliation, race or creed, and a concern that they themselves would hope for. In this vein, a special tribute to the former, unofficial, mayor of our neighborhood, Kevin Moore, Jr. He epitomized his parents' compassion and walked our community's streets talking to everybody and helping anybody with tasks great and small. A victim of neoliberalism's most recent scourge, he is only the latest of beautiful canaries sacrificed to a dysfunctional economy haunted by "surplus" souls.

Finally, my family, as always, has had to pay the steepest price for time spent researching, writing, reading and revising. To my wife, Deborah Milbauer, and my daughters, Bailey and Ruby, who so graciously gave me the space and time to work through the difficult task of making sense of the world around us while simultaneously living daily in that same world. Nothing will ever make up for the days spent hunkered down in Priceline hotels and bookstore cafes, but you have my undying love and sincere promise to miss fewer date nights and soccer games. To my parents, as always, for giving me a critical edge and a loving heart; this book is for you.

Introduction: In My Life

> Nowadays people often feel that their private lives are a series of traps. They sense that within their everyday worlds, they cannot overcome their troubles, and in this feeling, they are often quite correct. What ordinary people are directly aware of and what they try to do are bounded by the private orbits in which they live; ... [But] neither the life of an individual nor the history of a society can be understood without understanding both. (C. Wright Mills, "The Promise," from the *Sociological Imagination*, 1959)

In many ways this book is a political history and analysis of my own life. In it, I examine the contours of American politics and culture over the last half century in an effort to understand what went wrong. For those of us "late boomers" born to Kennedy's new frontier and reared in the bosom of the suburban middle class, the world seemed full of progress and possibility. My father marched for civil rights and change came. He protested against the war in Vietnam and it ended. My mother chaired the local Parent—Teacher Association (PTA) and a corrupt principal was fired and more resources allocated for teachers. The world had many problems, but if people organized and fought for progressive solutions, they could change things for the better. By the time I reached high school, my American History teacher's mantra, "there is no retrograde step to democracy," seemed to be the social and political law of the land.

Yet, even the best of what American imperialism offered its citizens after 1960 could not help but be ripped apart by its own contradictions. Moving commodity production and its attendant exploitation overseas eventually degraded wages and working conditions everywhere. Spreading "democracy" through barbarity may have protected "friendly" dictators but it also inspired nationalist and fundamentalist blowback. Conflating values of progress and prosperity with religious piety, patriotic arrogance, and mass consumption made the stalwart of America's 20th-century identity—the middle class—only more nervous, frustrated and, ultimately, depressed. Global brutality and suffering combined with creeping fear and guilt at home kept everyone from sleepwalking too comfortably through the end of the American Century. The nightmare was the reality; the dream a myth.

By the time I reached college in 1980, the world already seemed different. The oil crisis and economic malaise of the late 1970s had made people in my community uneasy. Unemployment and uncertainty broke through the once confident concrete sidewalks of suburbia. Love Canal and other environmental catastrophes suggested that some of our most dangerous threats were invisible, lurking beneath our backyard barbeques or pouring out from our kitchen taps. Powerful and debilitating drugs had seeped into suburban schools and stories spread about pushers and dealers and addicts. The horror films of the late 1970s to the mid-1980s depicted a society of maniacal, gluttonous adults and spoiled, hedonistic youth witnessing their comfortable, self-satisfied, mostly white worlds implode. From *The Stepford Wives* to *Carrie*, from *Nightmare on Elm Street* to *Blue Velvet*, something was amiss in America's middle-class communities that, on film, literally devoured them from the inside out.

Meanwhile, as redlining, "block busting," speculation and racism fueled white fears and white flight, our once "integrated" neighborhood in Hempstead, Long Island rapidly became a majority Black and Latino community. In fact, for once mildly liberal whites, the conflation of economic insecurity and changing neighborhoods convinced some that perhaps civil rights had gone "too far" and their new neighbors were actually to blame for increased economic hardships in "their" towns, the growing influx of drugs in "their" schools, and the overall sense that the urban sprawl of social problems had ruined "their" suburban utopia. Something was going wrong—but, without a strong analysis of what and why, many middle-class white people simply moved further away from traditional suburbs towards an ever-elusive anti-urban landscape. But this time, they would be far less tolerant and far less liberal.

My parents vowed to stay in our neighborhood, but when my father lost his job and the family landed on food stamps, we followed him to new employment outside of Philadelphia in southern New Jersey. Within three years he would lose that job, too, and begin a downward spiral leading him and my mom towards forced early retirement and a debt-ridden, stress-filled existence in a coastal Maine trailer park. To make a few dollars, my dad started a newsletter of political ramblings called *The Dolgon Chronicles*—part insightful analysis, part polemic, part Borscht Belt schtick. He sold subscriptions to friends, family, activist colleagues, and like-minded acquaintances. He entitled his first, front-page editorial "Downsized!" and argued that one could witness the destruction of contemporary economic and public policy one life at a time—in particular, his—but that the trend towards increased oligarchic wealth for the few and increased poverty and powerlessness for the majority would soon mean that his story would be the norm. My dad never read *The Sociological Imagination*, but he always had one.

The radical transformation of American society between 1960 and the early 2000s was not only about the structural economic and geographic shifts that shape the volatile and stressful lives we lead in what is now called "the global economy." After all, my early lessons taught me that people could act collectively to address social problems and—with enough intellectual acumen, organizing ability, and political will—the world could be changed for the better. But the structural transformations of the late 20th and early 21st centuries were accompanied by a cultural, social, and psychological paradigm that leaves many people stupefied into paralysis or bamboozled into believing such changes are actually good for them. Many Americans support and even espouse an economy that creates hyper-inequality. We welcome policies that weaken public institutions and infrastructures, which for decades bolstered whatever real social-mobility workers ever had. And we cheer laws that decrease democracy and hinder opportunities to organize for change, despite our diminished ability to alter America's course and protect the public good. Such contradictions formed the cornerstone of Donald Trump's campaign and are at the foundation of what I call "kill it to save it."

Growing Up and Anxious

I came upon this trend towards self-defeating social policies as I tried to understand the changing ways in which my students thought about the world around them. After many years of teaching in higher education—at institutions both public and private, working class and elite—I noticed that college students aged 18–25 grew increasingly uneasy at the social contract they had entered into. Yet they seemed unaware of, and even antagonistic towards, thinking that such problems might have to do with structural changes or need to be addressed with collective political action. In the late 1980s and early 1990s, students could still believe that if they worked moderately hard and did above average in school, they would graduate with access to what then seemed a "comfortable, middle-class lifestyle." They expected a modicum of economic security, leisure, and consumption based on a public institutional landscape that ensured decent employment, education, health care, housing, and the possibility of working harder for more. My students had yet to really experience the impact that dismantling public institutions, privatizing collective consumption, and delegitimizing the very value of the public good would have on their futures.

By the mid 1990s, however, students were already facing an uncertain financial future. Despite Bill Clinton's "economic miracle," the prospects for many undergraduates had dwindled. For those in business and engineering, opportunities still seemed bright, but those in the humanities and social sciences already faced jokes about living in their parents' basements and flipping Big Macs. Unemployment reached historic lows, but the *kinds* of jobs most college graduates expected to get also changed significantly. Masters and professional degrees beckoned as mandatory. Meanwhile, Reagan Era cuts in public funding for higher education and the skyrocketing costs of colleges competing for students who could pay full tuition (luxury dorms, upscale food, service and athletic facilities, high-speed everything) increased the price tag for undergraduate degrees exponentially, leaving most graduates in serious, and now crippling, debt. The first decade of the 2000s witnessed a student body self-described as highly stressed and more likely to be emotionally unstable, economically insecure, and more worried about the future than ever before. Few expected to do better than their parents—even first-generation college students—and most had no idea how they would pay off their debts. Many never did and now never do.[1]

Despite these significant challenges brought on by global economic changes and federal policies that destroyed working- and middle-class confidence, students have no critical analysis or effective ideological framework to understand what happened. Resonating with C. Wright Mills' observation, Americans once again seem trapped (I would now add *threatened* and, as Donald Trump exposed, *increasingly angry*), but now lack a sociological imagination with which to escape. And with no one really to blame, students increasingly blame themselves, or they try to self-medicate or escape—alcohol and drug abuse are up on college campuses, as are psychiatric drugs and attempted suicides. And when students don't hurt themselves, they lash out at others in often violent and counterproductive ways that, when intertwined with toxic masculinity, racism and xenophobia, fuel the increase of sexual assault and hate crimes on campus.[2] My students' futures (and now presents) have grown dim, but they lack both the intellectual fortitude to figure out why and the instinct for collective engagement to change it. Ironically, they continue to support the same anti-public policies that destroyed the possibility of their middle-class aspirations in the first place. But why?

In Tom Frank's *What's the Matter with Kansas*, he contends that, despite the negative impact that ultra-conservative economic policies have on most working- and middle-class

Kansans, they support ultra-conservative politicians because they share common views on hot-button social issues such as abortion and creationism. Frank writes:

> Not long ago, Kansas would have responded to the current [economic] situation by making the bastards pay. This would have been a political certainty, as predictable as what happens when you touch a match to a puddle of gasoline. When business screwed the farmers and the workers—when it implemented monopoly strategies invasive beyond the Populists' furthest imaginings—when it ripped off shareholders and casually tossed thousands out of work—you could be damned sure about what would follow.
>
> Not these days. Out here the gravity of discontent pulls in only one direction: to the right, to the right, further to the right. Strip today's Kansans of their job security, and they head out to become registered Republicans. Push them off their land, and next thing you know they're protesting in front of abortion clinics. Squander their life savings on manicures for the CEO, and there's a good chance they'll join the John Birch Society. But ask them about the remedies their ancestors proposed (unions, antitrust, public ownership), and you might as well be referring to the days when knighthood was in flower.[3]

Frank's basic argument seems sound and his tour de force of cultural politics in the heartland offers some of the best social critique of the past decade or so. The salience of his explanation simply begs the question, "What's the matter with Oklahoma, Nebraska, Tennessee, Mississippi, Maine, Michigan, and almost everywhere else in the United States?"

But Frank's approach to the "how and why" of such social transformations rests primarily on an analysis of conservative political strategy and tactics. Essentially, he contends that a socially conservative electorate stands at the ready, ripe for the picking by neoconservatives. These neoconservatives, he implies, frontload a good controversy over the pledge of allegiance or late-term abortion every time they want to gather the troops to vote for corporate-pocketed candidates who will reduce taxes on the rich or privatize public institutions like schools or prisons. The *strategy* calls for mobilizing the white working- and middle class; the *tactics* call for identifying the right hot-button social issues for the right campaigns. Even better if political rhetoric can be racially coded and echo deep historical and cultural themes of white supremacy.

In many ways Frank assumes that a vein of false consciousness in American culture not only exists, but can also be easily tapped by devious right-wing political strategists. I don't disagree in theory, but the term "false consciousness" (popular among Marxist social critics) has always been complicated and rightly criticized as an elitist, a priori assumption that poor and working-class people are easily duped. Conversely, intellectuals know better what is in the interest of workers—who, once properly enlightened, would instinctively coalesce based on their structural position in, and relations to, capital production. It sounds right theoretically—but then, so does trickle-down economics.

Instead, I would contend that consciousness and identity are much more fluid and complex. As social critic Michael Apple wrote, "The first thing to ask about an ideology is not what is false about it, but what is true ... [ideologies] do not dupe people."[4] Thus, I argue that the same group of Kansans that once looked towards unions, populists, socialists, and radical collective action for solutions to their problems could do so again. And the reason they turned away from these allies and strategiesso drastically in the first place tells us less about their "self-denial" (as Frank puts it) than about a differently constructed sense of self and identity, which—while it has developed over the last four decades—is as old as the nation itself.

The conservative instinct now guiding most Americans' political choices comes from a bewildered yet leaden blood plodding through their patriotic veins, tightening in their chests, and haunting their dreams. In essence, "kill it to save it" represents a sense of individualistic freedom, entrepreneurial bluster, and post-racial complacency that Americans (especially white Americans) *want* to believe about themselves and their country—regardless of the facts, experiences, and political history that expose the fallacy. The resulting disappointment, fear, stress, paranoia, and cognitive dissonance clot any critical imagination and constrict any real social awareness. But they clearly fueled both Donald Trump's campaign, and The Democratic Party's paralysis in response. Using Mills' concept, "kill it to save it" is an ideological, psychological, and even physiological trap.

What is "Kill it to Save it?"

What I argue in this book is that the past half-century has witnessed a new ideological paradigm, which shapes political consciousness and decision making with a toxic blend of *corporate hegemony* and *hyper-individualism*. This cultural and political framework evolved over the last fifty years to legitimize the convergence of neoconservative and neoliberal policies among a vast swathe of primarily white working-, middle-, and professional-class voters, who once supported the New Deal and its emergent welfare state, but no longer. The power of "kill it to save it" emanates not so much from the strategic force or tactical acumen of right-wing spin doctors and charismatic gas bags simply duping the American public. Rather, this new ideology's durability comes from the realignment of narrowly constructed (but widely held) capitalist core values with a deeply mythological sense of who we are (and should be) as Americans. It represents the narrative battle over the cultural and historical hardwiring of American society that the New Left of the 1960s and 1970s eventually lost to the New Right of the 1980s and 1990s.[5]

This newly dominant cultural and political frame promotes the supposed resurrection of absolutely free individuals no longer enslaved by public programs or collective goods and responsibilities. Thus, the "it" being "saved" may have once been a "public" good—like education or health care—but, according to *kill it to save it* policy making, can only be maintained today by getting rid of the "public" part. For example, to save mass public education, it must be replaced by a privatized charter system in which individuals choose to buy and sell what becomes known as "educational services." Education becomes not a public mission (available to everyone) but rather a private commodity (purchased by each individual).

To save Medicare or Medicaid (both public systems of health care for poor, elderly and infirmed) we must privatize them for individuals to buy on their own. Even Social Security—the "mother lode" of welfare state policies that support and protect mostly senior citizens—is under attack. Politicians and marketeers argue that the only way to maintain this program in the face of an aging baby boomer generation is to supplant it with "personal retirement accounts."[6] But, as economists Dean Baker and Mark Weisbrot have written, "the only real threat to Social Security comes not from any fiscal or demographic constraints but from the political assaults on the program by would-be 'reformers.'"[7] Social Security is *eternally* viable, dependent only on political decisions to establish the revenue necessary to fund it. Despite the actual numbers that prove Baker and Weisbrot's case, privatization's proponents have the advantage of tapping into the polluted ideological stream of austerity economics and the desire to destroy any public program that suggests social commitments and responsibilities. "Choice" becomes the language of newly liberated services (now privatized commodities), with the underlying, value-added premise of people seeming to have "more freedom."

But the "it" being saved can also be the whole economic and political system. While globalization may have opened every earthly nook and cranny to commoditization, the ensuing explosion of wealth has reached fewer and fewer people. In part, "kill it to save it" represents the deregulation of environmental standards and the degradation of labor rights, all in the name of liberating markets for greater corporate profits. But neoliberalism has also meant reducing wages, working conditions, job protection, and health and safety provisions for workers and their communities, ultimately destroying any semblance of the working- and middle-class American dream.

As well as paying less for labor, health, and environmental costs, corporations have lobbied to pay fewer taxes in pursuit of national austerity and individual liberation from undue social responsibilities. To "save" the government and the economy, first we terminate government's ability to regulate, tax, and spend—essentially what governments are supposed to do. Second, we bolster an economic system that produces increased profits for the wealthy but is no longer charged with making sure that basic necessities and commodities are distributed to maintain the health and wellbeing of the larger society—essentially what economies are supposed to do. While one theme of "kill it to save it" policy emphasizes corporate hegemony (the social commitment to "what's good for business is good for America"[8]), the other suggests that corporate hegemony itself somehow liberates individuals to compete more freely without the albatross of social responsibilities and the public good.

One important contributor to the conservative hegemonic triumph of "kill it to save it" has been the right wing's ideological deftness with, and adaptability to, a technologically driven corporate world of social media and 24/7 news cycles. The general public's growing reliance on immediate and constant consumption of information prohibits serious reflection and nuanced debate. It is increasingly impossible to consider historical context, process conflicting news accounts, and arrive at any sort of complex analysis. Without the ability to weigh competing narratives, research and analyze data, or discern distinction between information and knowledge, emotion and fear have supplanted deliberation and reason. Thus, the power of a particular cultural hardwiring that permits intellectual shortcuts also makes the new conservative hegemony even more impermeable. The stories we tell ourselves about who we are, what is right and wrong in the world, and what we should do about it have become susceptible to Frank's sense of false consciousness—but they are not exactly the same thing.

The phrase "kill it to save it," originated as a justification for destroying Vietnamese villages and killing Vietnamese people to save the country from Communism. But the war in Vietnam always represented a desperate, cynical strategy invariably based on a criminal foreign-policy belief that nihilistic violence and almost total obliteration could stop the impending movement of people who, for centuries, sought self-determination and liberation. Such movements can never be stopped permanently. Americans, too, can shake off the intellectual and political shrouds that cover us like corpses—walking dead in our own lives. But we must do it together. In the wake of mass killings in Aurora, Sandy Hook, Charleston's Emmanuel AME church, Umpqua Community College in Oregon, San Bernardino, Orlando, and whatever mass shooting incident happened yesterday, our inability to address the absurdity of our policy-making debates seem ever more striking. We can't pass serious regulations on guns, address the poor quality and paucity of mental health care, or change the direction of growing poverty and suffering even after witnessing time and time and time again the effects of not changing public policies that are in fact killing us. Only strong, progressive social movements for economic and social equality will create the kinds of fundamental challenges needed to change our "kill it to save it" common sense. They are the only things that ever have. But how do we get there?

Structure of this Book

In Part 1 of this book, I present a historical and theoretical context for the idea of a "kill it to save it" approach to policy making. The violent irony of a term born from a military strategy that burned Vietnamese homes and villages to save the people inside was not lost during its importation to America.[9] In debates over U.S. policy making, "kill it to save it" inspires stories about how the only way to save *public* institutions is to *privatize* them; the only way to save an economy's ability to produce and distribute goods for its people is to place absurd amounts of wealth in the hands of a few; and the only way to save a democratic nation is to limit the capacity of its majority to participate effectively, or even vote at all—while simultaneously sanctioning the power of corporations to act as individuals with their own "inalienable" rights.

The first chapter is primarily historical and suggests that the importation of "kill it to save it" solidified over the decade or so between Nixon's demise in the 1970s and Reagan's rise to power in the 1980s. The war in Vietnam and its aftermath destroyed many of America's myths about itself, challenging new generations to generate new myths. As I suggested earlier, hope and optimism ensued from the possibilities inspired by the creation of New Deal social policies, progressive educational programs, social movements, and the public institutions they built. But the changing global economy and domestic social landscape required even more change; perhaps more change than many people were prepared to embrace. A conservative military industrial complex (the one that Eisenhower had warned us about) produced doubt, fear, panic and a sense of crisis at the very moment that Jimmy Carter called for greater reflection and insight, sacrifice and patience. Instead, Reagan offered a return to innocence and basic, old-time myths about freedom and greatness. Carter was doomed. The result? Foreign policy based on provincial jingoism and global corporate domination, and domestic policies based on blaming the victims of poverty and inequality for the failures of economic and social systems.

In chapter two, I try to understand the theoretical underpinnings of "kill it to save it" by examining how cultural and historical mythologies can be manipulated to create new ideological frameworks—in this case, ones that dismantle and discourage critical thinking and influence narrow conceptions of values, beliefs, and reality itself. I investigate how myths work and how Reagan could reconstruct them in such a way as to recreate what Antonio Gramsci called "common sense."[10] An Italian revolutionary, Gramsci (1891—1937) argued that Fascism and capitalism created a reactionary popular culture in Italy and shaped what he defined as "common sense"—a general idea and feeling about how the world works, divorced from the facts, data, and sometimes even people's own experiences. It's the gut feeling that comedian Stephen Colbert calls "truthiness".[11] The very nature of common sense is its impermeability to critique and counter narratives. It exists to justify the power of what is and who rules, while warding off questions about the injustice of structural inequality and violent conquest. "Kill it to save it" not only represents the contemporary rational framework for legitimate intellectual analysis and political decision making in America, it also represents an active response *against* critical thought, building an ideological resiliency to effective critique and political action.

In the rest of the book, I examine how a "kill it to save it" paradigm for public policy informs our common sense in a variety of institutional and policy settings. The best way to understand any society is by studying its institutions. French sociologist Emile Durkheim proposed that institutions represented and reproduced most of what he called "social facts:" the things that originate in the politics or culture of a society and effectively shape the behaviors and attitudes of individuals therein.[12] Rules, laws, customs, beliefs, and values all dictate a variety of ideas and everyday activities that can be studied to understand how society imposes itself on individual thinking and behavior. And most of these social facts are experienced through institutions.

To examine the impact of "kill it to save it" ideology on Americans' everyday life, I focus on institutions related to education (Part 2), health and safety (Part 3), and the economy and government (Part 4). The power of changing institutions within a "reform rhetoric" of privatization and hyper-individualism has revamped our common sense about everyday life: how we learn, how we eat, how we think, how we work and vote (or not) for what we want. Part 2 includes chapters on elementary, secondary, and higher education; Part 3 includes chapters on industrial food production, junk science and media, guns and the criminal justice system; and Part 4 examines our political and economic policy discourse as a whole. Finally, the book's epilogue examines ways in which "kill it to save it" has been exported and now appears to be gaining an audience on the world stage. Just as this common sense goes global, however, I want to suggest that it can be supplanted by a better sense or "good sense" and be defeated by popular movements armed with alternative politics, policies, and practices. But we need to tell better stories about a better world and what it might look like.

A Cautionary Tale About this Book

Many of my friends and colleagues who saw various parts of this book while it was being written warned me that periodically they thought about slitting their wrists or hiding in a closet. One person suggested I have sections about positive things happening that challenge the "kill it to save it" paradigm. Such things *are* happening and the recent campaigns of both Donald Trump and Bernie Sanders suggest serious rumblings against the status quo. But the almost polar opposite platforms of Sanders and Trump suggest that protest and change could lead us to a more democratic public welfare state or towards a more regressive, brutal oligarchy. Populism cuts both ways. Donald Trump's victory (fueled by an overwhelmingly white, male, working and middle-class electorate) suggest that "kill it to save it" will continue to be an even more violent and vitriolic movement against public institutions and the public good for years to come.

Unlike the "incoherent and fragmentary" common sense that can be easily marshaled to support the status quo stranglehold of the rich and powerful, we need what Gramsci called "good sense."[13] This mindset requires a "critical conception" of dominant thinking and a consciousness of who has power and how they use it. In other words, a good sense would inform the cultural mainstream with the critical tools to recognize the ways in which "kill it to save it" continues to empower corporate and other elite interests over the welfare of poor, working- and middle-class Americans—as well as the masses of working people around the world. We need strong yet accessible political and ideological critique focused on the sometimes subtle rhetoric (but often openly hostile policies) of those in power. Such contributions have always been the bone and sinew of a strong progressive Left and I am proud to offer the following as another salvo across the hegemonic bow of corporate America and its cultural minions.

Thus, the need for radical democracy and the redistribution of wealth and power will require that people have a clear and accessible narrative of how and why things are the way they are and how they got this way. This book aims to provide just such a story. I spend much of my life organizing in communities and educating students to use their intellectual and social skills to change the world. And I believe the only ways to change it are to be collectively active in the process of doing so. But I have watched too many people (myself included) spend too many hours and too much energy on projects whose impact proved negligible—not because the intentions lacked commitment or communities lacked talent, but because the framework for action and the theory of change failed to address the paradigm shift necessary to challenge the underlying ideological burden of corporate hegemony and hyper-individualism. A socially just world will not happen until people take to the streets and demand it; but I am convinced at this historical juncture that the prolonged movement necessary to create change cannot occur *until* we challenge some of the basic cultural precepts that now keep us from building such movements. This book is a story of who we are, where we are, and how we got here. I hope it can inform the next story about how we changed it all.

PART 1
The Strange Life of Kill it to Save it: Origins, Theories and Myths

overview: Why an Autopsy? The Politics of History

> Time in reality has no divisions, there is no thunderstorm or peal of trumpets at the beginning of a new month or year, and even when a new century begins it is only we humans who shoot off guns or ring bells.[1]

Countering Mann's observation, sociologist Talcott Parsons argued that some sense of "historical convergence" and an understanding of particular historical periods is necessary for people to move beyond the "anarchy of facts" towards a meaningful "concreteness" of historical narrative and theory.[2] In other words, without formalized manifestations of past ideas, actions, and intentions, we would have no meaning, no order, no identity, no social anything. Thus, despite a universe with no real predilection for any particular human purpose, men and women construct historical records by carving up seemingly meaningful slices of the past in order to say something significant about them for a present audience, often in hopes of impacting future social action. The kind of history one tells says much about the kind of future one wants.

My goal here is a political composition for the present as well as a historical narrative to understand the past—it's an autopsy with a purpose. Autopsies are done primarily to discover a cause of death and perhaps what the deceased's final physiological makeup might tell us about human conditions during his or her life. At times of dangerous epidemics or deadly biological contagions, such autopsies can inform immediate, vital reactions to stop the spread of plagues. And as we have all learned from *CSI*-type detective shows, postmortem research helps good guys catch bad guys and hold them accountable for their crimes. My own historical and political autopsy of what I consider the triumph of capitalism over democracy combines all three functions.

In general, this book dissects the history and politics of American institutions from the war in Vietnam to the present in an effort to better understand what toxic conditions evolved to destroy them. The resulting pandemic of neoliberal austerity and the degradation of democracy now threaten economic and social, as well as environmental, devastation on a global scale. This catastrophic disease must be stopped. And it can be stopped, because the current situation is not a natural condition created by the free-flowing evolution of knowledge, technology, markets, and human relations. Our current challenges result from specific policies designed and funded by specific people with specific interests in maximizing their profits, power, and control. Therefore, we must name the people and systems responsible for this condition, and more importantly the ideology that legitimizes it. We do this not only to hold leaders and their policies accountable, but also to organize movements that will change the systems that people in power create and exploit.

My own birth in 1961 conveniently frames this period but doesn't necessarily temper the complexity of historical periodization. For example, as I researched and read about the years covered here, I was especially amused at how many books on "The Sixties" covered years as early as 1945 and as late as 1980. When a decade lasts almost 35 years, it must have been very special. But such historical fluidity is more likely a reflection of periodization's inherent challenge. To proclaim "the age of" anything requires a satisfactory argument for why one chose a specific start and finish. And to provide an effective rationale means finding the age's origins in previous conditions and concluding with a picture of how the period's decline diffused into what came next.

One of my favorite books about years surrounding my own birth—Todd Gitlin's *The Sixties: Years of Hope; Days of Rage*[3]—opens with the author's most insightful and eloquent chapter on the 1950s and its influential role on the subsequent decade. Maybe it was Gitlin's growing up in the 1950s and coming of adult age in the 1960s that inspired his most passionate political and cultural analysis. In a similar way, perhaps, I try to avoid the pitfalls of *proving* a period's historical and political mettle by simply suggesting my own life is just as valid a demarcation as any other. Still, I *do* argue that a particularly devastating ideological framework for public policy and, in many ways, human life itself, has evolved (primarily during my lifetime) that must be examined historically and analyzed politically in order to comprehend it, challenge it, and ultimately change it. We need a good autopsy to create a healthy alternative. To perform such a procedure, I need to explain the historical and theoretical tools necessary for success.

Thus, I start by presenting what I consider to be key historical and theoretical frameworks for the rest of this book's focus on contemporary society and how we got here. I want to look at the specific historical, political and social underpinnings of "kill it to save it" ideology, which occurred in the declining years of America's war in Vietnam and the denouement of various social and civil rights movements in the late 1960s and early 1970s. I believe this moment demonstrated a uniquely interesting crossroads as the progressive promise of social movements and social change declined surprisingly rapidly, replaced by an equally quick rise of ultra-conservatism and its reactionary social policies and institutional practices.

In chapter one, I start with the declining years of Vietnamese victory and its impact on the United States politically and culturally. The seeming collapse of American arrogance and its subsequent ideological need to fill the void of collective identity resulted in President Jimmy Carter's "crisis of confidence" speech. The speech itself was a kind of autopsy for the American Empire that presented the nation with a devastating diagnosis about a decline in economic power, political hegemony, and—in some ways even more damning—cultural and social values. Carter had dissected the American character and found it rotting from within; a victim of political corruption and brutal imperialism, mass consumption and materialism, growing selfishness, and increasingly global ignorance and apathy.

Unfortunately, Carter had no medicine for his patient—one of the unhappy certainties of autopsy. But neither did he have a prescription for an American public in search of some spiritual, if not physical, elixir. Carter's inability to offer an effective regimen was born, ironically, from the same paralytic condition of American mythology that would ultimately inform his defeat. Carter had compared the problematic present to a mythological golden age of U.S. exceptionalism that could not be reproduced because it was never true to begin with. To regain the ghost, Carter suggested severe sacrifice, compassion, accountability, responsibility, and humility—values supposedly featured in the American character. His 1980 opponent, Ronald Reagan, argued more effectively that there was nothing wrong with Americans' values or character—the problem was that government (and the burgeoning New Deal, civil-rights welfare state) had squelched the nation's entrepreneurial and patriotic instincts, its mythic character. Unable to perform an effective autopsy that might have liberated Americans from their own arrogant delusions, Carter would lose to Reagan, who essentially doubled down on the mythology—resurrecting it as a false pretense and false promise to "make America great again."

In chapter two, I take a more theoretical approach to understanding "kill it to save it" by examining how Reagan established an ideological framework that allowed both hyper-individualism and hyper-capitalism to proceed almost unabated from 1980 to the present. Despite a rapid dismantling of New Deal policies and New Deal social and political sensibilities, Reagan and his predecessors continued to attack liberal shibboleths way past their shelf life—and have done so ever since with amazing skill and success. Why? Because they effectively created an instinctive set of ideological tools that support and protect "kill it to save it" in the minds of most Americans. It's not so much that hot-button social issues distract people's class consciousness, but rather that they now converge with a new social and cultural hardwiring. This hardwiring idolizes wealth and sanctifies trickle-down economics because of their promise to reward those "hardworking" individuals who were once held back by civic responsibilities, public commitments and social regulations.

What replaces the public good is a reactive sense of self-interest, fear, and greed. And as I conclude this part of the book, I propose a theoretical foundation for "kill it to save it" in the works of Georg Simmel and George Rizer. Both sociologists suggested that the historical advance of technological speed and human efficiency—combined with centralized wealth and power—created an increasingly rationalized society, driven and measured by profit and control. But such a society continually creates systems that destroy the possibility of maintaining a peaceful and thriving human condition. Social innovation and the production of knowledge under a "kill it to save it" ideology eventually dismantle social relationships and discredit any knowledge not aligned with direct economic value. Such is the triumph of capitalism over democracy. Such is the framework and practice for contemporary public institutions. And such is the ironic death wish of an American Empire.[4]

ONE

The Vietnamization of America

> Don't you know why God allows wars? God looks down from heaven and he sees a poor country with too many people and he says to himself, "Oh dear, think how much poverty and degradation these people are going to face because there are so many of them," and then he whispers into the President's ear at night, and then in the morning there is a war. When the war is over, there are fewer people, and these fewer people are happier … in a while there will be fewer of us, and we will all be happier.[1]

Bringing the War Home

Father McGillicutty's commentary about wars and poverty reveals a lot about the rise of irrationalism in modern society. Wendy Kaminer argues that our nation has come to "value emotion over reason" and "faith over fact."[2] Durang's screenplay suggests as much as he depicts the "dark farce" of both American innocence and arrogance after Vietnam. The play presents the convergence of our wounded pride, lost purpose, and newly recognized vulnerabilities—often dressed in dark humor and played for laughs. But losing the war in Vietnam played many a mind game with Americans, individually and collectively. As Jerry Lembcke writes:

> American identity is linked to the nation's position in the global order in ways that are uncharacteristic of most other countries. ... Few pillars in the American identity stood taller after WWII than the claim, "We're Number One!" So overpowering was it that the perceived need for some *other* way to think about who we are and what we stood for receded into the backs of people's minds.[3]

Losing in Vietnam, Lembcke concludes, resulted in a "loss of a sense of self on collective and personal levels." This book examines just who we Americans are, and think we are, at the beginning of the 21st century.

The title of this book, *Kill It to Save It,* goes back at least as far as the war in Vietnam. The American military's "pacification" strategy targeted small villages rumored to be sympathetic towards the North Vietnamese National Liberation Front—the Communists. The U.S. terrorized these communities with multiple acts of violence and destruction, often burning homes and public structures to the ground. As one military officer explained after the devastation of Ben Tre in February of 1968, "It became necessary to destroy the town to save it."[4]

The most infamous of these "kill it to save it" attacks came only a few weeks later in the village of Son My, where the small hamlet of My Lai witnessed U.S. soldiers executing hundreds of unarmed old men, women, children, and babies.[5] But according to journalist Richard Boyle in *Flower of the Dragon*:

> [The My Lai Massacre] was not the act of one man. It was not the act of one platoon or one company. It was the result of an ordered and well-conducted campaign conceived at high command levels to teach a lesson to the villagers of Quang Ngai Province. The killing ... is part of a definite political strategy usually described as the "pacification" of Vietnamese villagers.[6]

The continued campaign of murder, torture, and burning hamlets forced tens of thousands of Vietnamese to become refugees, often crowded into small camps that could be easily watched over or decimated again at any time. *As a policy*, the American military was prepared to destroy Vietnam and its people to save it, and them, from Communism.

The killing only intensified as the pacification strategy gave way to the "Vietnamization" strategy. Concerned about growing public dissent over a war with no apparent end, Nixon withdrew American troops in hopes that the South Vietnamese Army could contain the Viet Cong with only logistical and air support from the U.S. Contrary to a military denouement, however, Vietnamization was accompanied by massive U.S. airstrikes (secret and illegal) in Cambodia and Laos. These bombings killed thousands and eventually lead to a genocidal civil war in Cambodia, where millions lost their lives. On April 7, 1971, Nixon proclaimed: "Vietnamization has succeeded." But the war dragged on until 1975, killing over a thousand more U.S. soldiers, tens of thousands of Vietnamese, hundreds of thousands in Laos, and somewhere between 1 and 3 million people in Cambodia.[7]

Part of the antiwar pressure that had inspired Nixon's Vietnamization strategy came from varied groups of domestic radicals, who promised to challenge the history of imperialism abroad *and* colonialism in the U.S.—essentially "bringing the war home." While persistent racism, poverty, police violence, and despair had resulted in waves of urban uprisings between 1964 and 1969 (especially after Martin Luther King's assassination in 1968), the antiwar movement raised its militancy level, too. Activists became increasingly frustrated and horrified by the government's own violence against protestors—from the brutal beatings of demonstrators at the 1968 Democratic National Convention in Chicago and the 1972 Republican National Convention in Miami, to the political assassinations of Black Panther organizers Fred Hampton and Mark Clark in 1969, to armed government repression at Pine Ridge and Wounded Knee in the early 1970s, to the rising violence on college campuses around the country culminating in the killing of student protesters at Kent State and Jackson State Universities in 1970. Eventually, indisputable evidence would demonstrate just how far American government officials went to stifle, discredit, dismantle, attack—and, when necessary, kill off—the leadership of civil rights and antiwar movement organizations.[8] Protecting a supposedly democratic country apparently required the worst violations of citizens' democratic freedoms and human rights. *Kill it to save it.*

In response to such domestic tactics, one New Left leader explained, "We've got to turn New York into Saigon."[9] And to some extent, they did. In 1969, *Time* magazine reported that 61 bombings occurred on college campuses, targeting mostly ROTC [Reserve Officer Training Corps] and other war-related facilities. Meanwhile, half of New York City's 93 bomb explosions that year were classified as "political."[10] According to the FBI, over 40,000 bombings took place in the U.S. between the beginning of 1969 and the end of 1970 as violent attacks on sites of military, corporate, and university power became a serious strategy for *some* militant Left organizations.[11] Antiwar activity against imperialism abroad bled together with antiracist and anticolonial movements at home and created a sense—at least for a critical mass—that a revolutionary moment was at hand in the U.S., as well as elsewhere in the world.[12] While Gil Scott-Heron would rap "The Revolution Will Not Be Televised," many New Left radicals came to believe, as Berkeley activists Frank Bardacke and Jack Weinberg did, that:

> We are now no longer just a protest movement, we're not only a movement to end the war in Vietnam, but we are a revolutionary movement. … We identified with the student movement in Paris, there was the Prague Spring, and the feeling that revolution was in the air—East and West, Capitalism and Communism, it was all coming apart and a new spirit and a new way of liberation was in the air."[13]

The Morning After

But for most of America, weary of war at home and abroad, the period's social and political upheavals also created a yearning for some kind of normalcy. When Nixon's war crimes in Southeast Asia and campaign crimes at home culminated in articles of impeachment and resignation, the Left *and* the Right cheered. After Nixon departed the White House in August 1974 and the final helicopters left Saigon in April the following year, many wanted to agree with Gerald Ford's declaration that "our long national nightmare"[14] was over. Long-time critics of Nixon celebrated the peaceful transition of power, proclaiming that the system worked and a "restoration" would be possible. *The New York Times* wrote: "Out of the despair of Watergate has come an inspiring new demonstration of the uniqueness and strength of the American democracy,"[15] the peaceful transfer of power. Historian Howard Zinn explained that such proclamations brought "a cleansing sense of relief to the American people," regardless of how clean we really were.[16]

With relief, however, came malaise. The end of American supremacy had indeed caused the loss of faith and arrogance that Lembcke (2003) suggests. The American people still distrusted their government and questioned its authority and its agenda, even if they were not prepared to overthrow it completely. The post-Vietnam War economy fell into stagflation (rising inflation along with economic stagnation), inspiring new questions about the vitality and viability of an economic system and foreign policy based on the need for perpetual growth and domination. So serious were the rumblings about economic system failures that in 1976, Treasury Secretary William Simon worried:

> Vietnam, Watergate, student unrest, shifting moral codes, the worst recession in a generation, and a number of other jarring cultural shocks have all combined to create a new climate of questions and doubt. ... It all adds up to a general malaise, a society-wide crisis of institutional confidence ... [Americans] have been taught to distrust the very word *profit* and the *profit motive* that makes our prosperity possible, to feel this system, that has done more to alleviate human suffering and privation than any other, is somehow cynical, selfish, and amoral. We must get across the human side of capitalism.[17]

Jimmy Carter should have been a good candidate for such a task. His thoughtfulness, intellect, and piety combined with a playful admission to *Playboy* magazine in 1976 that, despite being faithful to his wife, he had committed "adultery in his heart," all suggested he was a serious yet pragmatic, hip yet folksy candidate. The Georgia peanut farmer promised old-school honesty and transparency while still predicting a return to national prosperity and global ascendancy. But Carter's foreign policy, which focused on human rights and peace initiatives instead of what he called "an inordinate fear of communism,"[18] drew virulent critique from Cold War hawks and defense industry dollars. His commitment to environmental conservation and alternative energy threatened oil company profits and drew their consternation as well. Meanwhile, Carter's support for nuclear energy (even in the wake of Three Mile Island) and his willingness to try to balance the budget by cutting social programs raised the ire of progressives and liberal democrats. Thus, complaints from Left and Right combined with continued inflation and increasing frustrations over oil shortages all doomed Carter's presidency as surveys and pundits depicted the country's mounting "malaise."[19]

In an attempt to analyze and address a national identity crisis and growing discontent, Carter held an extended "domestic summit" at Camp David with scholars, politicians, clergy, labor, and business leaders all discussing their readings of America's social and political pulse.[20] Afterwards, he gave a televised address where he quoted from summit participants and other citizens he had interviewed. He surmised that, "All the legislation in the world can't fix what's wrong with America," where the nation's "greatest threat to democracy" was the "growing doubt about the meaning of our own lives and in the loss of a unity of purpose for our nation." Carter pointed to the "erosion of our confidence in the future … threatening to destroy the social and the political fabric of America." He continued:

> Our people are losing that faith, not only in government itself but in the ability of citizens to serve as the ultimate rulers and shapers of our democracy. As a people we know our past and we are proud of

> it. Our progress has been part of the living history of America, even the world. We always believed that we were part of a great movement of humanity itself called democracy, involved in the search for freedom, and that belief has always strengthened us in our purpose. But just as we are losing our confidence in the future, we are also beginning to close the door on our past.[21]

Like most presidential speeches, one has to sift through certain mythical narratives and arrogant puffery about national greatness and destiny; but if this crisis was one of "confidence," Carter's concern with a collective sense of purpose did seem in order. Just what *did* Americans believe in and what did they want from their nation, their leaders, and themselves?

From the President's newly informed perch, the problem seemed to have been brewing for quite some time, the result of a whole generation of shock and tragedy. Compared to Simon's shortsighted call for simply restoring our faith in capitalism, Carter offered a more powerful and sophisticated analysis of the country's reflexive self. He explained:

> We were sure that ours was a nation of the ballot, not the bullet, until the murders of John Kennedy and Robert Kennedy and Martin Luther King Jr. We were taught that our armies were always invincible and our causes were always just, only to suffer the agony of Vietnam. We respected the presidency as a place of honor until the shock of Watergate. We remember when the phrase "sound as a dollar" was an expression of absolute dependability, until ten years of inflation began to shrink our dollar and our savings. We believed that our nation's resources were limitless until 1973, when we had to face a growing dependence on foreign oil. These wounds are still very deep. They have never been healed.[22]

But as America looked to its government for solutions to the problems of domestic and foreign policies gone awry—policies and events that ultimately and perhaps forever damaged the innocence of our national pride and enterprise—its leaders, according to Carter, had failed miserably. Washington, D.C. had become "an island ... isolated from the mainstream of our nation's life." More specifically, Carter believed the gap between Washington politicians and the average American citizen left the government "incapable of action." The final result was a:

> Congress twisted and pulled in every direction by hundreds of well-financed and powerful special interests ... every extreme position defended to the last vote, almost to the last breath by one unyielding group or another ... a balanced and a fair approach that demands sacrifice abandoned like an orphan without support and without friends.[23]

In a summary that could have been ripped from today's headlines, Carter concluded that the American government, once upheld as a great beacon of democracy and justice, had succumbed to "paralysis, stagnation, and drift." While all such political narratives contain unavoidable hypocrisies (Carter's own corporate sponsors and special interests, for instance), his analysis suggested that only a significant and fundamental change in the structures and practices of national governance could make a difference in the current crisis. And first, Americans had to face the truth.

Remembering to Forget: Surviving a National Hangover

In fact, Carter went even further to suggest U.S. citizens *themselves* were just as much to blame; they had accepted a flawed democracy and loss of political vision and values as part of a shallow and materialist bargain with corporate commercialism. Carter lamented, "In a nation that was proud of hard work, strong families, close-knit communities and our faith in God, too many of us now tend to worship self-indulgence and consumption. Human identity is no longer defined by what one does but by what one owns."[24] In such a society, greedy corporations and politicians had gotten away with their corrupt practices because public participation and vigilance are replaced by gilded comfort and endless commodities, intellectual laziness and infantile expectations. The energy crisis had exposed all of our national failings because it required focused attention, sophisticated global long-term analysis, potential sacrifice, and a commitment to an expanding sense of the public good.

Carter suggested Americans had reached a turning point in our history where we had to "face the facts" and choose between two paths. The President warned Americans to abandon the misguided path that lead to "fragmentation and self-interest." He explained, "Down that road lies a mistaken idea of freedom—the right to grasp for ourselves some advantage over others. That path will be one of constant conflict over narrow interests ending in chaos and immobility. It is a certain route to failure." Instead, Carter proposed a second course of action: "the path of common purpose and the restoration of American values—that path leads to true freedom."[25] The United States could be triumphant again if it regained its traditional values combined with a more nuanced and humble sense of global citizenship; a kind of pragmatic realism embracing hard work, sacrifice, and collaboration.

Such a strategy, however, suggested that capitalism and commercial enterprise had to be even more regulated and tied to a democratic, public enterprise. It suggested that wealth, prosperity, and progress might have its limits and may not be the best indicators of a good and satisfied society. Carter had gone so far as to say that Americans had "discovered that owning things and consuming things [can't] satisfy our longing for meaning ... [that] piling up material goods cannot fill the emptiness of lives which have no confidence or purpose." Carter's narrative proposed that a substantive structural, institutional, and ideological shift might be necessary to restore a sense of core values and American identity.

Whatever Carter's actual policy initiatives would be to accomplish these changes, he faced three serious obstacles to fundamental institutional and ideological change in the United States: 1) a public that by the late 1970s did not want to face hardships, be critically introspective, or sacrifice consumer-driven lifestyles, 2) his own inability to create a more engaging democratic dialogue or empowering plan for action outside of asking citizens to: "Let your voice be heard. Whenever you have a chance, say something good about our country," and 3) a presidential opponent who promised "morning in America" without sacrifice, soul-searching, the nagging burden of economic regulation, or the moral encumbrance of the public good gone global. As Historian Kim McQuaid suggested, eventually, "National amnesia was the best way to put Vietnam behind us."[26]

Ronald Reagan nurtured and then harnessed this national amnesia, thus succeeding where Carter had failed. Reagan's triumph did not come because he led the United States into a new national identity, more sophisticated and nuanced in its sense of global purpose and more democratic and transparent in its domestic policy making. Instead of offering a good government, Reagan promised as little government as possible. He proclaimed: "In this present crisis, government is not the solution to our problem; government *is* the problem."[27] Contrary to America's leadership towards a global, integrated economy and a period of cooperative democracy and access to fundamental resources (food, clothing, shelter, education, and healthcare) as inalienable *human* rights, Reagan relied on the primacy of unrestrained markets and a reinvigorated myth of rugged individualism borrowed from his Hollywood experience.[28] And contrary to the sophisticated analysis and expansive sensibilities needed to inform a *new* national identity, what Reagan did was restore an old sense of provincial arrogance, cockiness, and certitude about America as a "shining city on a hill."[29]

Ironically, at the same time that Reagan declared a return to American supremacy, he effectively dismantled most of the social and economic policies that had fueled the nation's sense of greatness, its confidence in mission, and its virtue in purpose throughout the 20th century. The expansive American dream, built on Franklin Delano Roosevelt's New Deal agenda and Lyndon Baines Johnson's War on Poverty programs, would now be deferred by Reagan's policies to destroy the public welfare mission of the American government—all in the name of restoring freedom, liberty, and prosperity.[30]

In fact, Reagan blamed the social welfare agenda itself for ruining both the economy and our national character in the first place. The practice of blaming the victims of bad social policy and economic dysfunction for having caused them became part and parcel of Reagan's storytelling and policy making. To address America's diminished international political and military standing in the wake of anticolonial revolutions in Vietnam, Nicaragua, Iran, and elsewhere, Reagan blamed antiwar activists and Carter's "weakness" in seeking disarmament and human rights treaties. To rid us of the "Vietnam syndrome," Reagan—and then Bush—would carry out unnecessary, and arguably illegal, wars in Grenada, Panama, and Iraq (as well as counterinsurgent "secret wars" in Central America and Africa). Meanwhile, they conducted psy-ops campaigns such as Operation Yellow Ribbon to delegitimize and diminish dissent at home.[31]

More importantly, extinguishing the Vietnam paradigm was about "rewriting history" and revitalizing American mythologies about supremacy and power, virtue and destiny. As Lembcke writes:

> It was not the loss of the war, not the massive destruction of Vietnam itself, not the death of 58,000 Americans or 1.9 million Vietnamese, not any of the myriad other things the war was more evidently about that was at issue. The Aura of Vietnam [was about] the level of support soldiers and veterans had received from the American people.[32]

Also at issue was the very idea that the U.S. had lost both the war itself, and its own cherished images of virtue and invincibility. Despite the overwhelming evidence that most U.S. citizens had come to oppose the war in Vietnam, that increasing numbers of Vietnam veterans and soldiers opposed the war, and that the North Vietnamese had actually won the war, Reagan would promote the narrative that we lost Vietnam because America's hands were tied by an antiwar "liberal media" and "activist minority"—the people Vice-President Spiro Agnew once called "long-haired hippies" and an "effete corps of impudent snobs who characterize themselves as intellectuals."[33]

Myth: Villains, Heroes and Hyper-Individualism

On the domestic front, Reagan blamed poor people for their own poverty and for causing the federal government endless budget woes. Despite the fact that his "welfare queen" examples were fabricated and that welfare programs comprised miniscule amounts of federal spending, reality rarely got in the way of the President's domestic mythmaking.[34] In fact, cuts to public housing, food, health, and antipoverty programs made it increasingly difficult for poor people to obtain the education and support they needed to "get off" of welfare.[35]

Similarly, Reagan blamed unions for unemployment, inflation, and the degradation of the American work ethic, despite workers' inability to stop deindustrialization, manufacturing losses, and a growing trade deficit. Meanwhile, union membership and strength had declined so dramatically during the 1970s that it would have been impossible for the labor movement to be responsible for much of anything. Reagan's campaign to deregulate the economy and liberalize markets only further primed the pump for relocating factories overseas. Massive unemployment and falling wages resulted throughout the United States.[36] But by demonizing the poor and working class, Reagan could blame a racialized, feminized, and organized working class as the *cause*—not the victims—of economic inequality. "They" were behind the resulting social problems for the rest of "us."

The flipside of this demonization process required positive mythmaking. If racialized and feminized poor people and demasculinized union workers had "held back" the country's economy, who would *save* the nation?[37] In Reagan's America, heroes were needed—preferably ones that looked and sounded like the characters he had portrayed (or wanted to portray) in Hollywood.[38] These brave people (like Rambo, the celluloid soldier "held back" from winning the war in Vietnam) had been restrained from using their power and creativity to improve their own finances and, by logical conclusion, the whole American economy. In his first inaugural address, Reagan argued:

> If we look to the answer as to why for so many years we achieved so much, prospered as no other people on Earth, it was because here in this land we unleashed the energy and individual genius of man to a greater extent than has ever been done before. ... It is no coincidence that our present troubles parallel and are proportionate to the intervention and intrusion in our lives that result from unnecessary and excessive growth of government.[39]

Too much regulation, too much tax burden, and too many handouts to the "undeserving poor" caused our economic stagnation and national malaise—not oil dependency or globalization, hyper-commercialism, self-interest, corporate greed, or citizen apathy.

Inaugural addresses are all about narrative and mythmaking—manipulating sacred and historical symbols that already exist in a nation's culture and psyche as deeply and dearly held elements of collective identity. The idea of American individualism—the freedom of citizens bestowed by the Bill of Rights and chronicled by social observers from Alexis de Tocqueville to John Dewey—is a key philosophical component of American identity. But from the concept's very origins, "individualism" contained problematic and contradictory strains. Individualism might be a distinguishing national characteristic, but it is one fraught with tension and eccentricity.

De Tocqueville, a French social scientist, wrote one of the first examinations of political culture in the United States, *Democracy in America,* in the late 1830s. In it, he compared American *individualism* with Europe's culture of *egotism*:

> Our [European] fathers were only acquainted with egotism. Egotism is a passionate and exaggerated love of self, which leads a man to connect everything with his own person, and prefer himself to everything in the world. Individualism is a mature and calm feeling, which disposes each member of the community to sever himself from [others] so that, after he has thus formed a little circle of his own, he willingly leaves

> society at large to itself. Egotism originates in blind instinct: individualism proceeds from erroneous judgment … Egotism blights the germ of all virtue; individualism, at first, only saps the virtues of public life; but, in the long run, it attacks and destroys all others, and is at length absorbed in downright egotism.[40]

In other words, *egotism* results in an arrogance that *requires* social integration and, while public virtue is driven by self-interest, a certain level of mutual interdependence remains necessary, welcomed and even cherished as one needs other people to shape, identify, celebrate and even bolster one's own ego. *Individualism*, however, threatens to descend into egotism *without* any sense of, or concern for, the public. It could, in fact, destroy the very social nature of its own existence because individuals have no identity without social relations, without other people.

Yet, de Tocqueville argued that such socially destructive egotism could be avoided (or at least checked) by the power and privilege of local, participatory governance. Participatory citizenship tamed the parasitic excess of egotism and:

> remind[s] every citizen … that he lives in society … impressing upon his mind the notion that it is the duty, as well as the interest of men, to make themselves useful to their fellow-creatures; and as he sees no particular ground of animosity to them, since he is *never* either their master or their slave, his heart readily leans to the side of kindness.[41]

In other words, the balance of ego and public *could* be managed by the practice of collective and participatory democracy premised on a sense of equality. And a "civic man's" ritual performance of social acts eventually becomes a habit of heart and mind, as: "Men attend to the interests of the public, first by necessity, afterwards by choice: what was intentional becomes an instinct; and by dint of working for the good of one's fellow citizens, the habit and the taste for serving them is at length acquired."[42] It's a beautiful image and a great story—but a myth, nonetheless.

In fact, this process of moving from individualism to social responsibility was fraught with obstacles. American history does feature examples of such public behavior and grassroots engagement, but these have usually been movements *against* the mainstream, the majority, the powerful—and they have been exceptions, not the rule. More often we've witnessed, and been rapidly overwhelmed by callous self-interest, unbridled competition, and "others be damned" attitudes. De Tocqueville's confidence in individualism has proven badly misplaced.

As Roland Barthes and others have argued, mythologies—while steeped in historical origins and context—appear to be *natural* and *ahistorical*. Myths, especially "identity myths," present themselves as immutable and biological—a part of a nation's DNA. Thus, cultural myths are inherently ironic; they proclaim to be "a natural image of reality," but in fact distort and obscure their historical evolution and the very political context within which they are born and employed.[43] In the U.S. after the defeat in Vietnam, Lembcke suggests that the "myth of the spat upon vet" (he argues that no evidence exists of antiwar protestors *ever* spitting on returning Vietnam soldiers) was "less about something that did or did not happen than about the *belief* that it did."[44]

Individualism, for Reagan, was not about a complex process of socially constructed identity or the inevitable tensions between ego and public, but rather about the *natural* condition by which Americans had always existed and, to personal and national detriment, had only recently been prohibited from exercising. Thus, Reagan called for a return to the kinds of rugged individualism he believed had made America the nation it once was and could be again. As Haynes Johnson wrote in *Sleepwalking through History: America in the Reagan Years:* "At a time when Americans desperately wanted to believe again, Reagan presented himself as the political wizard whose spell made everyone feel good."[45] The nation would succeed if only American citizens could be unfettered by government regulations, unburdened by taxes, and freed from supporting or participating in social programs that sapped the middle class's ability to spend and invest.

To make such arguments without the slightest irony required an immense historical amnesia. The golden age Reagan celebrated was actually *born* of massive public spending. The middle-class American dream sprouted from huge public allocations for education (G.I. Bill and mandatory, free public K—12 schools), health care (public hospitals, health and safety regulations, and protections of food, water, and other commodities), transportation infrastructure (public transportation as well as highways, bridges, and so on), and subsidies for homeownership and pensions. But to simply ignore the role of cause (government-funded public goods) and effect (upward mobility and economic growth for working and middle classes) suggests more than simple oversight. Reagan helped rewire the American mind, creating a cultural and political instinct *against* the public good supposedly *for* the benefit of the public good. *Kill it to save it.*

In 1985, only four years after Reagan took office, Robert Bellah and his coauthors published the sociological classic, *Habits of the Heart: Individualism and Commitment in American Life*. In the book, they mapped out the social and political contours of our nation's long relationship with individualism, describing four major types: *biblical*, *civic*, *utilitarian* and *expressive*. For each of these types (represented by John Winthrop, Thomas Jefferson, Benjamin Franklin, and Walt Whitman respectively), the authors argued that either religious faith, civic governance, pragmatic interdependence, or a romantic sense of collective unity maintained the difficult balance between individual ego and public identity. But Bellah's research also found that a more contemporary radical or *hyper-individualism* threatened to upset the balance and eventually destroy the potential for individualism and democracy to coexist.[46]

The nuance and tension these strains of individualism suggested were both absent and hauntingly present in Reagan's mythology. For example, the inherent dilemma of individualism can be understood as the unavoidable tension between de Tocqueville's "civic man" and J. Hector St. John de Crèvecœur's "economic man." Crevecoeur, a French immigrant who became a successful businessman, farmer, author, and U.S. citizen in the 1770s, first published the fictional *Letters from an American Farmer* in 1782. In the most famous of these letters, the author celebrates the "new American man" who, shorn of European aristocracy and subservience, "becomes resourceful and enterprising, energized by the ability to keep the fruits of his own labor." American farmers were invigorated by their freedoms and the accessible abundance that surrounded them. He concludes: "Everything has tended to regenerate them: new laws, a new mode of living, a new social system. Here they are become men … the idle may be employed, the useless become useful, and the poor become rich."[47]

But even Crèvecœur's rugged individualist required context:

> We are a people of cultivators … united by the silken bands of mild government, all respecting the laws, without dreading their power, because they are equitable. We are all animated with the spirit of an industry which is unfettered and unrestrained, because each person works for himself … We have no princes, for whom we toil, starve, and bleed: we are the most perfect society now existing in the world. Here man is free.[48]

In other words, individualism (with only the most modest 'silken bands' to government) existed primarily because *equality* (or at least equity) also existed. And with general equity came measure and a sense of, or faith in, justice.

The evolution of individualism in the United States, however, was accompanied by ever-growing economic and social stratification to degrees unimaginable to Crèvecœur. Still, Reagan would harness the historical and ideological *feel* of rugged individuals and claim that Americans' own "energy, genius and creativity" had been and would be enough to guarantee success for those who deserved it. While the real evolution of a 200-year-old economy *had* created captains (if not princes and kings) of industry with huge economic disparities between workers and owners, by revitalizing the myth of individualism, Reagan also revived the legitimacy of *believing* in an 18th-century agrarian capitalism, recast by 19th-century industrial robber barons as laissez-faire capitalism for the 20th (and now 21st) century. Thus, on the one hand, inequality was natural—most people competed effectively and earned success; "others" didn't. On the other hand, government interference (social programs, public infrastructure, welfare, and so on) and regulations (health and safety, workers' rights, environmental, and so on) only atrophied personal determination and innovation. Despite the indisputable evidence that 19th-century laissez-faire capitalism had resulted in massive inequality and a gilded age whose greed and despair were legion—and despite the irreplaceable role of working-class movements, social welfare policies, and government intervention in *mitigating* such hyper-inequality (thus creating the modern American dream in the first place)—Reagan effectively demonized the very ideas of collective organizing, social welfare policies, and the government acting for the public good. The myth of rugged individualism survives only without historical context and historical facts.

In many ways, however, both de Tocqueville's and Crèvecœur's analyses were even more problematic because they required a willful blindness to the obvious historical realities for so many of the nation's early inhabitants. What seemed like interesting comparisons between European society and the new "American man" ignored the very large population of African slaves, indentured servants, Native Americans and women.[49] By now, such a critique is old hat and almost quaint, as even America's first Black president can capture American individualism as part of his own mythmaking. But the national obsession with individualism as a "core value" ingrained in our cultural DNA was born illegitimately and deformed—on the backs of the imprisoned, enslaved, and disenfranchised masses. For them, the freedom and ability to partake in the "animated spirit of industry" would not occur until the spoils of two centuries of economic growth and exploitation had already been divvied up.

In the end, Reagan's individualism (or hyper-individualism, as Bellah, in *Habits of the Heart*, would describe it) sang mythic but myopic—an all-encompassing elixir for the symptoms that ailed Americans without addressing any of the root causes of the nation's real maladies. Thus, his policies dismantled the very federal institutions once created to craft middle-class consciousness and envision "the American dream."[50] During his two terms in office, Reagan dramatically shifted the nation's tax burden from the wealthy to the poor and middle class, cut programs that supported economic and social mobility for the working class, and set in motion the kinds of privatization and levels of inequality we now associate with neoliberalism—all in the name of freeing individual enterprise and economic markets for the masses and middle classes. *Kill it to save it.*

But even more detrimental was the new narrative framework, which not only legitimized what Bellah called "neocapitalism"—the complete commitment to free markets economically, politically, and culturally—but also delegitimized, and even demonized, any possible critique. The resulting constriction of civic discourse and social action left many Americans yearning for an effective public-sector policy but with no intellectual or cultural tools to create it. Contemporary political discourse descends into the most absurd debates over our first Black president's birthplace and religious affiliation, while we can't figure out the best way to protect the health, education, and welfare of most American youth—let alone the next generations of youth around the world. And the policy decisions we do make are killing us.

TWO

Mourning Again in America

> Spurred by Reagan's gospel of progress and prosperity, Americans happily indulged themselves. ... Shopping became the great American religion, with advertising jingles uniting Americans through a common liturgy. Loudmouths in stadiums would shout "Tastes great," echoing a popular [Miller Beer] commercial for light, spelled lite, beer. The Pavlovian crowd would respond: "Less filling!" Malls sprouted like mushrooms across the landscape, creating huge, homogenized, artificial environments, killing off main streets and helping franchises gobble up individual entrepreneurs. Reagan's rhetoric made this prosperity patriotic—and transcendent. (Gil Troy, p 3)[1]

Of Toxic Soup and Suicidal Blends: Neocapitalism—an Elixir for the Pain

In the new Preface of Bellah et al.'s second edition of *Habits of the Heart* (1996),[2] they included remarks on what they had ten years earlier called "neocapitalism." Initially, they believed that this extreme form of economic individualism and laissez-faire policy making would blend in with its opposite—welfare liberalism—and create a more regulated policy of economic democracy. Instead, neocapitalism grew ever stronger ideologically and politically as "criticism of 'big government' and 'tax and spend liberalism' mounted." Ironically, the ideological triumph occurred while *most* Americans *still* favored many forms of public provision—but only the ones that benefitted their own interests and identity groups, not those helping "others." Bellah continued:

> We clearly underestimated the ideological fervor that the neocapitalist position was able to tap—ironically for us, because so much of that fervor derives from the very source we focused on in our book: individualism. The neocapitalist vision is viable only to the degree to which it can be seen as an expression—even a moral expression—of our dominant ideological individualism, with its compulsive stress on independence, its contempt for weakness, and its adulation of success.

The Reagan—Bush years had ushered in a cultural transformation celebrating a neocapitalist, social, and political success that mixed a reverence for corporate hegemony, commercialism, consumerism, and economic growth with hyper-individualism and self-centered virtue.

But the ideological brilliance and subsequent surprising durability of the hyper-individualist myth is that it was able to "turn even its policy failures into ideological successes." As Bellah et al. concluded: "[Neocapitalism] has persuaded many Americans that the problems it has produced, such as quadrupling of the national debt since 1980, are really the result of welfare liberalism, even though welfare liberalism has not set the American policy agenda for over twenty years." Ironically, this ability to blame welfare liberalism for economic crises despite the almost complete absence of such policies—or even espoused policy positions—has persisted for yet *another* twenty years. In other words, we have had almost four decades of policies driven by corporate capital interests and promoted by hyper-individualist rhetoric, yet the resulting crises have been blamed on increasingly (and now almost completely) nonexistent social welfare policies.

Most notable in this ideological twist is that, since contemporary social narratives are based on myth, facts don't matter. Reagan and his cohort argued that successful New Deal programs such as Social Security and unemployment insurance—and War on Poverty programs such as Medicare, Medicaid and Head Start—were failures, had become too costly to support, and actually caused too heavy a reliance on government "handouts," thus sapping economic individualism and growth. Aside from indisputable evidence that these policies *were* immensely successful and that funding for such programs still paled in comparison to corporate welfare subsidies, most of the "blame social spending" narrative was just plain wrong. During periods of increased spending for social programming after the Second World War, economic growth also went up. As social spending declined in the late 1960s, so did economic growth. In fact, many economists argue that spending on social infrastructure and maintaining education, health, and the standards of other collective goods and services bolsters economic growth and development. Dismantling such efforts has weakened our global competitiveness and damaged our economy.[3]

And as Reagan's tax cuts for the rich went into effect, not only did debt continue to rise and growth become spotty at best, but economic inequality also grew significantly larger. From the 1980s to the present, even during periods of the greatest economic growth, the gains from that growth have gone almost entirely to the top 10% (and really to the top 5%—and increasingly the top 1%) of our society.[4] The economic policies promoted by neocapitalism (what we now call "neoliberalism") and ideologically moralized by hyper-individualism have destroyed the economy and decreased the ability of most individuals to succeed—and, in some cases, even barely survive. But ask who killed the U.S. economy and its attendant American dream and the mainstream mantra still proclaims: tax-and-spend liberals, social welfare programs, union workers, and welfare queens.

Similarly, despite budget cutting and public sector dismantling, Reagan still ended up with the largest national debt of all time. How was that possible? In part, as was suggested, welfare and most War on Poverty spending never amounted to that big a piece of the federal budget anyway—thus, cutting it barely made a dent in the deficit. However, cuts to public spending on health, education, roads, bridges, and so on continually restricted economic growth and reduced social mobility. Meanwhile, Reagan dramatically increased allocations for military defense and related "pet projects" (*Star Wars*, for instance), as well as huge corporate subsidies for global advertising and expansion, thus increasing overall government spending.[5] But massive tax cuts for the wealthy comprised the largest piece of the new government debt as it represented a huge slice of pie that Reagan could simply not make up with other revenue. Following his initial tax cuts in 1981, the deficit rose immediately by almost 150% to over 6% of GDP. This debt resulted in raising interest rates, frightening financial markets, and the worst recession (at that time) since the 1930s.[6] In many ways, we continue to live under the legacy of Reagan's deficits—not that of tax-and-spend liberals.

To address this, the President could have rescinded his big tax cut for the wealthy; but instead he created new regressive taxes on gasoline and cigarettes—the kind that generally hurt the middle and working classes. He then increased payroll taxes for Social Security, creating a huge surplus that he then used to pay down the debt created by tax cuts for the rich. In 1986, he further cut taxes for the top 5% while increasing taxes on middle- and low-income citizens. For the first time in history, middle- and upper-middle-class workers faced income tax rates of up to 33%—higher than the wealthiest tax rate of 28%. And while Reagan gave those paying capital gains taxes on stocks and bonds a big break, he began levying taxes on unemployment compensation. To explain "tax the poor to help the rich" policies, tortured rationalizations appeared[7] that argued poor people had to pay *some* taxes, otherwise they would be alienated from the "shared enterprise" of funding the government; they would not feel compelled to work for the good of others if not themselves. Reagan had essentially operationalized and justified a reverse Robin Hood redistribution of wealth upwards from the poor based on market-based psychology about self-esteem and self-worth.

Almost thirty years after Reagan, we have created a political logic that informs debates over public policy with a toxic blend of (mythic) hyper-individualism and corporate hegemony. In fact, the conflation of corporate bottom lines with individual freedom and opportunity is now paradigmatic for almost all serious debate on social issues in the United States. The result is a seriously flawed way of thinking about and acting on public policy once designed to protect and improve the general welfare but now designed to intensify the wealth and power of an elite few. But Americans hardly consider the public welfare a legitimate goal anymore. Instead, we protect and improve the ability for individuals and corporations (which we've been told are "people" too[8]) to make gargantuan profits—the rest be damned.

Trickle Down Voodoo: "I am Poured Out Like Water, and All My Bones are Out of Joint"

To be fair, there are many who believe in "trickle-down economics:" that wealth made by millionaires and billionaires (now called "job creators") eventually leads to more investment, more employment, and a better economy overall for middle- and working-class people. And there is a "common sense" aspect to it. But as with most common sense, it isn't good sense because it isn't true. Some economic growth is better than others when it comes to whether or not growth actually leads to economic prosperity for everyone instead of just a few. While some increased wealth may go into the kinds of investment that create well-paying jobs and increase commercial activity, most of it (especially nowadays) doesn't.[9] The freedom to accumulate without limit leads to more for some and less for others. Great taste, less filling.

For instance, changing markets over the past two decades have resulted in massive investments in real estate and in the financial industry itself—rather than in, for example, manufacturing. Between 1990 and 2008, the American economy experienced tremendous growth, but little of it was shared growth. At the same time, tax rates for those making the most money were cut extensively.[10] In other words, lots of money was being made but little of it trickled down to working- and middle-class people. And because the growth came primarily from real estate shenanigans and financial chicanery, very few things were being produced, either. Fewer and fewer jobs were created while fewer and fewer people were pocketing more and more money. And when that money was made, it just as likely ended up in offshore accounts to *avoid* its trickling down.[11]

To best understand how wealth can be created for some while actually destroying the economy for others, consider one of the Democratic Party's favorite whipping boys from the 2012 campaign season: Bain Capital. Bain Capital is a venture equity firm. In other words, it makes most of its money by taking over businesses that still have some value and figuring out how to create more value from them. Sometimes it means restructuring or downsizing companies, resulting in layoffs and closures. But sometimes these companies do survive to increase their profitability—for Bain. Bain then sells them at a tremendous profit. If these companies continue to thrive, they might hire more workers, but rarely the same ones as before and even more rarely at the wages and benefits of previous workers. Unions rarely survive. Pensions and other benefits rarely survive. In other words, Bain and perhaps new owners and stockholders benefit, while previous workers lose decent or good jobs and new workers get crappy ones. More often, however, the work of venture equity firms results in companies being shut down and sold off. In many cases, Bain found that the highest profit came from taking companies that were still making money and decimating them to make more money by selling the skeletal remains, piece by piece. Portioning off and selling business scraps and bits created more profits for Bain than maintaining decent companies with good jobs at status quo profits. Bain made its money out of the bones and rubble of the companies it destroyed and the workers it let go. *Kill it to save it.*[12]

Other groups support the individual and corporate pursuit of profit over all other values—not because of a misinformed faith in trickle-down economics, but because they have a devout commitment to a mythical sense of "freedom" as unveiled by a supposedly laissez-faire economic system. Instead of the more pragmatic (albeit wrong) belief that the economy works better when it creates at the top and trickles down to the bottom, this group doesn't really concern itself with the efficiency or effectiveness of the system—these folks are driven by pure principles of political (constitutionalists) and economic (libertarians) freedoms. While this version of "survival of the fittest" might be enough to make Darwin roll over, the actual policy implications are equally startling. What would our country look like if government did *not* regulate health and safety, education and inequality, and the fundamental principles of democracy itself?

For a constitutionalist/libertarian like Ron Paul (Rand's dad), the major functions of government are: "to provide national defense, a court system for civil disputes, a criminal justice system for acts of force and fraud, and little else." He believes that the United States' "respect for individual liberty, free markets, and limited constitutional government produced the strongest, most prosperous country in the world."[13] A principled theory suggesting that unrestricted individuals and unregulated markets would produce the public good is an attractive vision, but one with little evidence of success. Individuals free from laws and regulations against manipulating markets have proven to produce mostly avarice and exploitation. If public goods like education, communications, transportation, and so on were left to the private sector and neoliberal markets, as Paul suggests, who would develop the systems of health and safety and schools and roads people need to actually compete—unless they turned tremendous profits? What is good for the general public's welfare is not always the most profitable for private industry, and vice versa. Later in this book, I demonstrate just how a libertarian, neoliberal approach to policy making in areas of education, health care and safety, government, and the economy itself actually destroys these systems' effectiveness.

Thus—for a variety of reasons and in a variety of powerful people's interests—we seem to have adopted a poisonous ideological blend of corporate capitalist ideology and hyper-individualism that, in and of itself, limits public policy discussions and leaves us with absurd laws and policy decisions. We pass food defamation laws prohibiting the critique of an increasingly unnatural and unhealthy food system, yet we refuse to adequately regulate campaign donations because—in the words of Senator Mitch McConnell, "money is speech."[14] We dismantle criminal pretrial release programs that in county after county successfully reduced overcrowded jails, kept people working, families together, and saved cash-strapped communities millions of dollars. Why? Because the bail bonds industry spent even more millions to protect their profits by supporting candidates who promised to end the program.[15] The protection of harmful practices or the destruction of productive public policies for the benefit of private sector profits all sold to and bought by a mainstream public under the guise of freedom from big government is the core of the kill it to save it paradigm.

From Killing Fields to Killing Us

On January 8, 2011, shoppers and bystanders witnessed the shooting of United States Congresswoman Gabrielle "Gabby" Giffords and 17 others, including a 9-year-old bystander who later died. The perpetrator, Jared Loughner, was a mentally ill man. He used a 9 mm Glock 19 semiautomatic weapon with a high-capacity ammunition clip. While the extent of his illness, political opinions, and so on have never been fully determined, his carnage raised two sets of important issues relevant to understanding how "kill it to save it" common sense not only pervades our culture and policy making, but is also an extremely dangerous mindset for making laws and shaping our society. And it is literally killing us.

First, immediately following the shooting, pundits began a heated debate about the influence that heightened political rhetoric (especially the kind of violent gun-related metaphors brandished, over and over, by prominent Republicans) may have had over the shooter. But little focus was given to either the current status of mental health care in the United States or the ridiculously easy access we have to violent assault weapons whose only function is to kill human beings. It's one of those perfectly American ironies—tens of millions of Americans cannot obtain mental health care, while most mentally ill people can get any gun with ease.

If the National Rifle Association (NRA) and its supporters are correct in saying that "guns don't kill people, people do,"[16] one might think it best to be extremely careful, erring on the side of great caution, to prohibit many people from having guns. The only federal restrictions that hinder gun purchases are: age (over 18); conviction for violent crime, domestic violence, or other felony; involuntary commitment to a mental institution or court-determined mental incompetence; dishonorable discharge from the military; renouncing of American citizenship; or being a fugitive or drug addict. While some states require licenses or permits to purchase and carry guns, others—like Alaska; Arizona; Arkanas; Idaho; Kansas; Kentucky; Maine; Mississippi; Montana; New Hampshire; New Mexico; Utah; Vermont; Wyoming, and West Virginia—don't. In many of these states, citizens can carry concealed firearms without restriction or permits as well. In perhaps the worst of all ironies, Arizona legalized the carrying of concealed firearms and other weapons without a permit at the same time that they cut state Medicaid coverage, leaving thousands of previously diagnosed mentally ill residents without health care. The same is now true of Alaska and Wyoming. Almost two-dozen more states are still considering legislation allowing firearms without *any* licensing or permit. Eight states (Colorado; Idaho; Kansas; Mississippi; Oregon; Texas; Utah; and Wisconsin) now allow concealed weapons to be carried on college campuses—and people worried about grade inflation before.

Second, regardless of any one politician's or pundit's violent rhetoric—and regardless of Loughner's actual political opinions and affiliations—one of the major targets of the "kill it to save it" mentality has been government itself. While Republicans long ran against "big government" or "too much government," Reagan's 1980 campaign solidified a kind of common sense about evil government liberalism, incompetence, and encroaching fascism. Regardless of facts about the government's role in advocating or protecting the public welfare, Reagan asserted over and over that government *was* the problem. More recently, George W. Bush emphasized this ideology in his efforts to dismantle everything from public education, food stamps, and the Environmental Protection Agency (EPA) to Medicaid and Medicare. But Bush's major target was the big daddy of them all: Social Security. As Nobel Prize economist Paul Krugman suggested, "privatizing" Social Security was mostly a euphemism for killing it.[17] Many of Bush's domestic policy architects, such as Stephen Moore of the Cato Institute, believed that: "Social Security is the soft underbelly of the welfare state … If you can jab your spear through that, you can undermine the whole welfare state."[18] Arguing that only the private sector could provide economic security, quality health care, education, and so on, Bush called for massive deregulation as a strategy for improving *all* domestic policies, not just financial ones. End government spending in all areas of government (except defense and corporate subsidies) and deregulate the private sector to empower its takeover of social welfare programs.

The strategy was (and is) an utter failure. Increasingly privatized health care not only left more and more millions of Americans without health insurance, but also meant that the insurance most people had cost more and covered less. The privatized school choice movement—so alluring in the 1990s and early 2000s—also lost some of its steam; charter schools failed at significant rates and private companies like Edison (in Philadelphia and San Francicsco) and White Hat (throughout Ohio) have been kicked out by dissatisfied school boards around the country.[19] But the biggest deregulatory flop has been in the financial industry itself, leading to the worst economic crisis since the Great Depression. The crisis was so bad that even Bush was forced to use government money to bail out the industry—not the kind of move antigovernment activists envisioned when they selected him. In the end, however, such actions always expose the hypocrisy of corporate hegemony and neoliberalism.

But antigovernment rhetoric only intensified with Obama's campaign. As Bush's failed strategies at home and abroad doomed Republicans in the 2006 and 2008 elections, they ratcheted up paranoid and mean-spirited vitriol even more. By the time Obama had won, the country's economy was *so* bad little could be done in the short run to stave off serious recession and unemployment. Yet, Republicans ramped up anti-government rhetoric and blamed Obama for everything. Meanwhile, Obama's biography allowed the antigovernment rhetoric to revive a variety of age-old, tried and true forms of ideological hatred. Obama was Black and his race alone stoked the still burning fires of white supremacy and hatred. Obama was a foreigner and a Muslim (neither of which is true—but why let the facts stand in the way of constructing a good anti-talisman?). He initiated policies suggesting that government should play a role in improving the general welfare (expanding health coverage, addressing climate change, regulating Wall Street banditry, and so on), so Republicans tagged him a communist, socialist, and "tax-and-spend liberal" (as if these were all the same thing). By the time the Tea Party took shape in the summer of 2009, it didn't take much to get a crowd of justifiably frustrated people all lathered up in fear of and hatred for a Black Muslim Socialist Terrorist President.

The angry vitriol against Obama eventually seeped down to other (primarily Democrat) officials. The repeated rhetorical violence from the mouths of many prominent Republicans and right-wing media personalities created a cultural legitimacy for such hatred, threats and harassment against congresspersons and senators increased as well. Such threats, in fact, rose over 300% in the first months of 2010 and dozens of congressional offices were vandalized after the historic March vote to overhaul health care policy.[20] Regardless of Loughner's political affiliations or ideology (if any), his act occurred at a particular historical and political moment at which the *idea* of killing government (and by extrapolation its human officials) in order to save America (or "take it back," as Tea Partiers would contend) doesn't seem so farfetched.

Since Giffords' shooting in 2011, she and many others have led campaigns to regulate handgun use, outlaw high-capacity clips, strengthen background checks, and introduce other legislative and policy initiatives to reduce gun violence in general and mass shootings in particular. And since the January 2011 shooting, Americans have witnessed dozens of mass shooting incidents with four or more people killed by one gunman in one event—including in Aurora, Colorado (12 dead, 58 injured); Newtown, Connecticut (27 killed, 1 injured); the Washington, D.C. Navy Yard (13 killed, 3 injured); Santa Barbara, California (7 dead, 7 injured); Charleston, South Carolina (9 dead, 1 injured); and Umpqua Community College (9 dead; 9 injured).[21] These cities and towns are now imbued with symbols of senseless violence perpetrated by emotionally disturbed men who had easier access to deadly weapons than they did to mental health care. But each incident quickly fades from the public's consciousness as contemporary media barrage the senses with rapid-fire images and information that actually degrades public memory and our ability to process and reflect on events.

When in Doubt, Shut it Down

I began writing this book on the heels of a government shutdown in October, 2013. For over two weeks, national museums, parks, and libraries closed; federal agencies charged with protecting people's health and wellbeing could not conduct reviews, inspections, or investigations; and the government itself lost billions of dollars in direct and indirect costs. According to the Office of Management and Budget, government workers were especially hard hit as "The shutdown followed a three-year pay freeze for Federal employees, cuts in training and support, and, for hundreds of thousands of workers, administrative furloughs earlier this year because of sequestration."[22] Most government workers live like most middle-class folks: paycheck to paycheck. Losing a couple weeks' pay—even if it's only "deferred"—can wreak havoc on family budgeting and grocery shopping. Even more devastating was the shutdown's impact on poor people, who depend on various programs and assistance. Meals on Wheels suffered cuts and some food programs closed down. Disability checks and other subsidies, such as the Special Supplemental Nutrition Program for Women, Infants and Children (WIC) and Temporary Assistance for Needy Families (TANF) were lost. Tens of thousands of Head Start kids saw their preschool classes cancelled—imagine the impact on their parents, who depend on such programs for childcare, too. Less measurable, but perhaps more cruel, was the intensification of stress from increased instability. As journalist Sasha Abramsky explained one week into the shutdown:

> We don't know how long the shutdown will last, and that uncertainty, too, is harder on the poor. The stress of not knowing what tomorrow will bring can be debilitating. If you're on food stamps … the prospect of not being able to pay for food in November is anxiety-provoking in a way that puts even more pressure on families that already have their fair share of it.[23]

According to Boston community organizer, Horace Small, cities around the country have homeland security and natural disaster plans, "but nobody was prepared for hundreds of thousands of poor folks who lost what little support they had to pay for food, heat, shelter, child care, and transportation back and forth to work."[24] It has been suggested, however, that the shutdown was not a natural disaster—instead it was a planned and purposeful event driven primarily by a former Republican presidential candidate, a large group of Tea Party activists, and their very wealthy benefactors. They believe the best way to save the country is by stopping the government from protecting and supporting the public welfare. But *how* do exclusive, powerful interests create mainstream ideological and institutional support among working- and middle-class people for policies that threaten to actually damage those people's lives? How are people convinced to support "kill it to save it" policies when they are, in fact, the ones being killed in the end?

By the time you read this book, you may not remember the shutdown at all—such is the state of a 1,440/24/7 news cycle. 1440 is the number of minutes in a day. Eventually, seconds will comprise an important part of our daily consciousness, resulting in an 86,400/1,440/24/7 cycle. In a text, Twitter, Tumblr, Instagram and Snapchat world, we may already be there. It may simply be intellectually and emotionally impossible to process information, analyze and comprehend its impact, and act accordingly.

Writing about the present poses a serious challenge to authors all too sensitive to the increasingly ephemeral lifecycle of words and things. A moment's "breaking news" ages quickly into "current events," ripens rapidly into "recent reports," matures immediately into "yesterday's news," eventually fades into the past and evaporates into a historical consciousness already made obsolete by the death of knowledge and reason. Thoughtful consideration and meaningful reflection surrendered long ago to data points, infomercials and a "this just in" appetite. The possibility for substantive debate, intellectual reflection, and evidence-based practice has been forcefully submerged by intake overload and the psychic need to deflect persistent images of suffering or avoid the constant inhaling of commercially saturated air. Call it strategic avoidance or selective amnesia, but even cognitive dissonance results in enough discomfort that folks realize something is wrong. Not so much anymore.

Sociologist Georg Simmel warned that the overstimulation of early-20th-century metropolitan life resulted in a mental and emotional reaction characterized by what he termed "a blasé attitude." City life, Simmel suggested, "Agitates the nerves to their strongest reactivity for such a long time that they finally cease to react at all." He continued:

> In the same way, through the rapidity and contradictoriness of their changes, more harmless impressions force such violent responses, tearing the nerves so brutally hither and thither that their last reserves of strength are spent; and if one remains in the same milieu [these nerves] have no time to gather new strength. An incapacity thus emerges to react to new sensations with the appropriate energy. This constitutes that blasé attitude.

Brought on by the intensification of mental, emotional, and physical stimuli, individuals respond—they *must* respond—by blunting any effective sense of discrimination. It is easy to understand why we prefer not to act rationally—it's too damn hard.

Simmel concluded:

> This does not mean that the objects are not perceived, but rather that the meaning and differing values of things, and thereby the things themselves, are experienced as insubstantial. They appear to the blasé person in an evenly flat and gray tone; no one object deserves preference over any other.[25]

Meaning and knowledge are replaced by information and shock, but even shock doesn't last long enough to do more than add calloused layers of anti-intellectual and anti-emotional epidermis. (Gil Scott-Heron once claimed that "America leads the world in being shocked."[26]) Time moves constantly, but stands still. The irony of modern life for Simmel was that the intellectual essence of human life—the ability, if not the actual basic human *need*, to discern and discriminate—lay dying amid the contemporary miracles of mankind's technology, architecture, and engineering. We had created the very physical and psychological circumstance that would eventually destroy us.

Nearly a century later, another sociologist, George Rizer, would tackle a similar dynamic in *The Mcdonaldization of Society* (1993).[27] Rizer's thesis was that late-20th-century life had grown even more fast and furious, and an increasingly rationalized, cost—benefit hegemony now dominated almost all aspects of economic, political, and social life. The four main tenets of McDonaldization were:

1. *Efficiency*: The optimum method of completing a task; the rational determination of the best mode of production. Individuality is not allowed.
2. *Calculability*: Assessment of outcomes based on quantifiable rather than subjective criteria—quantity over quality. They sell the Big Mac, not the Good Mac.
3. *Predictability*: The production process is organized to guarantee uniformity of product and standardized outcomes. All shopping malls look the same and all highway exits have similar fast food joints and retailers.

4. *Control*: The substitution of more predictable non-human labor for human labor, either through automation or the deskilling of the work force.

But the ultimate logic of Rizer's theory was how it demonstrated the "irrationality of rationality." According to Rizer, "Irrationality means that rational systems are unreasonable systems. By that I mean that they deny the basic humanity, the human reason, of the people who work within or are served by them" (p. 154). Put another way, the logical conclusion of McDonaldization is to produce the most "rationalized" product. In the fast food business, this might be McDonald's Big Mac meal. But averaging at 1,100 calories with 50 g of fat and 150 g of carbohydrate, it is hard to imagine thinking of this as a meal; it does more damage than good to the body. Add eating this content to the sedentary, highly individualized, drive-thru lifestyle—with its immense carbon footprint to boot—and we have developed an irrational food system that promises to do the exact opposite of what food is supposed to do: keep us healthy and alive. Instead, our food production system and attendant lifestyle continue to make us sick.

Has America as a nation developed a basic common sense about public policy that suggests we must destroy things to save them? Have we become too overwhelmed by the flood of data to process and comprehend our own impending doom? Or have we become so blasé that we can't muster the passion and critical engagement to care? In the place of an active and engaged citizenry—dumbed down by corporatized and McDonaldized education and slothed into apathy by poor nutrition and sedentary telecommuting, the stress of low-wage, high-speed workplaces and the narcotics we take to deal with stress—we have nothing left to fight with and perhaps no sense of what we would be fighting for. Most of us have become a growing mass of people with an inkling that something is wrong but without the tools to analyze what it is or the moxie to try to do something about it.

In the wake of such inaction, the corporate hunger for profit—justified by a rationalized laissez-faire hegemony and simplified narrative that "they" are to blame, not "us"—allows mega companies, and their governmental and media minions, to destroy whatever may be in the public interest to save it as a potential marketplace for private profit, not as a thriving human society. The myth of individualism and the primacy of corporate hegemony have left us with a very narrow ideological framework within which to navigate a moral compass already falsely fixed on perpetual economic growth and Gordon Gecko's mantra, "Greed is good."[28] How else could we explain a large swath of the public deciding that the best person to save us from this hyper-capitalist, neofascist morass should be Donald Trump. In a final show of misdirected frustration and ill-informed anger, millions are voicing their discontent with corporate banditry and corrupt politics by getting on the boss's own bandwagon. Can we find a way out of this mess?

Perhaps. I hope so. But first we must examine deeply how and why our major institutions fail so miserably and consider both the causes of flawed structures and the possibilities to change them. The following three parts investigate myriad ways in which we continue to undermine the public good with policy aimed at destroying it—all in the name of saving our schools, saving our communities, saving our economy, saving ourselves, and saving our nation. And while an important part of such common sense requires the kind of demonization of "the Other" and mythologizing of "us" and "ours" that Reagan so ingeniously inscribed into our contemporary cultural lexicon, the most destructive yet pervasive messaging remains the insidious sense that people *can't* really do anything to change the problems we face. We can! But only if we comprehend the scope of our problems and dismantle the hegemonic ways of thinking that keep us apathetic and paralyzed—yet perversely engaged in and supportive of the toxic lives that are killing us.

PART 2
Learning American Style: The Life and Death of American Education

overview: History of Learning American Style

> Universal education is the power, which is destined to overthrow every species of hierarchy. It is destined to remove all artificial inequality and leave the natural inequalities to find their true level. With the artificial inequalities of caste, rank, title, blood, birth, race, color, sex, etc., will fall nearly all the oppression, prejudice, enmity, and injustice, that humanity is now subject to. (Lester Frank Ward, *Education*, *c.*1872)[1]

> A great general has said that the only good Indian is a dead one, and that high sanction of his destruction has been an enormous factor in promoting Indian massacres. In a sense, I agree with the sentiment, but only in this: that all the Indian there is in the race should be dead. Kill the Indian in him, and save the man. (Captain Richard H. Pratt, Founder, Carlisle Indian Industrial School, 1892)[2]

The truth shall set us free. But the educational system we designed to help us find the truth is severely damaged. How it got this way documents a labyrinthine tale of horrific hypocrisy and Herculean hope. Education in the United States has represented our darkest fears and deepest dreams about who we are, and should be, as a people. The ability to discover, learn, and apply knowledge in making a better world still informs our loftiest vision for universal education. Unfortunately, our current educational policies and practices are killing that dream—primarily because we have handed over the reins of educational reform to marketeers and Madmen.

In the mid 1990s, equity researchers at Lehman Brothers sited education as a potentially "hot industry," comparing it to the health care industry of the 1970s. With schools undergoing serious financial and social challenges and movements for educational reform growing around the nation, financial strategists concluded that privatization could be positioned as both a solution to real challenges and a formula for making multimillions in return. Educational maintenance organizations (EMOs)—private sector groups that would provide educational services ranging from school district management to charter school development and operations—could do for education what health maintenance organizations (HMOs) had done for health care. Lehman's "investment thesis" could not have been simpler or more brilliant; examining its claims offers unique insight into the assumptions and misconceptions of "kill it to save it" ideology as applied to education.

Lehman researchers wrote:

> The classic investment opportunity involves a company that has a systematic solution to a problem and how successful that company may become depends on how big the problem is and how well the company solves it. ... The shift we see [in education] is a system going from a government-run monopoly with little accountability and, by definition, no competition, to a market driven system that competes on price and quality. As in health care, the delivery of service and the change in funding sources will be critically interactive as an investment driver. ... [These shifts] do not occur overnight, but with the increasing discussion, consideration, and implementation of charter schools, school choice, private management of public schools and vouchers,

> we are certain that the traditional way education and child care have been delivered and funded will continue to change, and there is no going back. We believe that companies that offer innovative solutions in this changing environment will offer significant opportunities to investors.[3]

It is worth closely examining this passage because, despite the always haunting sense that investment brokers are trying to sell you something, a strategy research document suggests at least some objectivity and earnestness. One reads this with a feeling that the writers believed what they said. Thus, the opening statement about the "classic investment opportunity" argues that part of successful investment has to do with quality of the product—how well one "solves" the problem to be addressed. But EMOs have proven otherwise: despite mega failures in town after town, city after city, state after state, over twenty years of privatization has still produced billions of dollars in profit for the Edison, Mosaica and White Hat companies of the world—regardless of their utterly dismal performances in school district after school district.[4]

In part, the "problem" for Lehman Brothers and its investors was always more about "where to make money next" than how to solve educational institutions' greatest challenges. Compared to the example of Bain's venture capital approach, Lehman's "classical investment opportunities" failed to be upfront about capitalism's prime directive: making money. Profitmaking will always be the ultimate goal of any privatized system or institution. Corporations are hammers and the rest of us nails. For Lehman, solving the problem of poor education is merely a matter of finding out how to extract more profit from it. By definition, more profit is better.

To actually "fix" education first demands recognizing what we expect from it to begin with. What is education and what do we want from schools? Sociologists have long examined education as an institution responsible for the reproduction of a society's most pervasive values and necessary skills.[5] Schools teach children what they need to know to operate effectively in a highly stratified economic, social, and political system that precedes them. But education is also charged with providing students the critical and analytical tools to compete and innovate, create and change. By necessity then, American education as an institution and set of social practices carries with it two kinds of conflicts and contradictions.

On the one hand, education socializes students into the existing dominant culture and ruling ideas of the age. On the other hand, schools become a terrain on which opposing political and social sensibilities collide. Schools purport to teach all students the same ideas, facts, figures, and philosophies in an effort to "equalize" or "democratize"—as well as "Americanize"—our population. Yet, how can we equalize an already stratified nation when schools so effectively reproduce inequality based on funding mechanisms that discriminate between wealthy and poor communities and between public and private institutions as well? How can we democratize and empower individuals if we force them to deny their history and heritage, identity and culture? And how can we encourage students to compete, analyze, and innovate without recognizing that such education may *challenge* the same conventions, norms, and values we hope to reproduce in the first place? These questions have guided and often plagued the history of American education.

I begin Part 2 below with a historical look at schooling in America and the ways in which economic and social inequality always lay at the foundation of educational objectives. Assimilated immigrants, obedient workers, and an obsequious middle class comprised the education industry's finished product. Yet education remained, at least ideologically, the institution most responsible for fueling social mobility and economic prosperity. Thus, the persistence of poverty and inequality resulted in constant calls for school reform.[6] This section looks at how current efforts to reform education adopt the "language" of addressing inequality but in fact undermine the potential of education to be a public good by promoting budget cuts and privatization. Lehman Brothers' treatise on commoditizing education essentially wrote the script for today's educational reforms. In fact, "kill it to save it" policy making has degraded both educational institutions *and* the knowledge they create.

Learning Outcomes: A Brief History of American Education

From the outset, our national leaders had seriously conflicting ideas about education's potential to empower and disempower. On the one hand, early slave codes from the 18th and 19th centuries prohibited the teaching of reading and writing to slaves. North Carolina even outlawed "giving or selling books or pamphlets to slaves," explaining, "'teaching slaves to read and write, tends to excite dissatisfaction in their minds, and to produce insurrection and rebellion.'"[7] Education *could* play a role in liberating people, so Southern lawmakers banned it for Black slaves. Slave codes prohibiting education for the growing slave population helped draw distinctions between Blacks and poor whites, giving tangible meaning to the formation of race and racism in the U.S.[8]

On the other hand, from the early 1800s to the early 1900s, the U.S. promoted Indian Residential Schools to teach Native Americans how to be *Americans*, not Indians. As Captain Pratt's aforementioned comments suggest, government policy evolved from violent destruction, displacement and resettlement to a more cultural form of genocide in which "civilizing" native peoples required them to cast off their history and culture and adopt "individualistic" and "American" values. According to Indian Commissioner George Manypenny, assimilation mandated that Indians learn to say "I" instead of "we," "me" instead of "us," "mine" instead of "ours." However, many native communities resisted, as: "A significant body of tribal opinion saw white education for what it was: an invitation to cultural suicide."[9]

Similar educational forays into forced assimilation occurred in the southwest, as corporations and regional governments established Chicano/a boarding schools specifically designed to house, educate, and train young Mexican women. Not only did business owners and politicians hope to create an obedient and effective supply of female domestic workers, but policy makers also pursued women as the purveyors of cultural values and social practices in their own families and communities. The next generation of immigrant children could be purged of ethnicity and traditional culture. "Go after the women," wrote educator Alfred White, "and you may save the second generation for America."[10]

By the early 20th century, education as a form of "Americanization" played a large role in the expansion of public schooling around the nation. Despite three decades of massive immigration from Eastern Europe, Asia, and Mexico, Americanization remained largely about Anglo conformity and subservient assimilation. Thus, educational policy promoted schools as the institution:

> to break up these groups or settlements, to assimilate and amalgamate these people as a part of our American race, and to implant in their children … the Anglo-Saxon conception of righteousness, law and order, and popular government, and to awaken in them a reverence for our democratic institutions."[11]

The "Americanization Movement," according to historian Roger Daniels, "was an organized campaign to insure political loyalty and cultural conformity." Schools not only taught English and Civics, but promoted hygiene and fitness, "middle class values, and discipline more appropriate to the factory than the classroom."[12]

Yet cultural assimilation and creating a conservative, racialized American identity was not the only goal of early public education. Ultimately, American schools would mirror and buttress the rise of industrial production and monopoly capitalism. Most early support for mass education came from financiers and industrialists, who realized that schools promised an effective training ground in which new workers would be instilled with an "industrial morality." Early factory owners had struggled to transform farm girls, children, rural immigrants, and independent craftsmen into the efficient and obedient "hands" necessary to run machinery in the new factory systems.[13] Far from being concerned with the "intellectual" development of working-class youth, manufacturers—and the school boards they elected—espoused the "object of education" to be more than "mere intellectual instruction." Instead, they proclaimed the primary goal was "a life-long formation of character" composed of "habits" such as: "attention, self-reliance ... order and neatness, politeness and courtesy ... and [especially] punctuality."[14]

Mid-19th-century schools designed their classrooms and planned their curricula with the needs of industrial capitalism in mind. As one writer in *Massachusetts Teacher* explained, a proper curricula guaranteed that:

> the habit of prompt action in the performance of the duty required by the boy, by the teacher at school, becomes in the man of business confirmed ... what has been instilled in the mind of the pupil, as a principle, becomes thoroughly recognized by the man as of the first importance in the transaction of business."[15]

Lowell educational reformer Theodore Edson even designed "a special clock for classroom use which divided up the school day neatly into thirty-two ten-minute recitation periods."[16] The efficiency and rationalization—as well as the habits of deference and order—needed to prepare workers for industrial production would be provided by mass public education and primarily funded by public moneys for the benefit of private corporate owners.

Political economist Harry Braverman described the evolution of industrial production and monopoly capitalism as a process that deskilled workers, increasingly taking human activity and knowledge from labor and infusing them into the machinery, thus reducing labor costs as workers became interchangeable or dispensable.[17] But he also argued that a necessary component of industrial growth derived from manufacturers' ability to *manage* workers by placing the authority and discipline they wanted "under the cap" of the worker himself. This type of "manufactured consent" also lay at the heart of Horace Mann's mission to create dutiful citizens:

> A stable body politic and a smoothly functioning factory alike required citizens and workers who had

> embraced and taken as their own the values and objectives of those in authority. Schools might do better than to instill obedience; they might promote self-control.[18]

"Educated" workers not only became more effective, efficient, and obedient; they also saw their own futures linked to the authority and advance of their bosses in the workplace and their municipal leaders in the community.

Throughout the late 19th and early 20th centuries, the same scientific management principles introduced by Frederic Winslow Taylor to heighten industrial efficiency would find their way into the educational systema.[19] Increased rationalization and standardization accompanied the expanding curriculum necessary to train both a burgeoning industrial workforce as well as a growing professional managerial class of "brain workers." In the mid 1920s, Robert and Helen Lynd observed classrooms in Muncie, Indiana and reported:

> The school, like the factory, is a thoroughly regimented world. Immovable seats in orderly rows fix the sphere of activity of each child. ... Bells divide the day into periods [and] by the third or fourth year practically all movement is forbidden except the marching from one set of seats to another between periods, a brief interval of prescribed exercise daily, and periods of manual training or home economics once or twice a week."[20]

After the Second World War, education (especially higher education) was once again called on to establish a conservative American identity and to serve the changing economic needs of corporate leaders. The G.I. Bill sent millions of veterans to rapidly expanding public and private universities as preparation for the new economy.[21] Clark Kerr, Chancellor of the University of California—Berkeley (the pinnacle of America's research institutions and flagship for the nation's largest university system), explained that higher education would be called "to educate previously unimagined numbers of students; to respond to the expanding claims of national service; to merge its activities with industry as never before." He continued:

> Characteristic of this transformation is the growth of the knowledge industry, which is coming to permeate government and business, and to draw into it more and more people raised to higher and higher levels of skill … [as] knowledge production is growing at about twice the rate of the rest of the economy. What the railroads did for the second half of the last century, and the automobile for the first half of this century, may be done for the second half of this century by the knowledge industry; and that is, to serve as the focal point for national growth.[22]

Educational institutions would continue to serve a stratifying function by producing knowledge as a profitable commodity and knowledge workers who were efficient, obedient, and committed to corporate growth and commercial consumption.

Meanwhile, McCarthyism and the House Un-American Activities Committee (HUAC) targeted universities and those intellectuals and scholars who might be critical of corporate hegemony and arrogant affluence. In Washington and California, Boards of Trustees purged faculty who refused to sign loyalty oaths or had been members of the Communist Party. They rationalized that Communists could not "think freely" and thus were inherently "intellectually dishonest" and threatened academic freedom. In a twist on "kill it to save it," colleges censored their faculty to protect academic freedom. Nationwide, redbaiting resulted in 69 members of faculty fired for "political" reasons—almost half from the University of California system.[23]

McCarthyism's initial success—along with the massive postwar expansion of public education at all levels—seemed to suggest that education in the United States would be, everywhere and for everyone, a celebration of Cold War consensus, national and corporate triumphalism, unrestrained prosperity, and what Sociologist Daniel Bell called "the end of ideology."[24] But such a hegemonic convergence had its cracks and cranks. As early as 1951, C. Wright Mills condemned colleges that "partnered" with

CEOs and politicians to fill their "personnel needs" and create a "good future" defined and measured by success in the "great salesroom" of humanity. The finished product of the educational machine was "the successful man," a good employee within a "society of specialists."[25] Other social scientists suggested the period rife with "lonely crowds" of "organizational men" duped into complacency by advertising's "hidden persuaders."[26] By the late 1950s, Kenneth Galbraith warned that private consumption crowded out public goods and the country quickly became a society with state-of-the-art automobiles but crumbling subways and busses; luxurious suburban homes but resource-starved public schools. The precursor to "kill it to save it" policy making had already suggested that private gains were in the public's interest. But some were not so sure.[27]

HUAC had actually inspired massive protests on college campuses as students around the country recognized the hypocrisy of practicing paranoid censorship while promoting progressive education. Meanwhile, the Civil Rights Movement—fueled by *Brown vs. Board of Education* and bus boycotts, lunch counter sit-ins and Freedom Rides—heightened the critical imagination of students and teachers everywhere. As Clark Kerr aligned knowledge production with national prosperity and economic mobility, his own campus exploded with one of the largest student demonstrations in U.S. history. The Free Speech Movement (FSM) criticized America's triumphalism at home and abroad, embracing the Civil Rights Movement (and eventually the antiwar movement) as a great awakening. FSM leader Mario Savio made it clear, however, that the corporatization of higher education itself was the movement's primary target. Standing on the steps of Berkeley's Sproul Hall, Savio told a crowd of student demonstrators:

> if this [university] is a firm, and if the Board of Regents are the Board of Directors, and if President Kerr … is the manager, then … the faculty are a bunch of employees and we're [students] the raw material! But we're a bunch of raw materials that don't mean to … have any process upon us. Don't mean to be made into any product! Don't mean

> to end up being bought by some clients of the University, be they the government, be they industry, be they organized labor, be they anyone! We're human beings! There is a time when the operation of the machine becomes so odious, makes you so sick at heart, that you can't take part. You can't even passively take part! And you've got to put your bodies upon the gears and upon the wheels, upon the levers, upon all the apparatus, and you've got to make it stop! And you've got to indicate to the people who run it, to the people who own it—that unless you're free, the machine will be prevented from working at all!![28]

This sense of activism among students not only awoke the nation from a political slumber and gave way to revolutionary consciousness but also created a belief in—and even a commitment to—"putting one's body on the line." A radicalized education in the 1960s created a "movement" representing what Todd Gitlin called the "fusion of collective will and moral style." Gitlin claims: "The movement didn't simply demand, it *did*. By taking action, not just a position, it affirmed the right to do so … The New Left's first raison d'etre was to take actions which testified not only to the existence of injustice, but to the imperative—and possibility—of fighting it."[29]

Eventually, the social movements of the 1960s would result in sweeping changes to education around the nation, from kindergartens through graduate schools as well as new alternative schools such as "open universities" on dozens of colleges across the nation. Similarly, civil rights groups ran Head Start programs throughout the South while the Black Panther Party ran free breakfast programs and Freedom Schools for young children in New York, Chicago, Oakland, and elsewhere. The Student Nonviolent Coordinating Committee's own Freedom Schools taught adults literacy, civics, history, and the material they would need to know in order to register to vote.[30] Colleges and universities not only broke down a Eurocentric canon of colonialist and credentialed knowledge, but also adopted affirmative action policies that literally changed campus life forever. Institutions also increased their transparency in relation to military research, corporate connections, and FBI and CIA recruitment. The War on Poverty resulted in numerous educational programs for poor children and children of color. Again, the late 1960s through the 1970s promised progressive changes that could improve society and they would begin with educational equality for all—from cradle through college graduation.[31]

These policies, like the movements that inspired them, would disappear all too soon. Some diminished over time or morphed into market-based initiatives while others were attacked for being "too political" or promoting "reverse racism." Head Start, for example, began as a community action and organizing program in the mid 1960s, but by the 1970s morphed into a narrowly defined early childhood literacy project. Links to civil rights and other social movements that drove early Head Start success in the South were purged as racist Dixiecrats threatened federal officials and Ku Klux Klan (KKK) groups trashed project offices and intimidated workers.[32] Eventually, conservative court decisions and the growing "kill it to save it" mentality decimated much of what remained from progressive educational policies in the 1960s and 1970s. Still, attacking and destroying effective government subsidized programs and public education as a whole was ultimately about redistributing wealth and political power back to those who don't benefit directly from programs for the poor, working class, and even middle class. As 1960s educational reforms were defeated, market-based privatized "reforms" filled the gap. Lehman Brothers captured the spirit and language of this transformation and ushered in a wholesale turnover of public institutions to private profiteers.

THREE

How the Knowledge Economy Killed Knowledge, and Other Scary Stories Out of School

> In Hollywood films and television documentaries, the battle lines are clearly drawn. Traditional public schools are bad; their supporters are apologists for the unions. Those who advocate for charter schools, virtual schooling and "school choice" are reformers; their supporters insist they are championing the rights of minorities. … It is a compelling narrative, one that gives us easy villains and ready-made solutions. It appeals to values Americans traditionally cherished—choice, freedom, optimism, and a latent distrust of government. There is only one problem with this narrative. It is wrong. (Diane Ravitch, *Reign of Error*[1])

Lehman Brothers: From Planned Obsolescence to Educational Profiteering

While Head Start—a program proven over and over again to successfully address at least some of the educational challenges faced by poor children—barely survives, the privatization movement in education flourishes—despite little to no evidence that it works. To the contrary, growing experience suggests privatizing schools is an utter failure. Districts in Philadelphia, Las Vegas, Dallas, Baltimore, and dozens of other smaller towns and cities have famously booted Edison, one of the nation's largest EMOs. It's been reported that Mosaica, another major EMO, saw 27 of its first 36 contract schools shut down or taken back by local school districts.[2] Although mounting evidence declares privatized education a failure, school privatization experiences ever growing popularity.

Why? Because Americans *want* privatization to work. Combine what Ravitch calls "traditionally cherished values," such as choice and freedom, to the recently hardwired penchant to blindly trust the private over the public sector; evidence and experience pale in comparison to an irrational "kill it to save it" common sense. The contemporary public policy mantra is that governments are ineffective and wasteful, and corporate driven policies address problems with innovation, efficiency, and skill. In my own community, a recently successful candidate for school board ran on the slogan, "The last thing the school board needs is another educator." Thus, we should not be surprised that our "kill it to save it" mentality in policy-making heralds educational policies that have no proven track record, but appeal to base emotional levels of what has become "common sense." Privatization just feels right; it feels good. It's not about evidence; it's about effervescence.

The denial of evidence is a good thing for EMOs because most research continues to disappoint. Major studies demonstrate that the majority of private charter schools have *at best* similar results to public non-charter schools. Quite often, they perform worse. In one of the largest recent studies of charter schools, Stanford researchers again found little evidence to support the claim that they outperformed or even matched traditional public schools in similar districts with similar student populations. After more than twenty years of the charter school movement—which included privately run, publically run, and non-profit run charters—assessments continue to show *at best* mixed results on student achievements. And the positive steps seem related primarily to increased resources, longer school days, and longer semesters.[3]

Still, conservative think-tanks continue to promote privatization, charters, and "choice" as saviors for public education and poor children, and such programs even become a significant part of the Obama—Duncan "race to the top" policy as well. If charter schools don't outperform traditional public schools and result in the loss of democratic public oversight and accountability, why have they become the bipartisan golden boy of public education policy? The primary answer is money, but the rationale for privatization is its appeal to "kill it to save it" sensibilities—which, after all, have money at their root. In the overview of this section, I argued that corporate interests in mass public education helped shape the contours of early policy making. Everything from curriculum and instruction to planning and design fostered obedience and allegiance to the goals of American industry. In a nation in which capitalism trumps democracy and economic growth determines opportunity and mobility, corporate hegemony stands strong. Few argued with Calvin Coolidge when he pronounced that the "chief business of the American people is business."[4]

Although various progressive reform movements have promoted critical consciousness and democratic civic engagement as worthy educational objectives, today education's raison d'être is professional career training and marketable skill development. Students are again the raw material for corporate and government clients and teachers are judged on just how good the workers they produce ultimately perform. Even service learning and civic engagement are sold as useful items to have on job resumes and good experiences from which to build relationships with potential employers.[5]

Yet, while corporate hegemony has permeated almost every nook and cranny of educational institutions, the significant sea change has been the commodification of education and the privatization of schools themselves. Some of this dynamic can be traced back to serious cuts in public funding for education, resulting in part from major tax cuts for the rich under the Reagan and Bush administrations. Public schools in the 1980s and 1990s found themselves with less money to meet ever-growing demands, caused on the one hand by burgeoning technology requirements and on the other by increased poor, homeless, and immigrant populations that needed special educational services. But even more notable was the strategic acumen of Wall Street marketeers, who recognized that the "educational industry" was ripe for mega returns on investment. Enter Lehman Brothers.

Essentially, planned obsolescence requires something to take the place of obsolescence. In the case of American educational policy making, once public schools lost public dollars and could no longer perform traditional functions adequately, the private sector promised to step in and fix what they themselves effectively broke in the first—on purpose. Just as Bellah and his associates articulated genuine awe at the ability of neocapitalists to blame the excesses of their own economic policies on the welfare state they had destroyed, Lehman Brothers suggested that private EMOs could reform a system that privatization has destroyed. Enter Edison, Mosaica, White Hat, and dozens of other EMOs, who have taken this strategy and run with it.

Take White Hat, for example. Started by Akron businessman David L. Brennan in 1998, White Hat's Hope Academies and LifeSkills Centers are privately-run public schools funded by the state. According to *Pro Publica*'s Sharona Coutts, White Hat received over US$230 million to run schools throughout Ohio. But by 2011, only 2% of its students had achieved the progress expected under federally mandated education standards known as Adequate Yearly Progress (AYP). In fact, a major report by the National Education Policy Center (NEPC) concludes that White Hat schools across the country underperformed. Of the 51 schools White Hat managed in 2010, only *one* met the AYP measure. Gary Miron, Education Professor and coauthor of the NEPC report, thinks AYP may be a "crude indicator" of success, but it does at least show whether schools are meeting state standards. "When you compare 2 percent of White Hat schools meeting AYP, that's just something that cries out that there's something awry here," he said. "Even schools in poverty are going to have a much higher rate of meeting AYP." Eventually, ten of White Hat's *own* schools and their corporate selected boards sued the company. But such lawsuits in states like Ohio prove highly problematic.[6]

A charter school overhaul bill (House Bill 79) passed by Ohio's state legislature in 2007 made all property managed by EMOs—even when purchased with public money—the EMO's property. Thus, school boards may have to buy back buildings and other resources given to White Hat even if they win current lawsuits. Journalists Jessica Mason and Mary Botteri explain:

> White Hat's grip on the school's property—from buildings to the trademarked school names—made it impossible for the charter schools to simply hire a new operator. Charter schools had to change their names and find new locations to teach. They even had trouble recruiting staff, who were afraid of losing their jobs for even speaking to the "new" schools.[7]

White Hat continues to make a fortune while the schools they manage fail miserably.

Ohio's House Bill 79 looked curiously similar to the American Legislative Exchange Council's (ALEC) Next Generation Charter School Act. ALEC is a "bill mill" group created to unify conservative politicians, think tanks, and financial resources under one umbrella as an efficient conduit for creating and implementing neoliberal legislation. Passed in one form or another by dozens of states, House Bill 79 grants increasing power to private EMOs and allows governors to appoint commissions that permit charters to circumvent local authorities, school boards, and community accountability movements. ALEC has donated heavily to Republican state legislators around the country and, in return, their legislation on all matters of privatizing public institutions from schools to prisons has passed. Predictably, the move from what Lehman had described as a "government monopoly" to a "market driven system that competes on price and quality," has been operationalized as a 'democratic" system run by publically elected officials hijacked by private interests and their campaign-financed legislative partners.[8]

One of the major pieces of ALEC legislation—the removal of restrictions on the growth of charter schools—may be the most egregious violation of Lehman's claim that quality drives investment success. After all, research demonstrates overwhelming evidence that there is:

> *an inverse relationship between rapidly expanding the number of charter schools and the aspiration to lift student testing outcomes.* Quite simply, charter performance declines as the number of charter schools increases and oversight capacity grows more lax … Deregulation diminishes quality.[9]

But it doesn't diminish profit— contrary to Lehman Brothers' hypothesis. Investment returns for private EMOs, *despite* their reported failures, continue to grow into the hundreds of billions of dollars.

The rip-off of public funding for private profit has found other supporters outside the moneyed boardrooms of Wall Street. ALEC has been both a leading think tank—designing pro-private EMO legislation—and a campaign finance trough—raising billions of dollars to support politicians who advocate for those laws.[10]

Even more interesting, though, is the role that major foundations have played in the EMO movement. Gates, Walton, and Broad foundations (as well as many smaller foundations linked to conservative corporate agendas) seem to form the new funding sources that Lehman predicted. In the groundbreaking period for "kill it to save it," wealthy donors financed Reagan- and Bush-era conservative legislators who supported tax cuts for the rich. As tax resources diminished, so did the public institutions that counted on collective revenues, and the municipalities that provided services such as education. As the quantity and quality of services declined and right-wing think tanks and pundits complained about the inefficiencies and ineptitude of the now financially drained public sector, private foundations took the money they now saved from fewer taxes on their wealthy donors and invested in private-sector "solutions" to public services, thus making huge profits while claiming the withering public sector couldn't deliver.[11] In an overtly disingenuous moment, Lehman strategists explained this process as if they and their clients had nothing to do with the planned obsolesce of the public sector.

Lehman wrote, "The educational industry represents the final frontier of a number of sectors once dominated by public control that have generally failed to achieve the standards of quality and cost effectiveness that were originally intended."[12] But it was a manufactured crisis, in large part led by the foundations and their donors.

Take the Bill & Melinda Gates Foundation's first foray into public education. In 2000, Bill and Melinda Gates argued that students in schools with low test scores needed more individual attention in smaller schools with intense "learning communities."[13] Journalist Joanna Barkan wrote, "The foundation didn't base its decision on scientific studies showing school size mattered; such studies didn't exist." Instead, she suggests that Gates spent US$2 billion between 2000 and 2008 setting up over 2,600 schools in 45 states and the District of Columbia, and underwriting almost every small-school initiative, conference, or meeting in the country. By 2008, however, the Gates Foundation dropped most of their small-school initiatives, citing that the project had essentially failed. What Gates didn't mention, however, was the "gut-wrenching sagas of school disruption, conflict, students and teachers jumping ship en masse, and [the] plummeting attendance, test scores, and graduation rates" his policies had caused.[14]

Gates has moved on to high-stakes testing and merit pay for teachers as the key to reform, but other foundations continue funding the privatization bailiwick. The Broad Foundation funds mostly "pipelines" instead of "programs." While programming—such as the Gates' private, small schools initiative—comprise the bulk of foundation funding, "pipelines" train new educational managers, administrators, and policy makers, and place them in positions of power to advance foundation ideas and interests. Broad practices this "high leverage" strategy by sponsoring the Broad Superintendents Academy and the Broad Residency training program. As Barkan explains:

> The mission of both is to move professionals from their current careers in business, the military, law, government, and so on into jobs as superintendents and upper-level managers of urban public school

> districts. In their new jobs, they can implement the foundation's agenda.[15]

As of 2009, the Academy had placed program grads in over 50 urban superintendents or executive positions across 28 states, while the Residency had over 200 graduates in top positions at over 50 educational institutions and districts around the country. While few of these powerful educational leaders have advanced degrees in education or practical teaching experience, they now advocate and implement the EMO message about privatization regardless of evidence. But as my neighbor suggested, the last thing schools need to improve is more educators. What we need are more tests to measure success.

(Mis)Measuring Up: High Stakes Testing and Teaching Evaluation

> If the misery of our poor be caused not by the laws of nature but by our own institutions, great is our sin. (Charles Darwin, *Voyage of the Beagle*[16])

> Poorly served students don't die. … if the opposite were true, Americans would not have allowed the educational system to deteriorate the way it has. (John Golle, quoted in Lehman Brothers Report[17])

Perhaps poorly served students don't die immediately in a way in which trial lawyers could convince a jury that schools, education departments, legislators, or even foundations and EMOs committed the crime. But certainly something is amiss in contemporary public education, and many of these people and institutions share the blame. And while state legislatures, local school districts, and multibillion-dollar foundations continue to put out treasure troves to address the situation, they increasingly choose the worst methods to improve teaching and learning. Why?

Currently, most of the focus from elite educational think tanks, foundations and the federal government's own Department of Education pronounce high-stakes testing as the best way to improve schools, teachers, and student learning. Mandated in 2002 by George W. Bush's No Child Left Behind policy and recently reaffirmed by Barack Obama's Race to the Top program, schools must implement panoply of annual tests for children in order to measure student progress. These tests are then used to hold teachers and schools accountable, the premise being that good teaching results in higher test scores and higher test scores evidence successful schools. Yet, over the last century, educational researchers have heatedly debated the reliability and validity of such testing. Unlike climate change, where the scientific community has overwhelmingly decided that indisputable evidence exists to support the theory of manmade global warming and its planetary impact, the notion of discerning student achievement or intellectual growth (or even more dubious, effective teaching) based on high-stakes standardized tests enjoys no such consensus.[18] Why, then, are they so popular?

Intelligence testing preceded today's standardized tests as a way to determine educational acumen. These tests proved highly subjective in their construction and implementation, eventually falling out of favor because of inherently discriminatory and ultimately "unscientific" data collection and analysis. As biologist Stephen Jay Gould argued in *The Mismeasure of Man*, the method of divining natural intelligence as a single quantity to signify worth or predict outcomes harbors:

> two deep fallacies: 1) *reification*—our tendency to convert abstract concepts into entities such as the intelligence quotient (IQ) … and 2) *ranking*—the propensity for ordering complex variation as a gradual ascending scale.[19]

Both required the "quantification or measurement of intelligence with a single number" in order to objectively define and rank individual's intellectual value. In other words, the ability to take a complicated and often culturally specific concept such as intelligence and give it one numerical definition to compare it to other, overly simplified numerical representations doesn't yield much useful data. Gould went on to dismantle scientists' ability to adequately avoid their own prejudices in collecting and analyzing such data objectively. The definition of intelligence has too many variables and what one counts as evidence of intelligence has too many determinants. Ultimately, Gould suggested that what scientists established as evidence of intelligence and then used to measure it tells us more about the existing racial, class, gender, and ethnic prejudices of the scientists themselves than it does about the subjects of their studies.[20]

While IQ and other intelligence testing rarely surfaces as valuable information for educators these days, our inability to understand what testing does and doesn't really measure remains. And so does Gould's observation that our use of educational testing ultimately tells us more about the social prejudices and political motivations of those who employ them then it does about the successful teaching and learning of our youth. Yet, like the myth of private charter schools and EMO efficacy, the story about the power of high-stakes testing to promote better student learning, teacher performance, and school accountability continues to misinform educational policy making. Why? Because it fits so nicely into the "kill it to save it" paradigm.

Consider the premise. High-stakes tests promise us a chimera of truth and accountability. They suggest that we can easily and accurately measure the success of student learning and quality teaching. But given Gould's caution about our penchant for mismeasurement, we must examine what exactly high-stakes tests *do* measure, and what those measurements actually mean. Essentially, the only thing such tests could measure is students' success in taking those tests. Contemporary reformers suggest that teacher evaluations, pay, and status be determined primarily on their students' test results. Government policies suggest that schools be rewarded or punished based on test results. Thus, they encourage teachers and school districts to focus on teaching to the test. But we have no reliable evidence that adjusting curricula to improve students' scores on high-stakes testing makes for smarter or better educated students, unless we limit such things to overly simplified numerical calculations—thus making the mistakes Gould warned us about.

We do, however, have evidence that increased high stakes testing is *bad* for students in particular and education in general.

Burgeoning studies suggest that high-stakes tests increase student anxieties. Older students often feel increased pressure to perform, as they understand the importance of the exams—not just for their own futures, but also for their teachers' employment and their schools' rankings.[21] Teaching to the test often narrows the curriculum and encourages more simplistic and reductive sets of disciplinary lessons, while severely limiting teachers' creativity and autonomy in the classroom. And most importantly, high-stakes tests result in *increasing* dropout numbers and adversely impact poor students and students of color—exactly the population that most educational reform is targeted towards in the first place.[22] With most of the evidence to the contrary, reformers' continued love affair with testing may be a sign of their own prejudices, economic interests, and political motives; it certainly isn't driven by the science.

In fact, not only is the emphasis on high-stakes testing based on flawed understandings of science—and not only does increasing evidence suggest it is detrimental to educational progress—but also the very *process* of administering, grading, and analyzing the tests has proven grossly inadequate and in many cases highly corrupt. Educational scholar Wayne Au cites a National Center for Educational Statistics report, which found statistical error rates of 35% when using one year's worth of test data measuring teacher effectiveness, and error rates of 25% when using data from three years. Au continues:

> Other research in the U.S. found that one time, randomly occurring factors like whether or not a child ate breakfast on test day; if a window was open and a distracting dog was barking outside during the test; whether or not a child got into an argument with parents or persons on the way to school ... etc. accounts for 50—80% of any gains or losses on a given student's standardized test score.[23]

Sociologist Michael DeCesare has written about his own experiences in trying to create measures for 'teaching effectiveness," and laments that after many years and many dollars, his research group could not develop a consensus list of criteria that could be defined, adequately collected or effectively analyzed. There are just too many variables to effectively do this kind of testing.[24]

While collecting valid and reliable data has numerous challenges, the evaluation and analysis of tests expose the highest levels of educational and scientific scandal. As Diane Ravitch explains, the data itself is generated subjectively through the construction of questions and problems to be answered and then evaluated. Unlike thermometers or barometers that create data mechanically, non-multiple-choice questions are written and scored by human beings. In the best scientific practices, teams of evaluators that score qualitative data or code results for analytical purposes must go through a rigorous process of training and preparation. Key to such methodology is the experience and relevant skills of the individual coders and the repetition and discussion among researchers and evaluators to develop a valid set of standards and reliable (consistent) practice of scoring. The high-stakes testing industry lacks in all of these categories.

Recent books by people within the industry such as Dan DiMaggio and Todd Farley expose an evaluation process totally out of line with scientific best practices and designed to maximize industry profits, not the rigor and legitimacy of their product. Farley explains:

> I worked in the test-scoring business for the better part of fifteen years (1994—2008), and most of that job entailed making statistics dance: I saw the industry fix distribution statistics when they might have showed different results than a state wanted; I saw it fudge reliability numbers when those showed human readers weren't scoring in enough of a standardized way; and I saw it fake qualifying scores to ensure enough temporary employees were kept on projects to complete them on time even when those temporary employees were actually not qualified for the job.[25]

And who are these employees on the ground floor of educational reform? According to DiMaggio, test-scoring companies profit by employing low-wage, non-benefited, temp workers who, despite a bachelors' degree, rarely have any experience in writing, teaching, or even extensive reading.

DiMaggio describes the process of scoring as an inherently rushed affair in which "dozens of scorers sit in rows, staring at computer screens where students' papers appear" one after the other and workers must complete hundreds per day. Companies pay most scorers by piece-rate, thus inspiring employees making 30-70 cents per paper to read as quickly as possible—especially those working at home. He imagines that:

> most students think their papers are being graded as if they are the most important thing in the world. Yet, every day, each scorer is expected to read hundreds of papers. So for all the months of preparation and the dozens of hours of class time spent writing practice essays, a student's writing probably will be processed and scored in about a minute.[26]

Not only are results determined mostly by underqualified, ill-prepared, and poorly paid employees encouraged to rush through the scoring process, but the companies themselves then skew the results when they don't meet their needs. Again, DiMaggio describes the process: "Usually, within a day or two when the scores we are giving are inevitably too low ... we are told to start giving higher scores, or, in the enigmatic language of scoring directors, to 'learn to see more papers as a 4.'" Apparently, testing companies manipulate the evaluation process to maintain relatively consistent, "bell-curve" like distributions on an annual basis. Farley concludes ironically:

> The test-scoring industry cheats ... It cheats on qualification tests to make sure there is enough personnel to meet deadlines/get tests scored; it cheats on reliability scores to give off the appearance of standardization even when that doesn't exist; it cheats on validity scores and calibration scores and anything else that might be needed.[27]

So the answer to my question about why standardized tests form the cornerstone of educational reform is answered in much the same way as why we privatize schools—because there are fortunes to be made on the backs of children and parents and teachers. Our "kill it to save it" framework accepts and legitimizes the notion that private corporations can not only teach our students better but also evaluate the quality of that teaching and learning better, when all it really does is exploit them for profit. High-stakes testing further takes the skill and control over teaching away from mostly well-trained and highly skilled educators and their (now ideologically) discredited unions, away from publically elected school boards (and their public accountability), and turns the educational enterprise over to a new industry, in which it's not impossible to trace Lehman Brothers' economic strategy and ALEC's political maneuvering.

As we have seen, using high-stakes testing in the ways in which legislators and policy makers would like to use them is an intellectually and scientifically dubious proposal at best. But wrap them up in a corporate-driven framework that not only profits from bad knowledge, but also uses its profits to support pro-privatization and pro-high-stakes-testing candidates and then lobbies to pass policies expanding the private market place, and we essentially have institutions devoted to producing knowledge now responsible for destroying it. Of course, Lehman brothers failed, too.

The Color of Money: Race and the Origins of School-to-Prison Pipelines

Yet, perhaps elementary schools and high schools are less about producing knowledge and more about transferring values. While Reagan's "education czar," William Bennett, and his cohort argued that testing would enforce higher standards, they also tended to moralize about the importance of giving low-performing students "tough love." Throughout the 1980s and 1990s, Hollywood produced film after film celebrating the success that strict discipline and disciplinary policies had in transforming schools. The most mythic of these tributes featured

Morgan Freeman as "real-life" Eastside High School Principal, Joe Clark, in the still-popular film *Lean on Me*.

The basics of Clark's story are well known: he is brought in to save a school rife with students' misbehavior (fights, drugs, guns), demoralized staff, crumbling infrastructure—and, above all, bad test scores. Clark's tough love approach—emblemized by his patrolling the halls with a megaphone and baseball bat—eventually saves the school, transforms or eradicates "problem" students, and sends the message that truly committed, maverick, virtuous, hardworking, antiunion and discipline-focused educators can turn around schools in low-income and non-white communities. Here is how Bennett tells the story:

> Everyone was given a list of rules. If you talked back to a teacher, you were suspended for five days. If you painted on a wall, ten days. Clark introduced a dress code. "You've got Calvin Kleins on your behinds and nothing in your minds," he said. The school was cleaned up from top to bottom. Security guards were put in the stairwells. If a teacher was incompetent, Clark told them so to his face. Twenty transferred out. Three hundred juniors and seniors [around 10%] were expelled. "I'm not going to let three hundred hoodlums destroy the lives of three thousand students," Clark told them. As for drugs, he told drug dealers: "If you come around here, you just might get hurt."[28]

While Bennett makes much of Clark's compassionate and "soft" side, too, the message about what it takes to bring order, discipline, and ultimately success is about fear and draconian discipline, not whispered encouragements and subtle boosterism.

However, Eastside never showed much improvement during Clark's five-year reign. Even the slight rise in certain test scores came from expurgating 300 of the worst performing students, not from increased learning and education among those who remained. Clark's self-promotion and aggrandizement, though, combined with the film's powerful yet simplistic message, did work to solidify a conservative educational reform agenda based on demonizing youth, busting teachers' unions, and implementing high-stakes testing. Complaints about low standards, overly tolerant or ignorant teachers, and incompetent school boards have existed since the mid 19th century (Richard Hofstadter once called it America's "educational jeremiad"[29]). But the most recent incantations have resulted in a now three-decades-old movement to criminalize and punish students whose academic performance and behavior doesn't measure up. And as overwhelming research demonstrates, the majority of these students who suffer at the other end of tough love are young students of color.[30]

Inspired by Joe Clark mythologies, War on Drugs policing, and a panic following high-profile school shootings in the late 1990s, public officials responded quickly by militarizing their educational institutions. Local leaders translated the language of criminal sentencing laws by establishing "zero tolerance" and "three strikes" disciplinary policies. They embraced deputized officers (fully armed), security technology (metal detectors), and policing tactics (stop and frisk). And they removed students from school-based discipline—focused on reforming behavior and inspiring maturity—to criminal justice systems in which youth were increasingly tried and punished as adults.[31]

Meanwhile, research has long shown that teachers of all races and ethnicities treat white and non-white students differently when it comes to classroom performance and discipline. Lower expectations and less academic attention, along with more ridicule and harsher punishments, reproduce lower achievement rates for many students of color. Similar disparities exist in the current criminalization of non-white students, as youth of color are more likely reprimanded for minor offenses. With zero-tolerance policies, all demerits are equal and non-white students are being suspended and expelled at increasingly alarming rates around the country.[32]

Just what has been the result of what many now call the "school-to-prison pipeline"? Between 1974 and 2006, the numbers of suspensions almost doubled (1.7 million to 3.3 million) with Black students now 3.5 times more likely to be suspended than their white counterparts.[33] Since 2009, over 200,000 students annually are arrested *in school* and placed in the criminal justice system; almost 90% are non-white. Missed class time, increased stigmatization, and a variety of institutional and personal or emotional challenges result from "doing time" in adult prisons and reinforce poor academic performance and dropout rates among this population. Meanwhile, according to Harvard's Civil Rights Project:

> The adult prison and juvenile justice systems are riddled with children who have traveled through the school-to-prison-pipeline. Approximately 68% of state prison inmates in 1997 had not completed high school. Seventy-five percent of youths under age 18 who have been sentenced to adult prisons have not completed 10th grade. Within the juvenile justice population, 70% suffer from learning disabilities and 33% are reading below the 4th grade level. The "single largest predictor" of subsequent arrest among adolescent females is having been suspended, expelled or held back during the middle school years. Seventy percent of women state prisoners have not completed high school.[34]

Tough love has resulted in more prison and less class time, more punishment and less teaching, more criminal records and less high school diplomas. Where is the *love* part?

And in a perfect example of how "kill it to save it" works in today's schools, the advent of high-stakes testing has increased the numbers of students suspended or expelled. Because schools and teachers are measured on student performance and youth with minor and major disciplinary issues are more likely to be lower-achieving students, faculty and administrators find ways to keep these students from taking high-stakes tests. Thus, the impact of increasing the number and impact of high-stakes tests actually decreases the likelihood that struggling students will get the educational attention they need. The testing regime "kills" students' opportunities to even take—let alone pass—exams in order to "save" the quality of teaching and the reputations of schools.[35]

Ultimately, criminalization, testing, and blaming students, teachers, schools, and parents all allows politicians and the private interests that benefit from the policies examined in this chapter to avoid discussing the real cause of America's educational woes. We can ignore the decreasing real dollars of federal, state, and local revenue spent on public education. We can ignore the resegregation of urban and suburban school districts and the increasing likelihood that students of color will be enrolled in poorer schools, with lower paid teachers, harsher disciplinary policies, and fewer extracurricular and summer learning activities. We can ignore all of the economic and political causes of bad schooling by deploying a fear-driven, Hollywood depicted, corporate, hegemonic, "common sense" story about failing schools and who's to blame for them. But is there an alternative?

As scholar and activist William Ayers has suggested, real school reform requires liberating education from "its single-minded obsession with control, obedience, hierarchy—and everyone's place in it. Alas, the movies are of no help in this … On the contrary, the ready-made clichés and empty repetitions feed our collective powerlessness and manage our mindless acquiescence." He concludes:

> Common sense can be more dogmatic than any political party, more totalizing than any religious sect—it is insistent in its resistance to contradiction or even complexity. It wants to be taken on faith—there isn't room for either reflection or objection. Take it or leave it. Films on teaching fall into step … they are all about common sense and they immunize against a language of possibility—for students, teachers, parents and the public.[36]

Like Gramsci's critique of common sense, Ayers suggests that breaking through the ways that corporate hegemony has hardwired our political and cultural instincts creates a serious impediment to alternatives. "Kill it to save it" approaches to public education—from preschool through high school—have severely damaged our ability to develop, or even imagine, an educational system that could challenge economic inequalities and other forms of institutional discrimination and oppression. Schools have become reproductive hotbeds for growing inequality and prejudice, segregation and poverty. Yet we continue with corporate-driven strategies, misguided science, and draconian discipline procedures because they *feel right*—especially for a mostly white swath of working- and middle-class people who are frustrated with the status quo but see no alternative. Their support for Donald Trump, who instinctively ignores complexity and beckons blind faith by demanding "believe me" after every claim he makes, only demonstrates their growing levels of powerlessness and lack of critical awareness. From false claims about seeing New Jersey Muslims celebrating 9-11 attacks (they didn't) to absurd claims that he knows military strategy better than "the generals" and reads the Bible more than anybody, Trump's assertions are consistently debunked by fact checkers while his popularity rises among those who *want* him to be right and *feel* his statements to be true.[37] And nothing feels more right than our faith in *higher* education as the ticket to social mobility, equality, and a better future. Even if we can't get a job at Lehman Brothers anymore, Goldman Sachs is still hiring.

FOUR

The University Burns While the Knowledge Factory Hums

> Championed as a haven for open inquiry and scholarship free from the demands of special interests, [the modern university] finds this self-proclaimed ideal counterpoised by the need for financial and political support from those same interests. Under exemplary circumstances, independent administrators protect educational institutions from untoward influences while simultaneously soliciting private and public support. In the worst case scenario, the god of Mammon suffocates the gods of Spirit and Intellect, with the university becoming a handmaiden to industry. (John Trumpbour, Harvard University)[1]

In the almost 30 years since John Trumpbour published *How Harvard Rules: Reason in the Service of Empire*, it has become harder and harder for higher education to breathe. The role of colleges and universities in supporting the cause of American industry and empire is a story well told. Many writers have chronicled the importance of these institutions in producing military research, and principles and practices of scientific management and industrial design, as well as harnessing nuclear energy for both weapons research and mass consumption.[2] From the early to the mid 20th century, scholars such as Thorsten Veblen critiqued the role that business hegemony played in "higher learning" and Robert Lynd worried over the rise of profit-driven knowledge production by asking "knowledge for what?" Both "were regarded with considerable skepticism, [at best] accorded the status of respectable cranks."[3]

In the post-Second World War period, the marriage of higher education and industry became even more prominent. Expert-driven economies, technologies, and governance were promoted to manage the prosperity of the burgeoning knowledge economy and its attendant utopian cities of intellect. Eisenhower's "Atoms for Peace" speech preceded Nixon's kitchen debates in linking Cold War supremacy and military superiority with the science and technology necessary to fulfill dreams of mass consumption and a triumphant corporate capitalism. Such goals fueled the vaunting narratives of Clark Kerr as he espoused the "uses of the university" and its primary position in the economy of the future.[4]

Despite various social movements that challenged the militarism, racism, and patriarchy of higher education in the 1960s, Kerr's vision of the new multiversity, with its direct links to corporate profits and professional training, never lost legitimacy or steam. But the stagnation in federal funding for research and massive cuts in state and other public monies for higher education resulted in new "partnerships" in which corporations funded basic research and shared patents and other intellectual property rights. Not only did the private sector now shape the research questions asked by scientists, but they also profited from the findings, subsequent innovations, and other products. Faculty research quickly created "spin-off" companies, and teachers and researchers became CEOs overnight. In fact, new majors and curricula were crafted for corporate interests and supported by corporate dollars. By the 1980s and 1990s, privatization and other business philosophies dominated administrative reorganization and governance in higher education. And by the turn of the 21st century, universities not only provided knowledge and a trained cadre for private industry, but the institution of higher education had also embraced the language and mimicked the practices of corporations themselves.[5]

While the primary functions of higher education—research and teaching—still remain, the commodification of knowledge and students, and the industrialization of the academy itself, have resulted in the degradation of both scholarship and teaching. With the rise of online, for-profit, market-driven "content providers," cheaper and easier ways to get college and postgraduate degrees could run many traditional campuses out of business. Most colleges have tried to increase revenues by bolstering their online distance-learning classes and finding innovative ways to capitalize on their facilities through conference services and exclusive food and beverage contracts with Sodexho, Coke, and Pepsi—to name a few. They have also responded by upscaling dorms, fitness centers, and food services to compete for full tuition-paying students while downscaling the status and autonomy of faculty by recruiting part-time labor, speeding up the work process with larger course loads, class sizes, and contact hours. Meanwhile, more and more governance has moved from faculty control to the hands of an increasingly bloated administration. The result, according to Deborah Leigh Scott, has been the "wreckage of American academia."[6]

As early as the mid 1990s, Bill Readings referred to this devastation as "the university in ruins." He argued that globalization and late capitalism (read: neocapitalism or neoliberalism) had dismantled the "nation-state," while post-modernism and anti-colonialism had dismantled a unified, modernist (albeit arrogant and brutal) sense of Culture with a big "C." Readings explains:

> The University no longer has to safeguard and propagate national culture, because the nation-state is no longer the major site at which capital reproduces itself. ... The idea of national culture no longer provides an overarching ideological meaning for what goes on in the University, and, as a result what exactly gets taught or produced as knowledge matters less and less. (p. 13)

Replacing a commitment to national culture and state-driven imperialism, universities have adopted the language of "excellence." Yet, excellence means nothing except in the language of accounting and assessment, ranking and competition.

Because excellence has no meaning outside of comparison, the raison d'être of the academy is quantitative assessment that allows for pseudoscientific proof of better learning, quality teaching, quality research, prettier campuses, happier student bodies, and more marketable graduating classes. All of these suggest the need for cost-effective investments and proven effective outcomes. In the end, the university no longer simply *acts* like a corporation; it has *become* a corporation: "The University of Excellence serves nothing other than itself, another corporation in a world of transnationally exchanged capital."[7]

The growth of college administrations reflects the increased need to account and measure, plan strategically for increased efficiency, cater to customers' satisfaction, cut long-term costs and create something called "excellence." These strategies require attracting higher paying students and lower paid faculty and staff. They require outsourcing practically everything: from food, health, and custodial services to staff recruitment, retention management, and—ironically—strategic planning itself. Faculty members find their pedagogy and research degraded at the same time that work speed-ups result in them being assigned more administrative and bureaucratic tasks. After all, *measurement* is how we know teaching and learning has been achieved. Clerical workers once charged with handling the bulk of logistical tasks are now the first ones fired, and their vacancies left unfilled—resulting in ever-mounting administrative burdens for faculty and the few staff that remain. Eventually, more administrators result in faculty and staff doing more administrative work, not less.[8]

Noam Chomsky suggests that burgeoning layers of administrative and bureaucratic heft represent the necessary cost of control: "If you have to control people, you have to have an administrative force that does it." From a management end, corporations have always required increased levels of management to impede the autonomy and resistance of workers. In retail and service economies, managers must handle both employees *and* consumers, thus becoming more significant to maintaining profits and stability. But Chomsky also suggests another crucial element for corporate control: the *precarity* of labor. He explains: "If workers are insecure, they won't ask for wages, they won't go on strike, they won't call for benefits;

they'll serve the masters gladly and passively. … as universities move more towards a corporate business model, precarity is exactly what is being imposed." Thus, the market ideology of contemporary higher education not only permeates the labor process, but also creates a "market McCarthyism" that keeps graduate student teaching-assistants and adjunct faculty from complaining or organizing.[9]

Automation has historically helped industry manage workers with threats of obsolescence. The university has also adopted these practices. Increasing technologies such as Massive Open Online Courses (MOOCs), "courses in a box," and other educational innovations encroach on academic freedom and critical pedagogies by rationalizing and standardizing both the process and content of higher education. Back in 1998, David Noble warned:

> the distribution of digitized course material online, without the participation of professors who develop such material, [may be] justified as an inevitable part of the new "knowledge–based" society … [but] in practice is often coercive … It is not a progressive trend towards a new era at all, but a regressive trend, towards the rather old era of mass production, standardization and purely commercial interests.[10]

Almost two decades later, faculty increasingly become "content providers" and students "platform users."With the hopes of greater automation and increased docility, college and university administrators now routinely impose market McCarthyism on whole departments and programs whose cost—benefit bottom line can't justify their jobs. Faculty at almost every institution can point towards instances where class size, numbers of majors, or grant dollars determined curricula decisions, faculty hires, and even tenure cases. Over the last two decades, the number of American Association for University Professors (AAUP) censures of higher education institutions has nearly tripled, primarily due to faculty firings (tenured and untenured) based on supposed financial crises and economic exigencies. In most cases, the AAUP could not find convincing evidence of either, and censured institutions for their exaggerated claims and faulty calculations. In the case of the University of Southern Maine, administrators predicated 60 faculty firings on "projected" shortfalls (which, it's been suggested, they had a long history of overstating) and cost—benefit calculations about majors and course enrollments that have been heavily contested.[11]

But the worst victims of such academic carnage may not be university faculty and staff; it may be the students themselves. Early entrees into corporatizing higher education promised students a vaunted position as customer. The irony of such an identity was not lost on faculty, who asked how, if the customer was always right, could they be charged with teaching students and evaluating their work. Many of us who teach experience that ironic jolt every time we see our students' teaching evaluations. And because these evaluations often weigh heavily towards promotion and tenure, we sometimes skimp on rigor and quality to appear more user-friendly—thus getting better evaluations, encouraging bigger enrollments, and impacting our own modicum of job security. It's sort of like test scorers at Pearson "learning to see more papers as a 4." Again, not only is the work process degraded, but so is student learning. In our neoliberal "kill it to save it" society, however, the role of consumer or customer has been degraded just as the worker's labor has been degraded. ATMs allow us to be our own bank tellers, shoppers are now asked to checkout their own groceries, drivers fill their own tanks, and travelers make their own reservations, check their own bags, bring their own food, and in the case of an emergency, remove windows and clear aisles. For students, it's no different. They are expected to register for their own courses, create their own majors, determine the quality of their courses and instructors, and navigate the myriad financial aid quagmires necessary to pay tuition. While college faculty have long tried to encourage students to be independent learners and critical thinkers, we continually dumb down curricula to make them happy while we require they perform more of the selecting and dispersing of services and monitoring and evaluating of employees and logistics.[12]

As students navigate the changing demands of higher education, they face increasing emotional and financial obstacles.

According to numerous studies, most notable the work of UCLA's Higher Education Research Institute, student stress levels are at an all-time high. In 2011, only a little over half of all incoming students described their emotional wellbeing as above average or better. This number dropped 3.4% from 2010 and has declined steadily since 1985, when over two thirds reported feeling above average or better. Reasons for increased stress (despite students reporting spending *less* time on academic studies than their predecessors) are probably many, but exponential increases in time spent on social media, extracurricular activities, and wage work certainly contribute to this dynamic. So, too, does the volatility and hyper-aggressiveness of campus social life.[13]

Above all, however, financial insecurities (especially since the fiscal crises of 2007 and 2008) weigh heavily on students. Over half of first-year students used loans to pay for college, with almost 40% borrowing US$6,000 or more during their first year. Meanwhile, almost 60% of seniors graduated with debt in 2010, with an average accumulated debt of $33,000 each. According to Andrew Ross, over 40% of 2005's graduating class is either delinquent or in default of their student loans, leaving him to wonder if we shouldn't compare student debt to indentured servitude. He writes, "In a knowledge economy, when a college degree is considered a passport to a decent livelihood, workforce entrants must go into debt in return for the right to labor. This kind of contract is the essence of indenture" (pp. 10-14). Like developing nations bound to unsupportable International Monetary Fund (IMF) or World Bank debt, student loans force young people into their own structural adjustment programs—choosing majors and careers based on their ability to pay back loans, not on their own desires to do meaningful, creative, or autonomous work. Regardless of lower unemployment rates for college grads, "the promise" of a college degree is fading faster than Obama's "Hope" posters.[14]

The depressed desperation of students, degraded and frustrated faculty, hungry caterpillar administrators, and institutions more concerned with enrollment management than critical knowledge production may represent the final whimper in a society searching for some glimmer of possibility—some last gasp before the final demise of education as a site for democratic deliberation and social justice. But our "kill it to save it" society may have convinced us that participating in such a system is not only in our best interest, but also the inevitable pathway to enlightenment and liberation. We produce the knowledge that tells us we shouldn't be bothered with knowledge in the first place.

The Vietnamization of Higher Education and the Night the Sun did Shine

In a wonderful (albeit sometimes shrill) essay entitled, "How the American University was Killed, in 5 Easy Steps," Deborah Leigh Scott argues that the attack on higher education resulted from the radical student and faculty movements of the 1960s. She begins with the post-Second World War period, when campuses surged with G.I. Bill beneficiaries and the children of the growing professional, middle, and even working classes. She writes:

> This surge continued through the 60s, when universities were the very heart of intense public discourse, passionate learning, and vocal citizen involvement in the issues of the times … colleges had a thriving professoriate, and students were given access to a variety of subject areas, and the possibility of broad learning. … Of course, something else happened—the uprisings and growing numbers of citizens taking part in popular dissent — against the Vietnam War, against racism, against destruction of the environment in a growing corporatized culture, against misogyny, against homophobia. Where did much of that revolt incubate? Where did large numbers of well-educated, intellectual, and vocal people congregate? On college campuses. Who didn't like the outcome of the 60s? The corporations, the war-mongers, those in our society who would keep us divided based on our race, our gender, our sexual orientation.[15]

Recognizing that the corporate, military, power elite could not just shut down the universities (even in a pseudo-free society, one can't manage by fascistic fiat), they responded by transforming them into different entities altogether. *Kill it to save it.*

According to Scott, they succeeded in accomplishing this goal with five easy steps:

1. Defund public higher education;
2. Deprofessionalize and impoverish the professors;
3. Develop a managerial/administrative class who take over governance;
4. Move in corporate culture and corporate money;
5. Destroy the students.

Scott concludes:

> Within one generation, in five easy steps, not only have the scholars and intellectuals of the country been silenced and nearly wiped out, but the entire institution has been hijacked, and recreated as a machine through which future generations will ALL be impoverished, indebted and silenced. ... Looking at this wreckage of American academia, we have to acknowledge: [The corporations] have won.[16]

Scott's version does seem somewhat reductive. After all, the corporate influence on higher education has been around since the beginning of America's higher education system. McCarthyism certainly cast an ideological pall over academic freedom many, many years ago— and even today, hundreds of faculty and thousands of students protest and demonstrate not only against racism and military interventions, sweatshop labor, and global warming, but also over the policies of their own institutions. Yet so many of these yawps against the academy are fragmented, incoherent, temporary, and easily avoided, assimilated or expunged. The day-to-day realities of student, faculty, and staff experience is such that few prolonged struggles have much impact. Whether movements have successful small outcomes or not (better recycling, fair trade coffee, more inclusive harassment policies, renaming college buildings, and so on), the overarching framework for dealing with social problems is by addressing them as personal troubles—making more money, taking stronger medications, or finding the right affinity group.

Like the other institutions we will look at in the rest of this book, one wonders why more Americans haven't revolted against the relatively few groups of CEOs and political and cultural elite who benefit from "kill it to save it" policy making. But such a movement, such a rebellion, would require a revolutionary consciousness that contemporary colleges and universities can no longer foster. Why? Because long ago they fell victim to the absurdity of producing knowledge for corporate power in return for the promise of corporate enlightenment and an expert-driven vision of eternal life, liberty, happiness and hope through consumption.

In 1950, the University of Michigan (U-M) Broadcasting Service aired a radio play developed as a promotional piece for the Phoenix Memorial Project—one of the nation's first postwar university programs for atomic energy research. The story began with Cacique, chief of the fictitious Santana Indian tribe, describing a nuclear test explosion in the desert:

> It has not been so long, since the sun did shine at night … All was blackness out there in the desert … and suddenly the sun itself did shine! After the White men had gone, the young men of the pueblo rode forth into the desert with great excitement to see for themselves the place where the sun had shone.[17]

Once the young men return, Cacique tries to convince a skeptical Jose that they had indeed witnessed a "piece of the sun." Jose had brought back a "hunk of green stuff" and the Chief asked if he had ever seen anything like it in the "white man's school." Jose replied that a chemistry teacher taught them, "if you could heat sand, it would melt into glass, but it would need terrific heat. Where could such heat come from?" To which Cacique proposes, "A piece of the sun."[18]

As the play continues, the tribe hears from the "talking box" that the U.S. dropped an atomic bomb on Japan. The newscaster speculates: "we might be on the threshold of a new world for science and mankind." Cacique leaves the community house to consider the possibility that the explosion was an omen of things to come. Suddenly, he is transported to a city where white people, too, are concerned about the danger of atomic power. Cacique tells one woman who has expressed her fears, that he is not afraid. She responds, "But then you are too stupid to be afraid ... you aborigine.[19]

Back at home, Cacique is perplexed by his own tribe's fears as well. He counters Jose's hysteria by explaining, "The sun is good ... It lights our way, nourishes our crops along the river ... and puts warmth in these old bones. [The bomb and the sun] are the same for I have seen them." He then conveys a legend about the Santana's first introduction to fire. Two tribesman had witnessed a great storm where lightening had lit the forest ablaze and destroyed their hunting grounds. After traveling a long time they came upon strangers who used fire to cook food, but the Santana men were afraid. Their hosts explained, "Fear not. It is *our* slave. It cooks our meat ... and lights our way in the darkness." The Santanas counter, "But it is bad. We have seen fire destroy the jungle—our hunting grounds." The host replies: "Ay. But if you seek danger, the water you drink has danger. [It] is dangerous for drowning, but it is good for drinking."[20]

Jose is not sure of the fable's relevance, so Cacique leads him in a Socratic dialogue:

Cacique:	Is fire good or bad?
Jose:	It depends.
Cacique:	Now, the Atom Bomb?
Jose:	That's Bad.
Cacique:	But *we* got it! We not aborigine any more with fire. We know fire. Even so, kill plenty of people. Scare plenty of people. Same with bomb. The night the sun did shine, all people became aborigines once more.[21]

In 1950, this radio play helped frame the university's evolution—not only as a center for capital production, but also a site for the cultural rationalization synthesizing scientific research, pro-growth philosophy and new forms of mass consumption. Today's universities provide similar narratives necessary for new capitalist formations and a new corporate hegemony of "kill it to save it."

Obvious from this radio play is the use of Native Americans to link atomic energy to "natural" human processes and traditional and authentic wisdom. As Jean-Jacques Simard argued, most images of American Indians represent archetypes: "Spontaneous, Natural, Timeless, and Original have been the most common ways of characterizing the *True Indian* as human beings.[22] By comparing atomic energy to a "piece of the sun," the play invites the audience to consider "the bomb" as not only part of nature, but also something ultimately beneficial. Far from being afraid of or resigned to atomic energy, Cacique's wisdom offers us the promise of better things to come because *we* got it and *our* experts will harness it.

What makes the play so effective is that Cacique's wisdom is not only his link to traditional authenticity, but also his willingness to defer to the white man's experts: it's the white man's school that explains converting sand to glass; it's the talking box that explains the bomb's significance; and it's "strange people they had never seen before" who teach them how to tame fire for good. Thus, at the same time that Cacique's sagacity claims a certain privilege for experience and common wisdom, it clears a path for a new common sense about the role of experts whose scientific intellect can transform this great natural power into a manageable source of human productivity. As Cacique tells Jose, "the rabbit gains wisdom when he learns not to fight bobcat." The chief's climactic claim that atomic energy has made "all people aborigines" reinforces not only the need to rely on expert knowledge about atomic energy, but also the need to support the Phoenix Project, whose experts work for mankind's benefit.

Even more poignant than naturalizing atomic energy and the wisdom of deferring to expert-driven benefits is how the play addresses just what those benefits might be. In comparing atomic energy to fire, Cacique stresses the importance of harnessing sometimes-dangerous forms of energy into providing safety, warmth, healthy food, and drink. Fire is necessary for customary ways of home and hearth: "Within the pueblo our women use it to prepare food we eat and the mate we drink."[23]

Elaine Tyler May has written that the 1950s American home represented a site of security and fulfillment in an atomic age rife with disruption and alienation.[24] This play, framed by the need to quell fears as well as inspire donations to the Phoenix Project, focused on the potential for atomic energy-driven convenience and improvements in the home.

As the last embers of Cacique's campfire faded, an announcer jumped in to conclude the U-M Broadcasting Service presentation. He confirmed Cacique's conclusion that all people "everywhere" were now Aborigines of the atomic age. Yet, he continued:

> We aborigines have the privilege of blazing the trail into the future when our children's children will perhaps sit at night in their homes ... switch on an atomic powered lamp, carefully adjust the atomic powered air conditioner, put the supper dishes in an atomic powered washing machine, and remind junior that tomorrow he must clean the family's atomic powered air-car.[25]

Like Eisenhower's "Atoms for Peace" speech some three years later, The Phoenix Project promised to "better mankind" by rising from the ashes of the Second World War with a renewed spirit of commercial capitalism. But it also promoted the unification of university knowledge production and mass consumption with a pro-growth ideology that not only shaped Cold War discourse but also itself became a master narrative for the period. As such, universities formed crucial sites for producing both knowledge for corporate production and ideological rationalizations—the new common sense—that would buttress the new capitalism. Ironically, the U-M created such a narrative not by killing Native Americans, nor by simply killing what Indian was in the man, but by promoting a supposedly natural hybridity of traditional wisdom with modern capitalist production and consumption.

Today, colleges and universities have become corporations themselves, and perhaps Scott is right that the result is the dying husk of academia. But it is more likely that institutions of higher education still play a key role in providing the cultural and ideological legitimacy for neoliberal Earth. In 1991, U-M President James Duderstadt—an engineer by training—would declare that "an aristocracy of university-based innovators had become the arbiters of economic prosperity and social well-being."[26] Yet his predecessors had already laid the groundwork and framework for such an appraisal some four decades earlier. And the impact of Aborigines embracing experts to hardwire mass consumption and corporate hegemony into our contemporary "kill it to save it" common sense suggests we may need to revisit what potential still exists in the halls of our educational institutions.

Alternatives do exist. Increasing discontent over academia's historical roots in America's slave economy and the increasing inaccessibility of decent pay for meaningful work may have stirred the student masses—and may explain why a 74-year-old Democratic Socialist seemed so popular among young men and women over 50 years his junior. Permanent loan forbearance and free public higher education could go a long way towards addressing some of today's class inequities. And a truly liberated and fairly compensated professoriate may be empowered to redesign a more democratic and public-oriented process and product. But if all our colleges and universities teach is neoliberal pabulum and hyper-corporate individualism, then neocapitalist icons like Donald Trump will be the future of our country.

PART 3
Junk Food, Junk Science, and Junk Freedom: Life and Death in America

overview: History of Health in America

> All I maintain is that on this earth there are pestilences and there are victims, and it's up to us, so far as possible, not to join forces with the pestilences. (Dr. Bernard Rieux in Albert Camus, *The Plague*)[1]

Sociologists see sociology everywhere—it is an occupational hazard. Back in the late 1980s, I attended a meeting with my father, who had sued his previous employer for age discrimination because he was fired only a few months before being eligible for retirement. The company took this action following years of good work and good evaluations, and after asking him (unknowingly) to train his younger, lower-paid replacement. A pretrial meeting to discuss a settlement took place at the company lawyers' swank offices on Park Avenue in New York City. As I stepped into the men's room before the meeting, I noticed a sign above the urinals: "In Case of Emergency Call Corporate Care Unit," with a phone number following. My curiosity led me to ask one of the attorneys what a corporate care unit was. He explained that the firm paid handsomely to have one of the best hospitals in New York helicopter to the roof in case of emergencies, with the best-qualified medical personnel available, and make sure that employees got priority care and the best facilities if and when they arrived at hospital. While I had long observed the ways in which inequality negatively impacted poor people's health (bad food, poor shelter, more pollution, more stress, and little or no access to quality care),[2] it had never occurred to me that there was a medical doppelgänger where wealthy people could pay more for luxury, priority care. Being rich can save your life.

And not being rich can kill you. The role of racial discrimination and class inequality in determining one's health and safety is nothing new. Social scientists have studied the impact of inequality on health, illness, and crime for generations. The United States has long accepted and supported policies aimed at damaging the health and safety of poor, working-class, non-white populations while protecting the health and increasing the wealth of rich, white people—from the dumping of smallpox-infested blankets on Native Americans[3] to the imprisonment and exploitation of recently freed Black men as convict labor after the Civil War in the South;[4] the Tuskegee syphilis experiments and the use of prisoners on which to conduct medical trials;[5] the mass internment of Asian Americans during the Second World War;[6] the disposal of toxic waste on Native American reservations and in poor and predominately non-white communities in the rural South and urban North,[7] and the more recent mass incarceration of non-white, immigrant, and youth populations providing the necessary raw material for privatized prisons[8] The very institutions and policies designed to provide health and safety for American residents continually provides just the opposite for so many—by design.

This section begins with an overview of America's approach to health and health care. In particular, I look at how issues of corporatization, professionalization, and patriarchy influenced the movement from a more integrated and cultural understanding of *health* to a more bureaucratized and commoditized vision of health *care*. The following chapters then examine institutions responsible for health and safety—two of the most vital functions performed by any society. In particular, I look at how institutions charged with keeping us alive and well—as safe from disease and harm as possible—have been reshaped in contemporary America to result in serious harm to all of us. I also look at the ways in which knowledge *about* health, safety and the environment has been contaminated and manipulated by the same corporations that profit from doing harm. We have reached a point at which the irrationality of our highly rationalized systems of economic and social reproduction has taken over.[9] In short: the food we eat and air we breathe are killing us; the drugs we take to cure us are making us sick; the science we hope will enlighten us too often lies to us, and the criminal justice system we expect will keep us safe from harm doesn't.

Who Cares? A History of Health and Health Care in the United States

Even the earliest of societies had individuals who—for various reasons, traditions, customs, and so on—were looked upon to provide care in the case of illness or to support natural and biological processes like childbirth. In most societies, it was women who initially took on "health provider" roles and, through family teachings and oral tradition, passed down various knowledge, remedies, and rituals around healing and nature. In some places, shamans or medicine men arose to maintain and control the power and knowledge of bringing back good health. The use of plant or other natural materials (insects and so on) comprised the dominant resources for addressing illness, with religious rituals or "magic" also used in many societies. Health and health care were integrated and infused into the daily rituals, practices, and values of local customs and everyday life.[10]

From Antiquity onward, formal education and training—with attendant discoveries about anatomy and the inventions of new tools for surgery and discovery (such as microscopes)—would revolutionize, and then institutionalize, the study and practice of medicine. From barbers and their leeches to herbalists and midwives, more local, indigenous, and traditional health treatments did continue, but served increasingly less urbanized, poorer, and more isolated communities. Meanwhile, doctors and hospitals evolved in growing cities, especially from the late 18th to mid 19th centuries, many of which treated the rich and rising professional classes. Physicians' own wages, however, usually left them in the working and lower-middle classes.

As the sciences of biology, chemistry, and anatomy developed and the application of these sciences fostered the professionalization of medical doctors, societies wrestled with the question of who should have access to more formalized medicine. But by removing the questions of wellness or illness from families, customs, and communities to the realm of knowledge experts and credentialed practitioners, health became more about treating sickness and disease and less about how people lived day-to-day—the food they ate, the air they breathed, their shared beliefs about nature, and their real links to natural processes.

Let me be clear: the point here is not to disparage the amazing advancements brought on by scientific knowledge and applications. What we still call "modern medicine" has resulted in extending and improving most human life on the planet. Its development, however, has not been without costs; and the monetization and professionalization of health care has created an "unhealthy" separation of medicine (and health in general) from both natural and cultural lifestyles. One historical exception was the late-19th and early-20th-century American fitness craze led, in part, by Teddy Roosevelt's bullishness for exercise and outdoor sports. "Expert knowledge" proclaimed good health in special exercises and leisure activity. But just as prevalent was the mass popularization of *using* "good health" to market medicinal elixirs and "snake oils." Hamlin's Wizard Oil Company and the Kickapoo Indian Medicine Company were just two of many traveling medicine shows featuring both phony doctors and faux Indian acts to attract paying crowds and sell bogus potions and salves. The ironic symbolic integration of Native Americans as naturally healthy and pure with the most modern and scientifically trained doctors and their medicines captured the historical and cultural nuances of late-19th-century thinking about health and healing.[11] But the increasingly obvious con of most products and their pitchmen simply made seriously trained scientists and physicians seem that much more legitimate, professional, and safe. More and more, people depended on accredited physicians for health—but only *after* they got sick.

In the United States, the history of health care as a social institution was characterized by the growth of formalized study and practice in medical sciences. The subsequent professionalization and marketization of these expanded rapidly and resulted in massive resources allocated for research and training, and the building of medical schools and hospital networks across the nation. But it was also about the centralization of power and knowledge and the struggle over markets and authority. And it also included a highly gendered struggle for power—initially over religion and patriarchy, but eventually over markets and professional legitimacy (and still patriarchy). One of the best ways to understand these converging power struggles is to look at how Americans thought of pregnancy and childbirth.[12]

For example, some historians have referred to medicine in 17th- and early-18th-century America as the "age of the midwife." Yet, in many quarters, women healers were "especially vulnerable" to charges of witchcraft. Local religious leaders didn't care for treating illness without penance, as most believed sickness related to misbehavior and the hand of God or the Devil. Similarly, while midwives handled the bulk of childbirth assistance, clergy grew increasingly concerned about their role in baptizing the newly born. During the late 17th century and 18th century, midwives and women healers drew harsh criticism from both male clerics and the rising number of male physicians. Historian John Demos suggests that at least a quarter to one third of all women persecuted for witchery in New England became targets because of "making and administering special remedies, providing expert forms of nursing, or serving in some regular way as midwives."[13] In a proto-moment of "kill it to save it," the religious, social, and political purges of these "healers" had detrimental effects on communities as male physicians battled for medical hegemony. Religiously driven harassment and witch trials, combined with new standards and laws determining who could and could not treat patients, eventually left women healers marginalized and discredited. Yet, male doctors—especially in the realm of childbirth—had much poorer records on health and safety than midwives.

Historian Polly Radosh writes:

> The most serious problem associated with the increased use of physicians over midwives was an increase in mortality, both maternal and infant. Male physicians were more likely than midwives to employ instruments in delivery, and prior to discovering the need for antiseptic precautions (circa 1860), interference by physicians with instruments was extremely hazardous.[14]

This frequently led to puerperal fever (blood poisoning) and the death of the mother. Such conditions led Ehrenreich and English to conclude that:

> male physicians were both more dangerous and less effective than female lay healers … [The witch hunts represented] a sheer waste of talent and knowledge. The victims, besides the individual women who were tortured and executed, were also all the people who were consequently deprived of their healing or midwifery skills."[15]

While the religious persecution of women healers and midwives diminished (as did the role of the Church itself), the rising importance of legal and professional legitimacy maintained pressure on women in medicine. Male-dominated professionalization—formalized in the founding of the American Medical Association (AMA) in 1848—all but guaranteed highly trained, elite, and male control over knowledge and authority in health care. While doctors maintained a poor record for successful childbirth, a new specialization in obstetrics sought to overtake the entire field, and the AMA declared war on midwives, fighting hard against their desire to gain more professional training and education. While European countries created a dual system in which midwives were trained and certified to handle "normal" childbirths and doctors called in only to address complications, the AMA refused to cooperate. Instead, they argued that hospitals were the *only* safe place for doctors to deliver children, and prohibited midwives from practicing in them.[16]

In 1920, Dr. Joseph B. DeLee wrote "The Prophylactic Forceps Operation," in which he described his routine of "active control over labor and delivery, attempting to prevent problems through a sequence of medical interventions designed to save women from the 'evils' that are natural to labor."[17] Obstetricians sedated women from the onset of labor; allowed the cervix to dilate; applied ether at the second stage of labor; cut an episiotomy; delivered the baby with forceps; extracted the placenta; gave medications for the uterus to contract, and then repaired the episiotomy. This routine could only be conducted in hospital, which DeLee and his cohort strongly advocated. By the mid 20th century, almost all deliveries were handled by doctors and pregnancy became a "pathological condition" of illness, not a natural process of reproduction.[18]

At the same time, health care systems were being professionalized and institutionalized throughout the United States—not only for the wealthy but also for the middle class. Churches and social workers helped poor and working-class people gain access to formalized health care, too, as the number of religious-based and public hospitals increased. Workers had established benevolent societies to help pay for funerals, medical expenses, and other emergencies among their memberships as early as the start of the 19th century. These organizations supported labor organizing; many unions eventually took over the functions of these benevolent societies, suggesting that health care and other compensation should be collective bargaining issues.

With the growth of federal systems of transportation and communication in the early 20th century came a call for the development of a national health care plan. Although supported by progressives and labor, effective opposition from medical professionals (the AMA) and insurance companies blocked these efforts, leaving unions to either create their own health insurance plans or include them in labor negotiations. Dallas Teachers became the first union to negotiate successfully for health insurance in 1929, and Blue Cross began in the early 1930s as the first major national health insurance company.[19]

But as the country fought its way back from the damage of the great depression and the carnage of the Second World War,

Franklin D. Roosevelt (FDR) included the "right to health care" in his famous Second Bill of Rights speech. To establish the highest standard of living in U.S. also meant addressing anyone who is "ill-fed, ill-clothed, ill-housed, and insecure." Thus, FDR proclaimed:

> [T]rue individual freedom cannot exist without economic security and independence. "Necessitous men are not free men." We have accepted a second Bill of Rights under which a new basis of security and prosperity can be established for all—regardless of station, race, or creed.

Along with rights to "a useful and remunerative job" paying enough for "adequate food, clothing and recreation" and "a decent home," FDR included "the right to a good education," protection from fears of old age, sickness, accident, and unemployment, and the "right to adequate medical care and opportunities to achieve and enjoy good health." He concluded: "All of these rights spell security. And after this war is won we must be prepared to move forward, in the implementation of these rights, to new goals of human happiness and well-being." Yet, FDR could not pass a national health plan as part of Social Security. Vociferous resistance from the AMA, private insurers, and other conservative free-market interests threatened to defeat the entire social security bill if national health care was included. FDR dropped it.[20]

It wouldn't be until Johnson's War on Poverty that Medicare and Medicaid would provide basic health insurance for Senior Citizens (over 65), younger people with serious disabilities (Medicare) and the poorest families and individuals (Medicaid). These policies resulted in a steep drop in the percentage of U.S. citizens without health coverage—from about 25% in the early 1960s to less than 10% in the late 1970s.[21] Still, the majority of U.S. citizens had insurance from employers or through private purchasing. While a variety of proposals for national coverage rose and fell, small gains were made for seniors—and especially for children, through the 1997 Children's Health Insurance Program (CHIP), which provided free care for many low-income youth. But from 1980 until 2010, the number of uninsured Americans rose to over 15%—or almost 50 million people. Much of this increase came as a result of Reagan—Bush-era cuts to public health institutions, the decline of organized labor, and the rise of health care maintenance organizations (HMOs).[22]

The Patient Protection and Affordable Care Act of 2010 (ACA; known commonly as "Obamacare") changed some of the ways in which health care is delivered to people. The ACA did away with most insurer restrictions on preexisting conditions, instituted a variety of subsidy programs to help low-income people acquire insurance, and provided funding for states to expand Medicaid. Yet many states—for overtly partisan political reasons linked to "kill it to save it" ideology—aimed to make Obamacare a failure. They refused funding to expand Medicaid, negatively impacting their own citizens' health in hopes of scoring political points. While many flaws—from technology gaffs to bad budgeting—have plagued the ACA, the new policy *has* reduced the number of uninsured Americans and provided billions of dollars for preventive health care for the first time in American history. But the ACA did not provide universal coverage, single-payer, or even a public option for health care in the United States. In many ways, the ACA only further entrenched the nation's inability to conceive of health care outside of insurance companies and HMOs.

In fact, until recently, most debates about health related to the accessibility and effectiveness of insurance. Yet, most basic issues about Americans' poor health, and how a "kill it to save it" ideology shapes them, are not about access to health care *after* we get sick. The greatest challenges come from our inability to avoid getting sick in the first place. Our most dangerous policies relate to the ways corporations encourage and profit from poor food, water, air, and overall lifestyles that literally kill us. Meanwhile, we get increasingly more disinformation about health and safety, curtailing our ability to change institutional practices on a structural level. Instead, we are limited to healthy "lifestyle choices," if we can find or afford them.

These conditions germinated in the spaces left behind by traditional lifestyles that included fresh, local and unprocessed foods, physical, outdoor activities, and active and diverse (albeit physically hard and often exploited) work and leisure. First convenience and then the necessity of fast-paced occupational and domestic lives paved the way for increasingly industrialized, processed foods; sedentary car-, phone-, and computer-based work and leisure; and the technology and mass commercialization to provide these new ways of life.[23] The history of health care in the U.S. suggests that with the annihilation of traditional knowledge and customs by the hegemonic rise of a scientific, technological, rationalized and corporate model of medicine also came a reliance on experts, engineers, and marketeers to determine the meaning of health and the delivery of care. In many cases, this triumph was driven as much by profit and markets as it was by the actual ability to provide better health, greater comfort, and longer lives. But profits over people's health shapes policies that impact everyday life even *before* we *need* medical help. Nowhere is this clearer than in the area of food production.

FIVE

Industrialized Food and Industrialized Farmers

"What an extraordinary achievement for a civilization: to have developed the one diet that reliably makes its people sick!" (Michael Pollan, *The Omnivore's Dilemma*[1])

Accounts of the now thousands of children who have died from foodborne illnesses over the last three decades can induce shivers and tears from even the coldest sociologist. I paused often as I read the heartbreaking stories of 6-year-old Lauren Rudolph, 4-year-old Riley Detwiler, 2-and-a-half-year-old Kevin Kowalcyk, and 2-year-old Michael Nole, who all died painful deaths from E. coli-contaminated hamburgers in 1993. Over 700 people (mostly children) fell ill after eating tainted beef in undercooked burgers from Jack in the Box. Franchises in western states were struggling to meet an overwhelming demand for their special promotion "Monster Burgers" (their slogan: "so good it's scary"). Harried workers routinely undercooked burgers for insufficient times at too low a temperature to kill bacteria. E. coli O157:H7 destroyed these kids' internal organs and, in a separate case, so ravaged another child, 6-year-old Alex Donley, that only his corneas were fit for organ donation.[2]

Many government and food industry leaders believed these 1993 outbreaks "woke up" the public and the industry, leading to numerous changes in beef production, food regulation, and the fast food industry as a whole. Yet it wasn't the first outbreak caused by the deadly combination of industrialized beef production and fast food chains—nor would it be the last. In fact, from 2006—2014, the Centers for Disease Control and Prevention (CDC) investigated 22 different E. coli outbreaks, almost one third of which were due to beef producers and distributors. E. coli O157:H7, the pathogen most commonly associated with ground beef, causes an estimated 96,000 illnesses, 3,200 hospitalizations, and 31 deaths in the U.S. each year. In all, the CDC estimates that roughly 1 in 6 Americans (or over 50 million people) get sick, 128,000 are hospitalized, and 3,000 die of foodborne diseases *every year.* In 4% of E. coli cases, toxins contaminate the bloodstream leading to serious health conditions such as kidney failure, internal bleeding, neurological damage, strokes, and death. E. coli is the leading cause of kidney failure among American children. Yet, despite the overwhelming evidence that our contemporary food system is harming us, we continue to massively subsidize fast food and its impact on all food.[3]

The myriad options presented by ever more bucolic and pretty packages lining bountiful supermarket aisles obscure the fact that corporate consolidation and the increased use of artificial flavors and colors have actually minimized consumer choices and taste pallets over the past five decades.[4] Industrialized food production, highly processed foods, and intensely rationalized packaging and distribution create exactly the kind of McDonaldized system George Rizer first wrote about in the 1990s. Not only does the process rely on efficiency, standardization, and control, but the extremely effective and profitable business model succeeds at the *expense* of Americans' health—especially that of its youth. We subsidize, promote, and even celebrate the causes of obesity and bad health for our next generation—the irrationality of rationality, or "kill it to save it."

Between 1962 and 2010, the rate of obesity in this country nearly tripled to 37% of all U.S. citizens. Obesity in children aged 6-11 years more than doubled from 7% in 1980 to nearly 18% in 2012. Similarly, the percentage of adolescents aged 12-19 years who were obese quadrupled from 5% to nearly 21% over the same period. Between 1980 and 2010, the number of

U.S. citizens with diabetes more than tripled from 5.6 million to 20.1 million, with youth aged 10-19 experiencing some of the heaviest growth. These increases have caused the CDC to conclude that obesity and related illnesses are now epidemic.[5] With so many people getting sick (and it's fair to assume many more citizens don't seek treatment for symptoms such as stomach cramps, diarrhea, and other digestive maladies, and thus don't get counted in Food and Drug Administration (FDA) or CDC statistics), how did the health impact of our food production system get so bad? What comprises the basic underpinnings of our current "kill it to save it" food production paradigm?[6]

Have It Your Way? We Are What We Eat—And It's Killing Us

> So that's us, processed corn walking. (*The Omnivore's Dilemma*[7])

"The industrialization of food production" is a phrase that harkens back to the Chicago slaughterhouses and Upton Sinclair's *The Jungle*.[8] Sinclair's semi-fictional expose of filthy steaming carcasses and severed body parts moving along the killing floors inspired federal regulations such as the Meat Inspection Act and the Pure Food and Drug Act of 1906. Along with creating the Food and Drug Administration in 1930, federal, state, and even local health departments responded to Sinclair's work by passing laws regulating food safety and imposing strict inspection regimes during the first half of the 20th century. But the post-Second World War drive to maximize food production through increasingly industrialized and chemically-based synthetic methods meant that the bounty of American agriculture would simultaneously symbolize our innovation and naiveté, our arrogance and our vulnerability.

Cheap fossil fuels made the use of industrial fertilizers common practice. Chemical companies flooded the agricultural market with cheaper yet more powerful pesticides. Farmers no longer had to alternate fields annually to allow for soil regeneration and immediately doubled their harvest and changed farming practices forever. Mass production increased, as did the use of chemicals and preservatives in food, lowering the price and increasing the abundance and durability of supermarket shelves and processed foods sections. Single-family homes with fully stocked refrigerators and pantries fed the conceit of the postwar suburban middle class and fueled our sense of Cold War victory over the Soviet Union, especially Nixon's famous "knock out" of Leonid Brezhnev in the kitchen debates.[9]

As early as 1962, however, Rachel Carson wrote *Silent Spring* and introduced the harm that dichlorodiphenyltrichloroethane (DDT) and other pesticides posed to mainstream America. While chemical companies made billions in profits, both workers and consumers suffered the poisonous impact. As layer upon layer of hazardous production methods and waste products poked at the country's "end of ideology" complacency, more and more writers exposed the short and long term dangers of industrialized food production. By the 1970s, Frances Moore Lappe (*Diet for a Small Planet*), Wendell Berry (*The Unsettling of America*) and Barry Commoner (*The Closing Circle*) all wrote bestsellers about the harm of industrialized food production and related environmental hazards.[10] Finally, the discovery of Love Canal's toxic secrets buried in backyards and playgrounds betrayed the disastrous effect of chemical wastes on children and families (abnormally high rates of birth defects, miscarriages, chromosomal damage, and early death). Their tragedies awoke the nation's psyche to the deadly impact of hazardous chemicals. These same idyllic neighborhoods once promoted as America's utopian landscapes had become killing fields.

Yet as environmental groups won increased legislation to clean up toxic dumps (Superfund laws) and inform workers and communities of the dangers of toxic chemicals (Right to Know laws), the industrialization of food production intensified. Spurred on by Nixon's desire to drive down the cost of food, Agriculture Secretary Earl Butz changed federal farm policy from boosting prices for farmers to boosting the yields of commodity crops—mostly corn and soy. According to Michael Pollan, "The administration's cheap food policy worked almost too well: crop prices fell, forcing farmers to produce still more simply to break even, [leading] to a deep depression in the farm belt in the 1980s followed by a brutal wave of consolidation."[11] "Get big or get out" became agriculture's mantra, as family farms could not compete with burgeoning agribusiness. The average farm size more than tripled from 135 acres in 1940 to 435 acres in the late 1990s. Meanwhile, the number of farms shrank almost 300% during that same period, from 6.1 to 2.2 million farms (now fewer than 2 million farms; even that number is misleading given how many of those farms are essentially being sharecropped by farmers, whose livestock is contracted out by—and whose farms are in major debt to—the largest chicken and hog producing corporations). Food prices dropped, but mostly those of processed foods made from corn and soy—the cost of fresh produce has actually risen since the 1980s. Washington succeeded in eliminating food as a political issue of cost and supply, but the food produced and its means of production changed the very nature of how and what we eat.[12]

The most powerful forces behind the increased industrialization of food production have been fast food companies. Throughout the first decade of the 21st century, investigative journalists, food activists, and documentary filmmakers exposed the dangerous underbelly of fast food chains and how they transformed American society—*especially* how and what we eat. The rapid and massive growth of McDonalds, Burger King, Carl Jr's and Jack in the Box intensified a demand-led food production system in which a few companies sought increasingly large producers to fill their own highly standardized demands. The death of the family farm and the rise of agribusiness went hand-in-hand with industrialization, standardization, and consolidation in food. Fewer and fewer companies now control the bulk of production: the top four meatpackers control over 80% of beef, almost 70% of pork, and over 60% of chicken. The companies, however, are not the only things being consolidated—so are the cows.[13]

A Steer's Crappy Life

> My guess is that, could you interview a steer and ask him whether he'd rather be out in the pasture or in

> the feedlot, I think the vast majority of them would vote to be in the feedlot. (Bill Haw, CEO of Kansas City's National Farms and concentrated animal feeding operation (CAFO) operator[14])

The modern production of beef, pork, and poultry brings animals into larger and larger—yet closer and closer—quarters. Take the life of a steer. Born and raised primarily on rancher-owned farms, these cows are grass-fed for around six months before being moved from field to CAFO (Concentrated animal feeding operation). The Union of Concerned Scientists describes CAFOs as "characterized by large numbers of animals [anywhere between 1,000 and 100,000] crowded into a confined space—an unnatural and unhealthy condition that concentrates too much manure in too small an area."[15] At CAFOs, cows feed primarily on corn—lots of it—fortified with vitamins and healthy doses of antibiotics to ward off the bacteria caused primarily by feeding the cows corn and having them wade in their own crap.

And here is the greatest irony of the industrial production of beef. By consolidating cows into CAFOs and getting them fatter faster and cheaper by feeding them corn, beef producers *increase* the likelihood of producing beef with E. coli O157:H7 and then passing it on to dozens (if not hundreds, if not thousands) of other cows. Cows naturally eat grass—not corn. Research suggests that corn-fed cows are more prone to developing bacteria (such as E. coli O157:H7) resistant to natural acids. To ward off these now-mutant strains of bacteria, CAFOs feed cattle a variety of antibiotics—but the antibiotics themselves have serious impacts on consumers. As cattle stand around, ankle-deep in their own manure, one cow's sickness easily infects another's; this spreads out into almost every burger produced as multiple cows end up in each package of ground beef. And—to add injury to injury—cattle not only wade in their own feces, but they are routinely fed that very same shit.[16]

In one of those richly macabre "kill it to save it" moments of economic rationalization—and despite laws prohibiting it—cows now regularly eat other cow products, especially their manure. When "mad cow disease" (bovine spongiform encephalopathy [BSE]) made its appearance on the world stage, scientists quickly discovered its main cause came from cattle being fed BSE-contaminated brain and spinal-cord tissue from other cows. The U.S. government quickly passed laws that prohibited feeding "beef-based products" to cows. However, they didn't ban using cattle scraps, bone, tissue, and manure to feed chickens. Such cow leftovers are now routinely mixed with other corn and soy and antibiotics to create chicken feed. While these aspects of cattle raising and chicken farming may gross you out, the meat industry has also found new uses for what's left on the floors of chicken coops and broiler rooms once chickens have been harvested and processed for market. "Chicken litter"—a rendered down mix of chicken manure, dead chickens, feathers and spilled feed—is marketed as cheap food for cows. The beef industry likes it because it's even cheaper than corn and soy. An estimated 2 billion pounds are purchased and fed to cows each year.[17]

As if the idea of your burger being the product of manure, beaks, bones, and feathers isn't unsettling enough, about one third of the chicken litter concoction is spilled chicken feed, which frequently includes cow meat, manure, and bone meal used to feed chickens but legally off limits for cows. However, any cow that eats chicken litter may also be consuming various beef products intended for chickens—the very same feed products that caused the mad cow disease outbreak in the first place. And it's not only the spilled feed that's the problem; the infectious agent can also be passed through the chicken manure. By the time the cows have been fattened on corn, fed with antibiotics and animal feces, and finally killed, the slaughterhouses continue the shitstorm as wads of caked on manure fall from their hides or spill out when workers remove stomachs and intestines. All of this material travels down the conveyor belt towards final consolidation as the meat from myriad cows gets ground together. A U.S. Department of Agriculture (USDA) report found that 78.6% of tested ground beef contained microbes spread primarily by fecal matter. *Consumer Reports* (*CR*) found 100% of 458 ground beef samples possessed bacteria from fecal contamination. In the end, a single cow infected with E. coli or other diseases can contaminate tens of thousands of pounds of ground beef.[18]

Antibiotics and Nature's Own "Blowback"

> And until we get real evidence or evidence of people—I hate to say it—dropping in the streets, so to speak, from antibiotic resistance, that nobody's going to do anything about this. (Tom Grumbly, Former FDA Policy Analyst[19])

Chicken farming doesn't inspire much more confidence in what we eat. Tens of thousands of chickens in windowless houses creep and crawl through their own crap and past the dead and dying carcasses of other chickens (apparently soon to be cattle feed). *The New Yorker* writer, Michael Specter, visited a chicken house and claimed he was "almost knocked to the ground by the overpowering smell of feces and ammonia." He continued:

> My eyes burned and so did my lungs, and I could neither see nor breathe. … There must have been 30,000 chickens sitting silently on the floor in front of me. They didn't move, didn't cluck. They were almost like statues of chickens, living in nearly total darkness, and they would spend every minute of their six-week lives that way."[20]

While industry spokespeople will paint a picture of fat and happy poultry lounging on beach chairs sipping out of umbrella draped feeding tubes, the truth is that chickens don't lounge—they languish. They literally cannot move because their genetically designed, rapidly grown, big-breasted bodies overwhelm their bones, muscles, and legs. Most can barely slide a step or two. And their brief lives—steeped in chicken manure, fed on cattle scraps and poop, and pumped full of antibiotics—don't bode well for the meat they eventually become.

Towards the end of their journey, chickens are bathed or power washed with ammonia, chlorine, and myriad chemicals to kill salmonella and other bacteria (which they carry primarily a result of industrializing and rationalizing chicken farming to begin with). While manufacturers claim that using such chemicals and antibiotics in massive doses has no adverse impact on consumers, most scientists *not* paid by corporate money suggest otherwise. For almost twenty years, the FDA, the CDC, the National Academy of Sciences (NAS), and the World Health Organization (WHO) have criticized the overuse and abuse of chemicals—and especially antibiotics—in animal food production, concluding:

> There is clear evidence of adverse human health consequences due to resistant organisms resulting from non-human usage of antimicrobials. These consequences include infections that would *not* have otherwise occurred, increased frequency of treatment failures (in some cases death) and increased severity of infections.[21]

Of course, antibiotics are themselves a unique form of "kill it to save it."

Once thought to be the "magic bullet" that might rid humanity of most diseases, antibiotics have proven to be a most effective elixir against violent bacteria. Inappropriate and over usage, however, create drug-resistant strains of bacteria, leading the CDC and many other health organizations to encourage doctors and patients to use fewer antibiotics more judiciously.[22] Penicillin's founder, Alexander Fleming, predicted such a dilemma, imagining there might come a time when antibiotics could be bought over the counter and people would routinely "underdose" themselves:

> The time may come when penicillin can be bought by anyone in the shops. … [Then] the ignorant man may easily underdose himself and by exposing his microbes to non-lethal quantities of the drug make them resistant. Here is a hypothetical illustration. Mr. X. has a sore throat. He buys some penicillin and gives himself, not enough to kill the streptococci but enough to educate them to resist penicillin. He then infects his wife. Mrs. X gets pneumonia and is treated with penicillin. As the streptococci are now resistant to penicillin the treatment fails. Mrs. X dies.[23]

Today, we have created bacteria we call "super bugs" because they are resistant to almost all common antibiotics.

While the medical industry has worked hard to diminish the use of antibiotics and reduce the occurrence of resistant viruses, employing antibiotics in food production continues to increase. *CR* found a type of antibiotic-resistant Staphylococcus aureus (S. aureus) bacteria called methicillin-resistant Staphylococcus aureus (MRSA) on three conventional—CAFO-raised and antibiotics-fed ground beef— samples out of almost 300. MRSA kills about 11,000 people in the U.S. every year. *CR* also found "18 percent of conventional beef samples were contaminated with other superbugs—the dangerous bacteria that are resistant to three or more classes of antibiotics."[24] The growing industrialized food production system has itself become addicted to antibiotics, and each package of ground beef or chicken tenders that hits the supermarket shelves hooked on drugs poses increased risks to consumers' health. The magic bullet may now be aimed directly at us.

Normally, people would duck if such weapons were pointed at them—but people in the United States remain only dimly aware of the extent of these threats. In Europe, many countries have severely regulated and limited the use of antibiotics in animals. In Denmark, serious scientific research informed government policy and led to banning the use of many antibiotics (and ALL antibiotics commonly used in human medical therapy). The goal was to increase the health and wellbeing of both humans and livestock. These transformative policies did not result in massive rebellion among farmers, retailers, consumers, or corporate food producers. In fact, because most dairies and slaughterhouses are owned by farmer co-ops, producers willingly and with great pride took on responsibility for the nation's health and designed more efficient and healthy ways of producing food. For example, from 1992 to 2008, antibiotic use in pigs dropped by more than 50%, yet overall productivity increased from 18.4 million pigs in 1992 to 27.1 million in 2008. As Jørgen Schlundt, director of the Danish National Food Institute, explained, "We have more efficient production and less disease." Journalist Sharon Levy added:

> Many Danish farmers now allow piglets to stay with their mothers for a longer period, which allows them to build their immune systems naturally … [compared to those] separated from their mothers very early in life [who] are much more susceptible to infection.[25]

Schlundt recognized that Denmark's penchant for using scientific knowledge and evidence-based research for policy making doesn't always play well across the Atlantic. But he also sees the irony. "When I talk to people from the U.S. about this," he notes wryly, "I have to start by saying that Danes are not communists." The antibiotic restrictions in Denmark are a science-based policy change, he says, well supported by data from multiple sources. Schlundt points out that this kind of thinking is hardly foreign to the United States. "The Danish researchers doing [this] work in Denmark all had some level of training at [the CDC]," he explains. "All Danish work on risk assessment is directly impacted by U.S. thinking."[26]

But applying such scientific knowledge to policy making in the United States gets measured against the economic costs to production and the powerful corporate lobbies that spread their money around Washington to *stop* science from informing policy making. Improving public health has a price, and corporations prefer to ignore evidence and simply spend more money on lobbying. Or they throw money at hack scientists of their own, willing to provide inflated, flawed, faulty, and false knowledge to protect or promote their wealthy benefactors.[27]

The U.S has become a nation ruled by corporate interests and the chimera of deregulation as an expression of individual freedom, regardless of how sick we become. Protecting corporate hegemony, however, requires keeping American people both ignorant and antiregulation. One "kill it to save it" irony is that deregulation in agriculture has actually facilitated consolidation, while massive subsidies for pesticide use and genetically modified (GM) corn and soy helped destroy family farms. The hardworking farmers feeding their families and the country—promoted by Reaganesque myths of rugged individuals—barely exist anymore, driven out of business by "kill it to save it" policies.[28]—Denmark may not be a communist or socialist society, but—like most other industrialized nations--it is an educated society, committed to using scientific evidence to prevent as well as treat illness. It also protects family farmers for the better health and safety of all their people. In America, "kill it to save it" policy making does just the opposite.

From Killer Seeds to Chicken Tenders: What's Left of the Yeoman Farmer

> Those who labor in the earth are the chosen people of God, if he ever had a chosen people, whose breasts he has made his peculiar deposit for substantial and genuine virtue. (Thomas Jefferson, *The Agrarian Republic*[29])

> If farmers lose their rights to use their own seeds they will become serfs to the land. (Percy Schmeiser, Canadian farmer sued by Monsanto[30])

Radical critics of American democracy have long suspected that national elections don't make much difference anymore. Local contests, however, are characterized by more direct democracy and can have a huge impact on citizens' everyday lives. One might even suggest that an overlap exists between the conservative instincts for "states' rights" and the progressive commitment to local, participatory democracy. But one of ALEC's dedicated areas of legislative involvement focuses on designing and promoting bills that *limit* local democracy and the ability of towns, counties, and states to restrict, limit, or even identify GM food. Despite all of ALEC's Orwellian named "Truth In ..." legislation, the truth is the last thing this bill mill and its chemical and food industry members want to share. In state after state, county after county, ALEC legislation stops communities from knowing what's in their food and how it's produced.[31]

The debate over genetically modified organisms (GMOs) is a serious and sometimes complicated one, and there are reasons to believe that highly regulated and narrowly limited GMO use could be beneficial. But to have such a discussion requires unrestricted access to data about GMOs and the power to decide for or against their use. The ability to have that information and control some of the basic elements of how humans relate to their food and its safety is not only about what *consumers* eat (as discussed earlier), but also about what producers grow and how they grow it. ALEC's efforts deny most communities such democratic deliberation and decision making.

One of ALEC's most powerful corporate members, Monsanto, has been accused of creating some of the worst deadly chemicals ever introduced to our planet, let alone our food supply. What journalist Jason Louv calls Monsanto's "Greatest Hits" include DDT (a dangerous carcinogen with a deadly impact on humans and wildlife, eventually banned worldwide in the early 1970s), polychlorinated biphenyls (PCBs) (a deadly toxin banned by the U.S in 1979; the manufacturer never informed the public of the hazards, despite knowing PCBs could cause cancer), recombinant bovine growth hormone (rBGH) (a highly controversial substance that many argue causes breast cancer), and Agent Orange (a defoliant responsible for nearly a million deaths and birth defects among Vietnamese people, as well as myriad forms of cancer in tens of thousands of U.S Vietnam veterans). Most notable about all of these incredibly hazardous chemicals has been Monsanto's consistent denial of the products' dangers—despite knowledge of the dangers—and an absolute refusal to take any responsibility for harm done to people or the environment. Mitt Romney can say that corporations are people, and the law can equate corporate rights with individual rights, but in my opinion if Monsanto were a person, he or she would profile as a pathological serial killer.[32]

Aside from the dangerous toxins it's unleashed around the globe, Monsanto's ruthlessness can be seen in the ways it pursues farmers guilty of, well, farming. For generations, farmers have grown crops every year and saved the seeds from harvested plants to use the following year. This is what farming *is*. Farmers purchased seeds periodically, but the crops they grow and the seeds produced belonged to the farmer. More recently, however, companies like Monsanto have lobbied to make the practice of "saving seeds" illegal and even designed technology to make it impossible.[33]

Take, for example, Monsanto's Roundup Ready seeds. These seeds are genetically developed to survive being doused with Monsanto's herbicide, Roundup. Researchers have argued that Roundup's key ingredient, glyphosate, is a carcinogen and could be responsible for many kinds of cancer. Monsanto has contested these results and successfully kept various U.S. regulating agencies from further testing. What we do know is that Roundup can be so powerful it not only kills weeds but also other crops—and pretty much any living organism—except Monsanto-engineered soy, corn, or canola. Roundup Ready seeds guarantee that Monsanto corn and soybean seed will be the only ones not susceptible to Roundup herbicide.[34]

But Monsanto requires farmers to sign licensing agreements when purchasing Roundup Ready seeds, restricting growers from collecting, washing, saving, and replanting them. Essentially, Monsanto sells the seeds but claims patent ownership over future seeds produced in the process of growing and harvesting. As an "intellectual property right," Monsanto owns the seed patent; farmers must buy the seeds annually, or be open to lawsuits. Monsanto has successfully sued hundreds of North American farmers; some have lost their land and livelihood just because they replanted their seeds in traditional fashion. These cases make Monsanto's threats of possible lawsuits even more effective, as tens of thousands of farmers have gotten letters, emails, phone calls, and visits from Monsanto lawyers and private detectives telling them to cease replanting or else.[35]

One could argue that farmers freely enter into such agreements with Monsanto, but that's not entirely true. Monsanto has an all-out campaign to control the seed market—and has bought out many independent and small-business seed sellers around the country—so that farmers *can't* go anywhere else. Monsanto, sometimes along with ALEC, has helped design and pass legislation and pushed for FDA rules to criminalize seed cleaning operations, making it harder for farmers to store and reuse their own seeds. Obtaining the various loans needed to survive can be more difficult if farmers don't demonstrate using Monsanto or other GMO seeds. And then, of course, there is the case of Percy Schmeiser, who never intended on planting and harvesting GMO seeds at all.[36]

For fifty years, Schmeiser, a Canadian farmer from Saskatchewan, bred his own canola seeds, experimenting with hybridization and other traditional ways of developing better seeds. But a bad storm in the winter of 1997 dispersed GMO seeds throughout the region, where three other farmers had started using Roundup Ready. Schmeiser found that some of his own seed had been contaminated. He lost decades of his own work breeding canola seed because of the cross-pollination. Adding insult to injury, the following year Monsanto sued Schmeiser, claiming that he had planted Monsanto Roundup Ready seeds without permission and owed the company all of his previous year's proceeds. Despite the fact that Monsanto had ruined Schmeiser's *own* breeding efforts and, in essence, invaded his farm, the company claimed (and the courts subsequently found) that regardless of *how* Monsanto seeds infiltrated Schmeiser's land, the seeds belonged to the company. Schmeiser had violated Monsanto's patent.[37]

Instead of paying the US$100,000 judgment, though, Schmeiser appealed and countersued Monsanto for environmental contamination and ruining his own seed. This unleashed the now predictable side of corporate thuggery; company investigators began following Schmeiser and his wife, spying on their house and farm, calling them on the phone, and telling them to stop the lawsuit or face recrimination. Schmeiser explains: "They did everything to bring us down financially and mentally and that's what they are doing to financially and mentally break people. They are totally ruthless and they have no ethics, no morals; it's totally about the bottom line."[38]

In 2001, Canadian courts not only upheld the original judgment against Schmeiser, but also added a US$400,000 penalty to pay some of Monsanto's legal fees. The courts' consistent finding supported Monsanto's position that it does not matter how farmers are contaminated—by wind, birds, insects, pollen, and so on—GMO seeds (and any other plants that might be tainted) become Monsanto's seeds under patent law. Monsanto's licensing agreement stipulates that farmers *only* grow Monsanto seed and use Monsanto herbicides, that farmers can't replant seeds, and that Monsanto personnel must be permitted to enter the farmer's property and check bank and farm records. As of 2003, contracts now include a prohibition against *ever* suing Monsanto. Eventually, Schmeiser won a moral victory when Canada's Supreme Court maintained Monsanto's patent rights but wiped clean any financial judgment against him. U.S. courts have not been as favorable to farmers.[39]

Aside from the infringement on free speech rights and the right to due process that Monsanto extorts from their farmers, the overall methods Monsanto employ suggests that democracy, the Constitution and its Bill of Rights are all up for the highest bidder. Troy Roush, an Indiana farmer and Monsanto victim, advises growers threatened by the company. He explains that the first thing farmers must do is get independent, third-party sampling, because Monsanto falsifies its own findings. Roush goes on to explain that:

> The farmer most at risk is the farmer NOT growing GMO soybeans because he has to prove his innocence. That's the opposite of what people think our legal system does in America—innocent until proven guilty. Well, maybe so in a criminal situation, but … when you are in a civil fight with a company like Monsanto it is up to you to prove you did NOT do what they are accusing you of. … The majority of farmers I speak with don't have the financial wherewithal to fight these battles … and then you have these multinational corporations spending millions of dollars. They can prove whatever they want. Lady Justice is holding those scales and balances and the way the court system seems to work in America … is you pile money on the balances and whoever piles the most money on wins.[40]

It appears that Monsanto goes to great lengths to protect not only their patents but also their business model, which is based on keeping farmers financially indebted, legally liable, and physically and emotionally fearful of breaking with the company. Farming is almost dead—and so are the seeds. Monsanto has temporarily held back its most damaging strategies for keeping farmers enslaved to their seed. In one of the most obvious "kill it to save" metaphors imaginable, Monsanto has developed seeds with genetic use restriction technology (GURT). Known as "terminator seeds" or "suicide seeds"—or perhaps most accurately as "killer seeds"—these seeds produce sterile crops: plants with seeds that *cannot* reproduce. Monsanto claims not to have released this product on the market, but rumors of its use caused international protests. And there would be nothing illegal, per se, if the company did "commercialize" the product.[41]

The image of yeoman farmers as the bulwark of democracy is based on the notion that landowners who control their crops and their harvest will participate effectively and knowledgably in a democracy because the country—and literally the land—has intense, tangible meanings for them. Thomas Jefferson's lofty ideals of democracy, similar to those of de Tocqueville (1900) and Crèvecœur (1912) depended on the yeoman farmer. Jefferson wrote that the: "Cultivators of the earth are the most valuable citizens. They are the most vigorous, the most independent, the most virtuous, and they are tied to their country and wedded to its liberty and interests by the most lasting bands."[42] But while groups like ALEC create and disseminate legislation to prohibit democratic rights, access to information, and due process, farmers are degraded from icons of colonial democracy to modern-day serfs tending other people's seeds. And this is true not only for farmer's crops, but also their livestock.

At the beginning of the documentary *Food Inc.*,[43] chicken farmer Vince Edwards claims that "the chicken industry came in here [McClean County, Kentucky] and helped this whole community out … I have about 300,000 chickens." But the possessive here is a bit of a stretch; Edwards doesn't really *own* the birds. Tyson delivers chicks stamped with corporate I.D. and barcodes and Edwards cares for them until the company comes to harvest full-grown chickens a few weeks later. The chickens themselves have been genetically designed to grow breasts twice as large as—and in half the time of—natural chickens. Edwards explains: "[Tyson] has been growing chickens for many, many years … and it's all a science. They have it all figured out. If you can raise a chicken in 45 days, why would you want one you gotta grow in three months ... More money in your pocket."[44]

Unfortunately, very few chicken farmers have much money in their pockets; they are deeply in debt. And their debt has less to do with natural science than with economic science and exploitation. The "chicken belt" refers to areas throughout the South where tobacco farms gave way to chicken farms. Global competition, agribusiness-friendly farm policy, and the demise of domestic cigarette markets all made small tobacco farming unsustainable. From 1987 to 2012, U.S. tobacco farms declined over 90%. In Virginia alone, there were 8,444 tobacco farms in 1992 and only 558 in 2012.[45] In came poultry producers—now known as "Big Chicken." These companies advertised in local newspapers that they would help tobacco farmers convert to poultry farming. Pilgrim's Pride allegedly went from farm to farm in some regions with glossy brochures and representatives with calculators and fairytales about how much money farmers could make. Story after story from farmers recount how companies showed them "the numbers" they could take to local banks for the loans needed to start their businesses. One remembers how: "The banks make it sound good, the poultry companies make it sound good. They can paint a Rembrandt about how good this business sounds." Or as Dudley Butler, former head of Grain Inspectors Packers and Stockyards Act (GIPSA), suggests: "When [the chicken company marketers] get through talking to [the farmer], he can see Hawaii over the horizon."[46]

One farmer, Craig Watts (whose story is the focus of the documentary *Cock Fight*[47]), remembers being offered a dream deal. Now, he explains: "We're not farmers, we're sharecroppers, but you don't know this when you first get in. You're a little naïve and you think that they're gonna be fair business people." But after three years of working round the clock and getting close to paying off his initial debt of over US$200,000, Perdue reportedly convinced him to double his chicken houses to increase income. He quickly realized that he hadn't doubled his revenue—but he had more than doubled his expenses and debt. He claims the numbers he received were fictions: "I don't know where they got them from."[48]

Other farmers in the documentary *Sharecroppers*[49] remember similar lies and dubious practices that they fell victim to: "Everything's wonderful that first year you make good money ... The second year you make a little less and it just keeps coming down where you're like everyone else." As revenues go down, companies continue to demand increasingly expensive upgrades to chicken houses and equipment. The result? Chicken farmers go further into debt and have no viable option but to grow chickens, because leaving the business would result in having to pay back their debt in full. The Crutchfield family of Lamar, Arkansas needed what Farm Aid calls an "all-star lineup of attorneys and experts in food, farm and consumer rights organizations" from around the country just to help them file suit for bankruptcy and keep their farm. Few farmers can glean those resources; they can't leave the business, and thus they fall further under the control of the companies.[50]

It's undoubtedly a brilliant business model for the companies involved—but it's a devastating economy for the farmers, over 70% of who live near or below the poverty line. As in the case of Monsanto farmers, poultry "keepers" have also lost their Freedom of Speech, as well as their freedom to farm. Recent congressional hearings and documentaries feature testimony suggesting that "Big Chicken" retaliates against farmers if they try to speak out. The companies own the birds, make the feed, own the processing plants, and do the marketing. While company prices and profits have gone up over 70% since 2000, prices for farmers have risen only 11%—not enough to keep up with increased costs and upgrades. Some farmers have witnessed that if they complain to the company about mandatory upgrades or make public aspects of unfair contracts and practices, they no longer receive higher-grade chicks. Higher-grade chicks produce higher incomes for farmers, especially with companies that use competitive pay schemes such as the "tournament system," which pits farmers against each other. Growers are divided into groups and the company decides how much it will pay total for each one. Then, while the top one or two producers in a group may make decent money, the majority of growers don't. Getting lower-grade chicks guarantees farmers less money and greater hardships. So many farmers are too afraid to speak out.[51]

Other forms of retaliation have reportedly included physical and economic intimidation. When Watts first spoke out about the poultry industry practices, he received almost daily inspection visits and eventually written notices of violations and penalties. The Crutchfields stopped receiving birds from Tyson altogether. Aside from fear and financial retribution, the poultry industry lobbyists have been very effective in essentially criminalizing free speech. In 2008, the U.S. Farm Bill authorized a rule the USDA had worked on for six years designed to protect poultry, cattle, and pig farmers from industry retaliation. It also insured farmers would have better standing when negotiating contracts with "Big Chicken." But conservative lawmakers placed riders on the bill (and all subsequent agricultural legislation addressing the meat industry) that prohibited the USDA from spending *any* resources to enforce the rule. In 2015, Congress once again failed to fund a rule designed to protect farmers' First Amendment rights. It would be perhaps too obvious a point to make that the majority of lawmakers who lead the opposition to a rule that only enforces basic constitutional rights for poultry farmers also receive huge campaign contributions from "Big Chicken" and their trade group, the National Chicken Council. And these companies and trade groups can donate unlimited amounts of money because the courts have found that campaign money equals free speech. The scales of justice are heavily burdened by the weight of not only corporate dollars, but also infinite irony.[52]

Meanwhile, the very foundation of the constitution and the exercise of free speech wheezes in the dank hallows of chicken houses and ALEC conference rooms. The triumph of capitalism over democracy and the ability of rich and powerful individuals and the companies they own to destroy even a semblance of actual democratic governance and free speech goes mostly unabated. But perhaps that's because, while corporate-sponsored policies and politics consistently stifle information about possible health and safety risks, the false claims and junk science that corporate-sponsored scientists and public relations firms produce degrade both knowledge and information.

SIX

Junk Food, Junk Science and a Bad Case of Mad Truth Disease

> "Freedom is the freedom to say that two plus two make four. If that is granted, all else follows." (George Orwell, *1984*[1])

The video starts with a chunky, bearded white guy stating that for too long the popular media and the scientific press have suggested obesity comes from people eating high-calorie fast food, junk food, and sugary drinks despite "virtually no compelling evidence" that this is the case. We then see a relatively fit guy on a couch supposedly watching TV, eating chips and ketchup-drenched French fries, and surrounded by empty candy and snack wrappers. The chunky bearded guy, Dr. Steven Blair, is a Professor Faculty Affiliate at the University of South Carolina's Prevention Research Center and also Vice President of Coca-Cola's new Global Energy Balance Network (GEBN), the organization that made the film. He concludes the video introduction proclaiming: "Those of us interested in science, public health, medicine, have to learn to get the right information out there."[2]

Within months, GEBN had taken the video down from its website and Dr. Blair had issued the following statement:

> I have asked that my video addressing energy balance be taken down from the GEBN website. I regret that a statement I made in this video has been used by some to brand GEBN as a network focusing only on physical activity. This is not true and never has been true. From the beginning the mission of GEBN has been to study the *science* [emphasis added] of energy balance which involves both diet and physical activity. GEBN has some of the top nutritionist experts in the world who have published research showing the importance of diet and in particular of soda consumption in causing obesity. My dismissal of diet as a cause of obesity did a disservice to their work. I hope many of you can relate to feeling so passionate about an issue that you say some things that you later regret.[3]

Personally this statement reminds me of the ways in which precocious children and politicians offer "apologies" when their hands are caught in the proverbial cookie jar. After all, Blair does not say he "regrets" his statements, only the ways in which others have "used" them to distort his organization. Yet his original claim is very clear: "virtually no compelling evidence" to support high calorie intake as the primary cause of obesity. And what of the latter suggestion that he simply misspoke due to "feeling so passionate" about the issue? It seems unlikely that such a highly polished corporate video would not be carefully scripted: that every word was not purposely edited to convey *exactly* the message that Coca-Cola wanted. By claiming we need more data on "energy balance," what this video did was avoid the myriad data we already have on the *disastrous* impact of sugary drinks and junk food on obesity and diabetes, especially in children.

More than enough scientific studies exist to prove beyond any doubt that such food is just plain bad for us. But if GEBN can create the guise of its own "new science," give the field a new name ("energy balance"), and suggest that we need more studies on the impact of physical activity on calorie intake (much of which, again, we already know), then perhaps it can obfuscate or misdirect people into doubting what the scientific research already tells us. If GEBN is successful, people will discount their own knowledge, experience and instinct—now clouded by manufactured scientific uncertainty—and they will follow their gut desires to eat crappy food and drink crappy drinks and maintain Coca-Cola's bottom line. And armed with "new science" and "expert data," well-funded, corporate politicians can contradict public health campaigns and claims. And this, many suggest, is what Coca-Cola, Pepsi, and their industrial front groups—such as the American Beverage Association (ABA) and the International Bottled Water Association (IBWA)—have done.[4]

Aside from lobbying politicians, Coca-Cola spending millions of dollars to create GEBN and support "university-based research" follows a long precedent of corporations funding scientists willing to concoct theories and studies that support corporate profits. GEBN President, James O. Hill, also serves on the Board of Directors for McDonalds and General Mills and has received research support from the American Beverage Association and the Beef Council.[5] In other situations, Coca-Cola has gone to great lengths, and given funds to corrupt governments and dictatorships, in countries like the Philippines, Guatemala, Pakistan, India, and Columbia to protect anti-labor, anti-environmental agendas in these nations.[6]

Why not spend a few million here at home to convince people that, despite overwhelming scientific evidence that soda is bad for you, Coca-Cola has its own science that suggests otherwise? As if junk food wasn't bad enough, now Coca-Cola wants us to consume junk science.

The New York Times was primarily responsible for exposing Coca-Cola's GEBN farce. Reporters such as Anahad O'Connor followed the money to find out just how huge Coca-Cola's impact on producing false and misleading science had been. His stories forced Blair's retraction and an apology of sorts from CEO Muhtar Kent. In Kent's letter to the *Wall Street Journal* (pledging to improve transparency), he suggests that, "The characterization of our company does not reflect our intent or our values."[7] But what, then, are we to make of reports of the company allegedly violating environmental and human rights around the world? In

India, for example, one of its fastest-growing national markets, Coca-Cola drains drinking water from poor communities, releases dangerous effluents into groundwater, builds illegally on indigenous lands, and so on.[8] At home, they build playgrounds and support First Lady Michelle Obama's anti-obesity campaign while pouring millions into their sugary products. Arguably the beverage company even breaks its promises not to market directly to young children as cute cartoon polar bears and Santa Claus pushes Coke to kids.[9]

At my own college, a "ban the bottled water" campaign successfully changed the habits of many students, staff, and faculty. Students educated the campus and convinced administrators to place water spigots throughout classroom buildings and residence halls where people could refill reusable drinking bottles instead of buying bottled water. Many campus events now feature tap water in pitchers. But when the issue of removing bottled water from vending machines arose, Coca-Cola threatened to stop their annual institutional grants for exclusive vending machine rights. As was explained in the previous chapter, cash-strapped schools now rely on corporate money to compensate for public funding cuts. Aside from threatening to stop payments, Coca-Cola also produced videos criticising student movements to ban bottled water for stifling "freedom of choice" and threatening "one of the healthiest drinks on the shelf." We still have bottled water in vending machines where I work.[10]

Consider also that Coca-Cola ran a campaign *against* tap water, one of the most cost-effective and safe public resources still available. While reportedly polluting ground water around the world and supporting tax policies that degrade public infrastructure's ability to maintain and regulate free, healthy tap water at home, Coca-Cola feeds fears about possible health risks of tap water. They have even gone so far as to persuade restaurateurs to train their employees to stop using tap water and promote bottled water and other soft drinks instead. *Civil Eats* writer Andy Bellatti explores their "Cap the Tap" campaign, in which Coca-Cola suggests:

> Capture Lost Revenue By Turning Off the Tap. Every time your business fills a cup or glass with

> tap water, it pours potential profits down the drain. The good news: Cap the Tap™–a program available through your Coca-Cola representative–changes these dynamics by teaching crew members or wait staff suggestive selling techniques to convert requests for tap water into orders for revenue-generating beverages.[11]

Bellatti continues:

> "Cap the Tap" is a perfect example of the doublespeak that Big Food and Big Soda often employ. The carefully calculated veneer of wanting to be "part of the solution" and "offering choices" to consumers is negated by efforts like this one, which basically paints tap water as an "enemy to be defeated."

Kent concludes his own GEBN apology by saying: "As we continue to learn, it is my hope that our critics will receive us with an open mind. ... The one thing we all have in common—we care."[12] Given Coca-Cola's practices, even this claim is hard to swallow.

Kill the Messenger: Change the Message

For decades now, numerous chemical companies have used scientists to challenge critics of pesticides and genetically modified (GM) foods while simultaneously promoting the agricultural bounty they have produced. And certainly tobacco companies tried for decades to obscure or deny scientific evidence about the health risks of smoking while making commercials touting the social and psychological benefits of lighting up.[13] The documentary *Merchants of Doubt* explores the billions of dollars that fund the ruthless tactics of think tanks and public relations firms that try to prevent government and the public from demanding regulations to protect our health and safety. But perhaps the most egregious example of purposely creating junk science and attacking legitimate scientists occurred in the area of climate change.[14]

Early in George W. Bush's first year in office, he announced that the United States would not implement the Kyoto Protocol to meet global greenhouse gas reduction goals. His rationale was "The incomplete state of scientific knowledge of the causes of, and solutions to, global climate change." Bush wanted to not only make sure climate change policy would be "market-based," but also to wait until "all the science was in." For most astronomers, mathematicians, climatologists, and leaders in climate research, the science had been in for almost two decades—climate change was real and human activities (especially producing CO2 by burning fossil fuels) were primarily to blame. Yet, instead of actually looking to see if all the science was in, Bush got rid of the scientists.[15]

Heeding the demand of ExxonMobil's top lobbyist, Randy Randol, Bush conducted a housecleaning of Environmental Protection Agency (EPA) scientists and directed that climate scientists no longer be invited to partake in policy discussions on—you guessed it—climate change. As Dr. Rosina Bierbaum, former acting director of the Office of Science and Technology Policy (OSTP), explained: "The scientists [who] knew the most about climate change at OSTP were not allowed to participate in deliberations on the issue within the White House inner circle."[16] For his entire first term, Bush stalled any real effort to address climate change, claiming "we lacked the adequate scientific knowledge" at the same time as he refused to listen to his own scientists and what they knew.[17]

ExxonMobil's resistance to climate change policy seems peculiarly ironic because ExxonMobil itself had been on the forefront of scientific research and discovery about the dangers of climate change and fossil fuels' role in causing it. According to a recent investigation of the company's work on climate change from the early 1970s to the present, *InsideClimate News* concluded that, "Through much of the 1980s, Exxon researchers worked alongside university and government scientists to generate objective climate models that yielded papers published in peer-reviewed journals. Their work confirmed the emerging scientific consensus on global warming's risks"—and human activity's responsibility. In fact, much of the work to which ExxonMobil scientists contributed, and projects they led, resulted in climate models that have proven, thirty years later, to be highly accurate. During that period, ExxonMobil researchers suggested that while the rapidity and magnitude of global warming's impact could be debated, its existence and anthropogenic origins could not.[18]

But dropping oil prices in the mid 1980s resulted in massive cuts to ExxonMobil's climate science research program. By the late 1980s, newly selected Corporate President, Lee Raymond, seemed to be steering the company away from examining the impact of global warming. From the late 1980s through the early 2000s, no corporation spent more money than ExxonMobil on scientists and PR firms to deny the scientific evidence demonstrating climate change. Ironically, one of the first "science" groups to take up climate change was an organization named The Advancement of Sound Science Center (TASSC). TASSC had been a primary recipient of tobacco company money as cigarette makers fought against the mounting evidence that smoking was dangerous to people's health. According to Clive Hamilton, "the tactics, personnel and organizations mobilized to serve the interests of the tobacco lobby in the 1980s were seamlessly transferred to serve the interests of the fossil-fuel lobby in the 1990s."[19]

Former National Academy of Sciences President, Frederick Seitz—who earned well over a half-million dollars in the 1970s and 1980s as a consultant to R.J. Reynolds Tobacco Company—went on to chair groups such as the Science and Environmental Policy Project and the George C. Marshall Institute, both of which have been key players in efforts to "downplay" global warming. Working with Seitz was Fred Singer, who also made a fortune as a scientific hack for tobacco's Philip Morris. Seitz and Singer, along with a handful of other paid-for scientists, coauthored the Oregon Petition: a document published jointly by the Marshall Institute and Oregon Institute of Science and Medicine in opposition to the Kyoto Protocol.[20] The petition and accompanying *Research Review of Global Warming Evidence* claimed:

> The proposed limits on greenhouse gases would harm the environment, hinder the advance of science and technology, and damage the health and welfare of mankind. There is no convincing scientific evidence that human release of carbon dioxide, methane, or other greenhouse gases is causing or will, in the foreseeable future, cause catastrophic heating of the Earth's atmosphere and disruption of the Earth's climate. … We are living in an increasingly lush environment of plants and animals as a result of the carbon dioxide increase. Our children will enjoy an Earth with far more plant and animal life than that with which we now are blessed. This is a wonderful and unexpected gift from the Industrial Revolution.[21]

Up is down, white is black, and once again "there is no compelling evidence"—except for the overwhelming scientific evidence. Over 31,000 scientists allegedly signed the petition—but journalists quickly challenged the document, not only because of its absurd claims, but also because only 0.1% of signatories were actually climatologists and even fewer directly researched global warming. Meanwhile, most signatories were medical doctors and engineers (not climate scientists) and other names on the petition included the world-renowned—but deceased—scientist Charles Darwin, famous but fictional doctors Frank Burns, Hawkeye Pierce, and B.J. Honeycutt from the television show M★A★S★H★, and singer Geri "Ginger Spice" Halliwell (referred to in the document as a biochemist from Boston).[22]

The now-common practice of major corporations funding made-up science, and scientists with little to no expertise in a particular field, to prop up false claims by signing bogus reports or appearing as talking heads on television news programs continues to seriously damage our ability to keep the public informed, healthy, and safe. These "merchants of doubt," as Director Robert Kenner calls them, find no shortage of people to produce bad science. Nor is it hard to find public relations thugs who will viciously attack and intimidate real scientists, who speak out about climate change and the corporations who profit from our ignorance. As Marc Morano, right-wing attack dog, admits in Kenner's 2014 film:

> I am not a scientist, although I do play one on TV occasionally ... hell, more than occasionally. ... You go up against a scientist [in the media] and most of them are gonna be in their own little policy wonk world or area of expertise, very arcane, very hard to understand, to explain, and very BORING. ... Communication is about sales, keep it simple, and people will fill in the blank with their own, I hate to say biases. ... You can't be afraid of the absolute hand to hand combat; you've got to name names and you gotta go after the individuals. That's what I enjoy the most, going after the individuals.

In the film Morano frequently posts scientists' emails online and suggests they be harassed, attacked, and "publicly flogged." With regards to death threats that scientists received, Morano suggests he was doing the public a service: "I enjoy death threats. I think it was one of the healthiest things that could have happened in the climate debate. I still [post scientists' emails] and I enjoy doing it."[23] But if corporate scientists and media hitmen can't win the public relations battle, they try to intimidate and challenge through the legislative process and the court system.

Mad Truth Disease: What We Know and What We Think We Know

> *Howard Lyman:* One hundred thousand cows per year in the U.S. are fine at night, dead in the morning. The majority of those cows are rounded up, ground up, fed back to other cows. If only one of them has Mad Cow Disease, it [could] infect thousands.
> *Oprah Winfrey*: It has just stopped me cold from eating another burger! (Partial transcript from *The Oprah Winfrey Show*, April 16, 1996)

This segment of Oprah's show resulted in a multimillion-dollar lawsuit against Winfrey, Lyman, and the show's production company for violating "food disparagement" laws. Not much has changed since this episode, although it's quite possible that Oprah has had a burger since then—she did not respond to tweeted invitations for an interview. But 13 states still have one version or another of food hate-crime laws limiting what can and cannot be said publicly about food. Sometimes known as "veggie libel laws," this legislation emanated from a famous CBS News *60 Minutes* episode, broadcast in 1989, on the pesticide Alar.[24]

Alar—a trade name for daminozide, which regulates fruit size, color, and ripening speed— proved to be carcinogenic in many studies, including those conducted by its own producer, Uniroyal. Under pressure from corporations, the politicians they lobbied, and industry-funded researchers, the EPA did not outright ban its use, but suggested early in 1989 that it *might* issue a ban after more studies were completed. However, armed with a National Resources Defense Council (NRDC) study "Intolerable Risk: Pesticides in Our Children's Food," *60 Minutes* produced a program critical of both Alar and the EPA's lack of definitive action. Follow-up appearances by NRDC spokespeople in the media and growing concerns among consumers led grocery chains to halt sales of apples treated with Alar. The EPA eventually did ban the chemical—but not before Uniroyal terminated its production, as growers increasingly stopped using it because consumers wouldn't buy their fruit.[25]

The situation struck fear in hearts of corporate farmers, retailers, and the chemical companies that produced pesticides. Their response was twofold. First, they created food-libel laws that would punish public figures and media outlets who published or broadcast "false claims" about food. Then they lobbied to pass such legislation in over a dozen states. Second, chemical companies and agribusiness went on a public relations offensive of their own to generate the impression that the Alar case itself was an example of "anti-corporate" hype. And they succeeded in both strategies. Washington State apple growers immediately filed a US$250-million-dollar suit against CBS, claiming *60 Minutes* falsely disparaged their product. Eventually, CBS prevailed in both district and appeals courts as judges repeatedly found growers had failed to raise a genuine issue of material fact as to the falsity of the broadcast. But—as I have written about throughout this book—facts don't really matter when they contradict corporate interest and the "kill it to save it" ideological framework. The corporations and their minion just make it up.[26]

The PR firms hired by agricultural companies spread the word that essentially the growers had won and the Alar scare was a hoax. In fact, according to Elliot Negin—Senior Writer for the Union of Concerned Scientists—the Alar affair became "a favorite media symbol for a false alarm. Reporters and pundits repeatedly refer to it as a prime example of Chicken Little environmentalism and government regulation run amok." Negin continues:

> Like most media myths, this one includes a fact or two. There was indeed an overreaction to the *60 Minutes* report, as viewers confused a long-term cumulative threat with imminent danger. But Alar is a potent carcinogen, and its risks far outweigh its benefits. After extensive review, the [EPA] decided in late 1989 to ban it because "long-term exposure to Alar poses unacceptable risks to public health."[27]

Still, Negin explains that corporate PR campaigns have won the prolonged battle to leave the lingering impression on the public's mind that the entire Alar case was a media conspiracy against fruit growers and discredits the combination of so-called "bad science" and the "liberal media." Quoting David Rall, a physician and former Director of the National Institute of Environmental Health Sciences, the lasting sense of Alar among the general public is "a triumph of publicity over science."[28]

Of further interest regarding Elliot Negin's article on the Alar controversy (which appeared in a Fall, 1996 issue of the *Columbia Journalism Review*) was a letter to the editor in the following issue from Dr. Elizabeth Whelan, President of the American Council on Science and Health. Whelan wrote:

> All that really needs to be said about Elliott Negin's article attempting to justify the Alar hoax is to ask what planet he has been inhabiting for the last seven-and-a-half years. Since that time, virtually every reputable scientific body and leading scientist—ranging from the National Cancer Institute to the American Medical Association, the World Health Organization, and C. Everett Koop—has gone on record as saying that the use of Alar on apples never posed any risk to the health of either children or adults. Are we to dismiss all of these testimonies as a "concerted disinformation campaign by industry trade groups?
>
> Virtually the only scientists who still regard the Alar scare as genuine are those associated with the EPA—who, in doing so, are merely carrying out the agency's protocol that any substance that causes cancer in high doses in even a single rodent is therefore a "probable human carcinogen" (a standard that, if applied to natural substances, would lead to the banning of peanuts, honey, mushrooms, and tap water).[29]

Negin responded:

> The planet I live on has a long tradition of fact-checking, and most of Elizabeth Whelan's "facts" don't check out. While she's right about C. Everett Koop, she's wrong about the groups she cites. Neither the American Medical Association nor the National Cancer Institute has issued an official statement on Alar. Meanwhile, the World Health Organization's International Agency for Research on Cancer and its Joint Meeting on Pesticide Residues both concluded that UDMH—the major breakdown product created when Alar-treated apples are processed or eaten—is a carcinogen. ... Other prominent organizations (besides EPA) regard UDMH as carcinogenic, including the National Toxicology Program of

> the U.S. Public Health Service and the American Academy of Pediatrics, which urged the EPA to ban Alar ... Whelan also misstates the EPA's "protocol" for assessing cancer risk—despite the fact that the agency sent her a letter in March 1992 detailing its guidelines.[30]

Aside from the accomplishment of providing perhaps the most inaccuracies and distortions ever produced in a 172-word letter, Whelan's real success seems to have been her funding pedigree. While the American Council on Science and Health began with money from private foundations (most supported by corporate dollars), by the time of Whelan's death in 2014, almost half of the organization's funding came from the likes of American Cyanamid; Archer Daniels Midland; Chevron; the Dow Chemical Company; DuPont; ExxonMobil; General Mills; Monsanto; Pfizer; and Uniroyal—the company that not only manufactured Alar, but also conducted research that proved that Alar was indeed carcinogenic and potentially hazardous.[31] Food defamation laws are primarily intended to chill free speech and keep critics of industrialized food production from speaking out. Winfrey has never done a follow-up program on food safety and has often said, "I have no beef with beef."[32] But if corporations can't scare critics and don't win in court, they go after the critics with their own sham scientists. Groups such as Whelan's American Council on Science and Health seem to be hell bent on distorting science and criticising those with the courage and integrity to speak out. Contemporary environmental writers such as Sandra Steingraber as well as the authors of *Our Stolen Future* (1996) have been challenged by reviews published in professional and mainstream outlets but ultimately written by corporate-funded scientists.[33]

For example, the *New England Journal of Medicine* panned Sandra Steingraber's *Living Downstream: An Ecologist's Personal Investigation of Cancer and the Environment* (1997, Addison-Wesley), a book about the links between cancer and environmental contamination. But hers is also a book about the many kinds of silence surrounding cancer issues: personal and political, individual and collective, and the silence of scientists who fear loss of funding or corporate attacks. The *New England Journal's* reviewer claimed Steingraber's book was "obsessed" with environmental pollution and reminded him that environmental activists' jobs were to create controversy and panic monger. The *Journal* never acknowledged that the reviewer, Jerry H. Berke, M.D., M.P.H., was Medical Director for W.R. Grace and Company: the chemical manufacturers made famous in John Travolta's 1998 film, *A Civil Action*. The movie chronicles a real-life law suit against Grace, whose illegal dumping of toxics led to exactly the kind of neighborhood poisoning that Steingraber wrote about in her book. Steingraber's work has been widely lauded by scientists who *don't* have ties to chemical companies.[34]

Our Stolen Future received even greater vitriol as authors Colborn, Dumanoski and Peterson Myers provided evidence that endocrine disruptors can be found in a staggering list of synthetic chemicals common in pesticides, herbicides, and petrochemicals—as well as everyday household items like soaps and detergents, flame retardants, and the dioxins produced in pulp and paper mills. Science writer Laura Orlando explains that, "These chemicals can result in, among other things, severe reproductive tract deformities, declines in sperm count, elevated risk of cancer, and even behavioral changes." The industry attack on *Our Stolen Future* was instant and vicious. As Rampton and Stauber point out in their book *Trust Us, We're Experts!*, the chemical-industry-funded Advancement of Sound Science Coalition held a press conference at which almost a dozen scientists on the company dole labeled the book as "fiction." Even Whelan's group got into the act; having obtained a copy of the book in galley form before publication, they prepared an 11-page attack before it even reached bookstores. Not surprisingly, *The Wall Street Journal* referred to *Our Stolen Future* as an environmental "hype machine." But almost all reputable science since its publication has supported the book's findings.[35]

The organized public relations campaigns by corporations to encourage consumer loyalty and confidence—despite contrary scientific evidence and even the public's own experience—continue to be highly successful. The role of such advertising and media messaging has been exposed and deconstructed in numerous books and documentaries. Yet few politicians and policies hold corporations accountable. As communications and media scholar Stuart Ewen argued in the documentary *Toxic Sludge Is Good for You*: "Part of the job of corporations in a democracy is continuing to massage reality so that ordinary people see an identity between their own interests and the interest of the corporation."[36] Despite periodic wakeup calls to the dangers of industrialized food production, the overuse of chemicals and antibiotics in food and other consumer goods, and a variety of other ways in which our daily consumption-based lifestyle is bad for our environment and ourselves, corporations use PR firms to lull us back to sleep. Distortions and lies paid for by wealthy companies not only buttress "kill it to save it" policy making, but are also part and parcel of a "kill it to save it" approach to knowledge itself. However, nowhere is the distance between our experience and our policy making more disparate than in the areas of guns and crimes, explored next.

SEVEN

Junk Freedom, Broken Windows, and Black Lives Matter

> One only wishes Wayne LaPierre and his NRA [National Rifle Association] board of directors could be drafted to some of these scenes, where they would be required to put on booties and rubber gloves and help clean up the blood, the brains, and the chunks of intestine still containing the poor wads of half-digested food that were some innocent bystander's last meal. (Stephen King, *Guns*[1])

I had to return to the introduction of the book quite a few times while writing the remainder of it, in order to keep updating the part where I mention the most "recent" mass killing. In midsummer of 2015, white supremacist Dylann Roof shot and killed 9 African Americans in the Emanuel A.M.E. Church of Charleston, South Carolina. I had to substitute this shooting for the previous spring's Isla Vista killings in which a sexually frustrated misogynist, Elliot Rodger, had killed 6 people and injured 14 to punish women for rejecting him and sexually active men for being, well, sexually active. As I went back to this section of the book in Fall of 2015, Christopher Harper-Mercer had just fatally shot 9 people and wounded 9 others at Umpqua Community College in Roseburg, Oregon. Harper-Mercer had a history of mental illness and his mother had a large gun collection—a predictably toxic combination. Mrs Harper-Mercer often took her son to the shooting range.[2] In writings he left behind, Harper-Mercer praised Eliot Rodger and shared his own frustrations at being a virgin and social outcast. At this point I realized I should finish the book quickly.

But I could never have finished fast enough to account for the rapidity with which mass shootings occur in the United States. I complete the last revisions of this book as news circulates of another gun massacre in Orlando, Florida. In the worst single shooter incident of mass killings in U.S. history, Omar Mateen opened fire in a crowded gay, Latino nightclub, murdering 49 people and wounding 53 others. While perhaps unique because of its magnitude and links to both homophobia, racism and jihadi terrorism, mass shootings themselves have become commonplace in America. Extrapolating from the FBI's definition of four people murdered in one incident as a definition for "mass killing," the website www.gunviolencearchive.org uses the number of four people shot in one incident to determine a "mass shooting." Applying this definition, 372 mass shootings occurred in the United States in 2015—an average of just over one *every day*.

While mass shootings did not actually occur every day, over 70 days featured multiple mass shootings: 36 days had two mass shootings, 21 days had three, and 14 days had four or more. Particularly gruesome were the days of June 13, with 6 fatal shootings and 17 wounded; July 15, with 5 killed and 20 injured; and the week stretching from August 2 through August 9, with 18 killed and 63 injured during mass shootings. This week of violence began with drive-by shootings in Brooklyn, New York; Baltimore, Maryland; Chicago, Illinois; and St. Louis, Missouri; and ended with domestic-violence-related murders in Houston, Texas (eight dead); Barre, Vermont (four dead); and Gastonia, North Carolina (two dead, three wounded).[3]

In fact, in the week leading up to the Orlando killings in June 2016, 19 people were killed and 44 wounded in 13 mass shooting incidents. In Roswell, New Mexico, a husband and father shot his wife and four daughters; in Los Angeles, California, a man shot and wounded his former girlfriend and her son and killed her two daughters before turning the gun on himself; and separate shooting sprees at a Phoenix, Arizona hotel and a Cape Coral, Florida convenience store left five people dead and eight people wounded. In the latter cases, as in many mass shootings, no motives have been determined. But given that the number of gun-related deaths in the United States has increased over 13% in recent years—from 29,684 in 2005 to 33,636 in 2014—the number of shootings is close to average. What surprises people about shooting deaths in the United States, however, is that gun related *homicides* comprise only about one third of these incidents (just over 12,000), while *suicides* make up almost two thirds of firearm deaths. And most of these deaths are the result of handgun use.

As in all health-related phenomena in which government regulation might save lives but cost corporations a few bucks, lobbyists and spin merchants abound. The NRA's lobbying efforts to deny virtually *any* regulation of *any* type on carrying *any* gun remain legendary. While the organization's annual lobbying expenditures ranged between US$2 million and US$4 million dollars from 2008 to 2015, their election campaign contributions to candidates skyrocketed by 250%—from just over US$8 million to over US$28 million—during that same time period. With two of their own Super PACs and 501(c)(4) organizations the NRA itself will donate well over $30 million this 2016 election cycle, not to mention the wads of money they mobilize from their 5 million members' individual contributions. Despite the incredible and tragic impact that gun violence has on our nation's public health, politician after politician refuses to support even minimal regulations regarding background checks, waiting periods, or assault weapons.[4]

In part, the NRA succeeds in funding handpicked candidates who will adhere to the group's legislative agenda and infamous "scoring" system.[5] But the real impact emanates from the intimidation factor that their campaign war chests motivate. As one congressional aide, Chris Kofinis, suggested:

> Unlike some interest groups, where it is money that creates influence, here it is more the *threat* of response [emphasis added] ... The idea is that if you come out for any type of gun control, any type of commonsense reform, they are going to come after you,

> especially if you are a red-state Democrat. And they will paint you with a broad brush as being anti-gun.[6]

Even after the most recent mass shooting in Orlando, Democratic senators needed a 15-hour filibuster just to get Republican senators to allow a *vote* on gun-related legislation. The bills—one banning people on the government's terrorist watch list from obtaining gun licenses and the others expanding background checks to gun shows and internet sales—were both doomed to fail, given NRA opposition; and fail they did. But politicians prefer to keep such proposals from public votes because the majority of Americans support increased gun regulations.[7]

Not only does our nation's inability to address gun violence suffer from the same "follow the money" scheme as "kill it to save it" policies in education and food production, but the NRA and its investors also have their own information manipulators. Take, for instance, a 2013 study by the Bureau of Justice Statistics, which found that firearm-related homicides fell by 39%—from 18,253 in 1993 to 11,101 in 2011.[8] Later, in 2013, The Pew Research Center adjusted those figures to represent per capita rates, concluding that the incidence of gun-related homicides actually fell 49% during the same period. By themselves, these statistics look significant enough to suggest that gun violence is diminishing and perhaps concern about firearm regulation is misguided. In fact, the message of declining gun violence appeared far and wide in the right-wing media and was extremely loud on the tongue tips of many an NRA-pocketed legislator interviewed on mainstream media. Headlines in conservative media read: "Disarming Realities: As Gun Sales Soar, Gun Crimes Plummet" and "More Guns, Less Gun Violence Between 1993 and 2013."[9]

The evidence suggests a very different story about gun violence for a number of reasons. First, the report was not only about homicides; it was about *all* gun-related deaths, which were and are increasing. It is true that gun-related homicides declined, but just as *all* violent crimes declined. From 1994—2013, all violent crimes fell almost 700,000 (or over 37%) while the *rate* of violent crimes (factoring in population changes) fell almost 48%. All homicides fell from 23,326 to 14,196 (or almost 40%), while the per capita *rate* of murders fell 50%. Thus, the fact that gun-related homicides fell accordingly merely suggests that gun-related homicides fell at approximately the same rate (49%) as *all* murders committed with or without guns (50%). But the more notable statistical analysis suggests that most (if not all) of these major decreases occurred from 1993 to 2001, during the Clinton administration. While many theories have been generated to explain the large decline in violent crime during this period (demographic shifts, waning of the crack cocaine epidemic, improved economy, tighter gun control laws, and so on),[10] all of these trends may have impacted rates significantly. Regardless, however, the numbers are clear: from 1994 to 2001, violent crimes rates fell over 30%; from 2001 to 2013, they fell under 23%. Murders fell almost 40% from 1994 to 2001 and only 18% from 2001 to 2013.[11] Gun-related homicides fell almost half, from 7 per 100,000 people in 1993 to 3.8 per 100,000 people in 2000. But the number stayed flat throughout the 2000s, rising slightly to 4.2 in 2007.[12] While NRA and other gun-rights advocates have implied that the Bush administration's "pro-gun" policies and the massive increase in guns on the street from 2001 to the present *caused* the decrease in gun homicides, the greatest decline occurred pre-Bush and before big booms in gun sales.

Second, a more uncomfortable statistic suggests that while gun-related homicides declined alongside all murders and violent crimes, shooting deaths overall did *not* diminish—because gun-related *suicides* actually increased. Over the past 30 years, firearm suicides have exceeded firearm homicides even when homicide rates were at their highest in the late 1980s and early 1990s. Since 2006, though, the gap between the two has widened exponentially as gun-related homicides leveled off while gun-related suicides increased. And the relationship between guns and suicide continues to prove deadly. Although guns are not the most common method of suicide (drug overdose and poisoning are), gun-related suicides comprise the most *successful* suicides compared with all other methods *combined*. For example, drug overdose attempts succeed in only about 3% of cases, while handguns and shotguns succeed over 90% of the time. Meanwhile, the ease of accessibility (as well as the overall number) of guns available has serious correlations with gun-related suicides. According to the Harvard Injury Control Research Center, more guns equals more suicides, especially among teenagers and young adults. Youth firearm suicides often involve weapons found in their own homes. Researchers controlled for region; divorce; education; unemployment; alcohol use; poverty, and urbanization to demonstrate that the most statistically significant relationship between youth and suicides is the accessibility of guns.[13]

In 2011, economist Richard Florida conducted an exhaustive study of gun-related violence and a variety of psychological, economic, social, and political characteristics by state. His findings? Despite myths about mental illness, drug abuse, and even unemployment and other predictors of stress, none of these provided strong correlations with gun violence. Poverty and poor wages *did* have a positive correlation with gun violence, as did lower levels of education, less successful economic development, and—not surprisingly—whether or not states consistently voted Republican. Given these characteristics, it is even less surprising that states with stricter gun control laws had lower levels of gun-related deaths—homicides and suicides. Florida concluded:

> While the causes of individual acts of mass violence always differ, our analysis shows fatal gun violence is less likely to occur in richer states with more post-industrial knowledge economies, higher levels of college graduates, and tighter gun laws. Factors like drug use, stress levels, and mental illness are much less significant than might be assumed.[14]

Meanwhile, gun violence of another sort is also on the rise: that related to large-scale, public incidents in which firearms are involved. The FBI and other law enforcement agencies define these "active shooter incidents" as those in which "an individual [is] actively engaged in killing or attempting to kill people in a confined and populated area. Implicit in this definition is that the subject's criminal actions involve the use of firearms." Examining the years from 2000—2013, the FBI identified 160 active shooter incidents, noting they occurred in "small and large towns, in urban and rural areas, and in 40 of 50 states and the District of Columbia." And while most incidents occurred in business and school environments (70%), they also occurred on "city streets, on military and other government properties, and in private residences, health care facilities, and houses of worship." The report continues:

> The shooters victimized young and old, male and female, family members, and people of all races, cultures, and religions. The findings establish an increasing frequency of incidents annually. During the first seven years included in the study, an average of 6.4 incidents occurred annually. In the last seven years of the study, that average increased to 16.4 incidents annually. This trend reinforces the need to remain vigilant regarding prevention efforts and for law enforcement to aggressively train to better respond to—and help communities recover from—active shooter incidents.[15]

In other words, despite the significant decrease in violent crimes and murder between 2000 and 2013, the number of active shooting incidents and mass killings has risen dramatically. And we'd better get used to it.

The NRA and its gun proponents have their "researchers", too. Most notable and prolific is John Lott and his new Center for Crime Prevention Research. Lott's seminal work, *More Guns, Less Crime* (1998), argued that violent crime rates go down when states pass "shall issue" concealed carry laws.[16] In this and other books, Lott tackles most of the prevalent issues in gun debates: more guns equal less crime; good guys with guns stop mass shootings; guns are used more in self-defense cases than in committing crimes; mass shootings increase in "gun-free" areas; women's gun possession makes them safer, and low firearm murder rates in other countries are overrated and misapplied when compared to the United States. Lott has created large data sets to conduct highly sophisticated econometric studies. Unfortunately—as is often the case in such research—it doesn't prove what the researchers want it to prove and, as their research gets scrutinized, their responses get more outlandish and more wrong.[17]

For example, soon after Lott's book came out, a 16-member panel of the country's National Research Council (NRC) convened to examine whether right-to-carry (RTC) laws influenced crime rate. Their 2004 report, "Firearms and Violence: A Critical Review," looked at Lott's methods in detail and wrote:

> The committee found that answers to some of the most pressing questions cannot be addressed with existing data and research methods, however well designed. For example, despite a large body of research, the committee found no credible evidence that the passage of right-to-carry laws decreases or increases violent crime, and there is almost no empirical evidence that the more than 80 prevention programs focused on gun-related violence have had any effect on children's behavior, knowledge, attitudes, or beliefs about firearms. The committee found that the data available on these questions are too weak to support unambiguous conclusions or strong policy statements.[18]

Meanwhile, a 2010 reexamination of both Lott's work and the NRC's analysis not only supported what they called the NRC's "cautious conclusion," but also suggested the only *consistent* finding to emerge "is that aggravated assault *rises* [emphasis added] when RTC laws are adopted. For every other crime category, there is little or no indication of any consistent RTC impact on crime."[19] Such critique might have influenced Lott to note his limitations and to suggest that results are debatable and that science works best when people dedicated to its project continue to examine and collect data, in order to find the most accurate results and defensible conclusions possible. Instead, Lott continued to doggedly defend his initial research and his accusations of a scholarly witchhunt by the NRC. In a rare event, the NRC's Executive Officer publicly rebutted some of Lott's more absurd claims, but concluded with a very measured statement concerning the scientific study of gun law policies and what the initial NRC study suggested:

> [Lott's] column states that the panel ignored most of the studies that find a benefit in crime reduction from right-to-carry laws. The report contains an entire chapter and three appendices that address the rather large literature on these laws. The report cites both studies that do find positive effects and studies that do not find positive effects. On the basis of the very mixed evidence, the panel concluded that there was no basis for a conclusion that the passage of right-to-carry laws either increases or decreases crime.[20]

But when John Donohue and his colleagues revisited the NRC panel's findings, their conclusions went further in criticizing Lott. According to Evan DeFilippis, Donahue corrected Lott's dataset, which had several errors. DeFilippis continues:

> Also, the [NRC] panel failed to incorporate a number of proper criminal justice control variables and lacked clustered standard errors. ... Whereas the NRC panel found contradictory yet statistically significant results across most of the crime categories, Donohue and his coauthors found very few statistically significant effects of RTC laws on crime rates, but almost all of them, significant or not, show crime *increases.* The conclusion of the best and most sophisticated RTC study to date: these laws have no beneficial impact and may actually increase crime. Lott is wrong. It is no longer a question of whether RTC laws are beneficial, but rather if they are impotent or harmful.[21]

Most recently, Lott has been taken to task for using fraudulent survey data and reviewing his own books under fake names for Amazon and other websites. As his academic career spirals downward, he can still be found on Fox News and other right-wing propaganda websites like Brietbart.com. But so much of these discussions have gone beyond trying to really present facts and figures, scientific analyses and policies that would actually promote public safety. The power of "kill it to save it" is once again its ability to ignore uncomfortable facts and devolve into "truthiness" (accepting arguments that feel 'right' in the gut regardless of messy facts). In the case of firearms, regardless of how deadly and dangerous to the general public they prove to be, guns have become symbolic of "American freedom." To own a gun without restriction—or (since gun ownership has actually declined while opposition to gun control has increased) just knowing you *can* own a gun, any gun, and as many guns as you want without restriction—has become emblematic of our nation's gut definition for what freedom is. Freedom is not free education. Freedom is not universal, free health care. Freedom is not unrestricted access to decent jobs with living wages. Freedom is not a right to basic food, clothing, and shelter. In some states, freedom isn't even the right to vote anymore. None of the elements that Roosevelt included in his Second Bill of Rights to guarantee citizens' freedom speak to contemporary Americans' imagination of freedom. These phenomena do not make Americans *feel* free. But guns do. Individuals can hold guns. And since we can't really measure freedom, if guns make you *feel* free then the more guns we have, the more freedom we feel. And so we embrace them, fetishize them, rationalize their virtue, and defend them most virulently at those moments when they seem least virtuous—after every mass shooting in America.

From Broken Windows to Obama Care and Black Lives Matter: What's Race Got to Do With It?

> We could choose to be a nation that extends care, compassion, and concern to those who are locked up and locked out or headed for prison before they are old enough to vote. We could seek for them the same opportunities we seek for our own children; we could treat them like one of 'us.'" (Michelle Alexander, *The New Jim Crow*[22])

James Q. Wilson's and George L. Kelling's 1982 "broken windows" theory was brilliant in its simplicity: have police focus on "quality of life" crimes (public drunkenness, graffiti, vagrancy, and so on) and not only will people in a "neighborhood" *feel* safer, but small crimes also won't escalate to big crimes. The theory—based on some anecdotes, observations, and minimal research—caught the imagination of many conservative politicians and police officers tired of the 1960s and 1970s trends toward decriminalization and focus on "root causes." Despite the authors' caution against training officers to "manage street life," Wilson and Kelling did suggest their theory came from a Newark, New Jersey pilot program, in which more officers walking the beat resulted in new community standards of behavior. They explained:

> Drunks and addicts could sit on the stoops, but could not lie down. People could drink on side streets, but not at the main intersection. Bottles had to be in paper bags. Talking to, bothering, or begging from people waiting at the bus stop was strictly forbidden. If a dispute erupted between a businessman and a customer, the businessman was assumed to be right, especially if the customer was a stranger. If a stranger loitered, [an officer] would ask him if he had any means of support and what his business was; if he gave unsatisfactory answers, he was sent on his way. Persons who broke the informal rules, especially those who bothered people waiting at bus stops, were arrested for vagrancy. Noisy teenagers were told to keep quiet.[23]

This description suggests a collaborative effort between police and residents to maintain order while acknowledging certain liberties and even allowing small transgressions. Over time, however, these collaborations devolved into practices that encouraged beat cops to arrest primarily young men of color for the most minimal infractions. Exported around the country, a war on "quality of life" crimes combined with the 1980s and 1990s War on Drugs and effectively sent what some have called a "lost generation" of young men of color to prison.[24] How did this happen? With great fanfare, New York City Mayor Rudolph Giuliani and top cop William Bratton adopted "broken windows" in 1993.[25] But as geographer Neil Smith (2001) explained, operationalizing "broken windows" became a "zero-tolerance" policy driven by a revanchist (revenge) and racist framework regarding who did and didn't belong in 21st-century America. He wrote:

> The founding document of the new U.S. revanchism is undoubtedly the innocuously named Police Strategy No. 5 bearing Giuliani's and Bratton's names. … "A decent society is a society of civility," it begins, and then lists a litany of people and "behaviors" that have *stolen* the city [emphasis added] from its rightful citizens: street peddling, panhandling, prostitution, squeegee cleaners, boom boxes, graffiti, public drinking, loud clubs, speeding cars, litter louts, public urination, street artists, and "dangerous mentally ill homeless people." (The latter euphemistic convolution was forced by the fact that although homelessness is not a crime, homeless people, numbering perhaps 100,000 in the early 1990s, were the first targets of the new revanchism.) The document's subtitle tells the strategy: "Reclaiming the Public Spaces of New York." Less formally, Giuliani and Bratton vowed to "clean the city" of the "scum" that apparently "threatened" decent people walking down the street. Zero tolerance was passed off as an anticrime program. Actually, it is a social cleansing strategy.

And how, why, and for whom would this cleansing take place? Smith continues:

> The language of decency and civility in Police Strategy No. 5 was heavily overwritten by class and race norms. It was generally clear to poor New Yorkers and especially people of color and many

> immigrants that these norms expressed particular middle-class, white, often-suburban interests, ambitions, and identities. ... In fact, zero tolerance policing has led to an increase in police brutality and abuse, with a rash of police murders, shootings, beatings, sexual assaults, wrongful arrests, and various forms of corruption, suggesting a police force out of control. ... In two years, the Street Crimes Unit, a centerpiece of zero tolerance policing, made 45,000 street searches of disproportionately minority youths and made 10,000 arrests. Zero tolerance policing has encouraged race and class profiling that places a premium on street arrests of suspects while minimizing concerns about evidence. ... Operation Condor was another zero-tolerance social cleansing program. It stipulated arrest quotas for narcotics detectives working overtime, and officers would cruise the streets looking for people to pick up on petty infractions, or simply on suspicion. In March 2000, two undercover Condor officers with their quotas almost filled approached Patrick Dorismond, a Haitian immigrant and off-duty security guard, and asked to buy marijuana. When Dorismond retorted angrily that he was not a drug dealer, the officers got into a fight with him, drew a gun, and killed him.[26]

The media criticized these units and their tactics. Referring to "the Mussolini of Manhattan" and the "Hitler on the Hudson," some journalists questioned the racial and class intentions of zero tolerance.[27] After Guinean immigrant Amadou Diallo was shot dead by four police officers and 41 bullets, even police officers themselves complained that "zero-tolerance tactics" have become a "blueprint for a police state and tyranny."[28] As Neil Smith (2001) concluded, "When the police are exercised about an imminent police state, we should presumably take notice."

Of course, these policies did not end in the late 1990s or early 2000s. Courts only recently agreed that "stop and frisk" violated civil liberties and New York City Mayor, Bill de Blasio, only recently began reforming police practices—all leading

The New York Times to report that "'Stop-and-Frisk' is All but Gone From New York."[29] But such policies swept the nation throughout the 1990s and early 2000s, not only crowding the burgeoning prison industrial complex but also resulting in increased shootings of young Black men by police. The list of these murders over the past decade is too long to include here, but zero-tolerance policies and police practices like Operation Condor have left behind a Black and Brown body count crisscrossing the nation—from Eric Garner in Staten Island and Michael Brown in Ferguson, to Tamir Rice in Cleveland and John Crawford in Dayton, Ezell Ford and Dante Parker in California, Walter Scott in Charleston and Freddie Gray in Baltimore. And these are only a few of the more well-known, unarmed Black men killed by the police in 2014 and 2015; hundreds of others have met similar fates since then.[30]

The mistake would be to blame these social phenomena on "a few bad cops." As *Slate* columnist Jamelle Bouie writes:

> In this environment, where police are empowered to stop anyone for the faintest cause, violence is inevitable. Last month, Eric Garner was the victim, but it could have been anyone, because senseless deaths are a *predictable* cost of broken windows policing. It's the trade-off. We'll stop petty "disorder," but at the price of dead bodies. And given what we know about our biases, those bodies will almost always be brown.[31]

It has become an epidemic inexorably linked to the operationalizing of "broken windows" as a zero-tolerance policy of social cleansing. Young men of color are imprisoned or killed to "save" the streets and city for the rest of "us."

Even Kelling, one of the original authors of "broken windows," recently asked people not to "blame my theory for poor policing," for zero-tolerance practices and the mass arrests and shootings of young Black and Brown youth. He explains that, "Broken windows was never intended to be a high-arrest program. Although it has been practiced as such in many cities, neither Wilson nor I ever conceived of it in those terms."[32]

And to Kelling's credit, he and Wilson did carry the following disclaimer in their original 1982 *Atlantic Monthly* piece:

> The concern about equity is more serious. We might agree that certain behavior makes one person more undesirable than another but how do we ensure that age or skin color or national origin or harmless mannerisms will not also become the basis for distinguishing the undesirable from the desirable? How do we ensure, in short, that the police do not become the agents of neighborhood bigotry? We can offer no wholly satisfactory answer to this important question. We are not confident that there *is* a satisfactory answer except to hope that by their selection, training, and supervision, the police will be inculcated with a clear sense of the outer limit of their discretionary authority. That limit, roughly, is this—the police exist to help regulate behavior, not to maintain the racial or ethnic purity of a neighborhood.[33]

This seemingly throwaway disclaimer eventually undermined the entire theory and has ended in both failure and tragedy. For most, the implementation of "broken windows" policing has been discredited; contemporary criminologists, sociologists, and economists write overwhelmingly about its flawed assumptions and poor application.[34] But, as Bouie reminds us, "If broken windows were just a waste of resources, it wouldn't be a huge concern. But as a policy, broken windows has also had the effect of terrorizing Black and Latino communities."The recent turn towards social cleansing, towards terrorizing communities of color, is of course the dark underside of "kill it to save it." Part of this nation's rewired cognitive functioning graduated from welfare queens in the 1980s, to gangbangers in the 1990s, to any person of color driving, walking, shopping, or simply waiting in a shopping mall in the 2000s. As we "kill" public institutions and any real semblance or conception of "the public" in order to "save" the nation, what is left to save remains this toxic blend of hyper-individualism and corporate hegemony, often woven together with the historically strong thread of racism. When Michelle Alexander wonders why we can't treat Black and Brown youth "like one of us," the answer may be that white America (and the non-white parts of America with enough class privilege to "pass") no longer knows or cares to know (or perhaps knows all too well) what "us" means. This dynamic has been at the heart of the Black Lives Matter movement. While some, predominantly white, politicians, and pundits claim "All Lives Matter" and cry reverse racism about "special" attention to African American deaths by police, the last three decades of intensified and militarized policing in urban communities of color has resulted in movements challenging the ways in which white supremacy and neoliberalism have devastated poor, non-white neighborhoods. The degradation of education and local economies, combined with mass incarceration and unindicted police homicides, has inspired a mass movement.[35]

While the Black Lives Matter movement has focused on police shooting and police brutality in general, it continues to expand outward and offer both a critique of current racist and neo-liberal policies, as well as create a vision for a different ideological premise for public policies. In "A Vision for Black Lives: Policy Demands for Black Power, Freedom & Justice," movement leaders explain the cultural and political landscape that inspired protest, but also set out demands to address the underlying economic and racial dynamics that makes solving racism and economic inequality so difficult. As Historian Robin D.G. Kelley argues: "Demilitarizing the police, abolishing bail, decriminalizing drugs and sex work, and ending the criminalization of youth, transfolk, and gender-nonconforming people would dramatically diminish jail and prison populations, reduce police budgets, and make us safer." "A Vision for Black Lives" explicitly calls for divesting from prisons, policing, a failed war on drugs, fossil fuels, fiscal and trade policies that benefit the rich and deepen inequality, and a military budget in which two-thirds of the Pentagon's spending goes to private contractors. The savings are to be invested in education, universal healthcare, housing, living wage jobs, "community-based drug and mental health treatment," restorative justice, food justice, and green energy." But such policies invariably meet up against kill it to save it opposition that repels any efforts to create new public policy intended to address poverty, inequality and racism.[36]

The obvious case in point for such a dilemma has been the design and implementation of the Patient Protection and Affordable Care Act (ACA), which has come to be known as "Obamacare." Addressing the inadequacy of our health care system, especially the fact that over 40 million citizens had no health insurance, newly elected President Barack Obama pledged to change it. But his campaign for health care reform, more than almost any other policy or position he's promoted, incurred the wrath of conservative pundits and politicians. Health care reform debates seeded the 2009 summer of anger and frustration as masses filled town meeting halls flailing their arms and shouting, "Americans have lost our government," "we've lost our country."[37] The birth of the Tea Party during those hot, hazy days made for interesting political theater as automatic-weapon-bearing protesters carried signs like: "The Zoo Has An African Lion and the White House Has a Lyin' African;" "ObamaCare: Coming to a Clinic Near You" (with a large picture of a stereotypical tribal medicine man superimposed with President Obama's face); and a whole host of banners with pictures of monkeys, watermelons, fried chicken, and dozens of other racist images.[38]

Recent research demonstrates the impact of race on opposition to the ACA.[39] Prior to 2009, racial attitudes had little influence on white Americans' opinions about whether "health care should be voluntarily left up to individuals." But the Tea Party's summer of discontent resulted in greater racialization about health care reform. As Judy Lubin explains, "Antiblack stereotypes, which had no independent influence on preference for governmental insurance in March 2009, became a strong predictor of views on this issue by September of the same year." Other researchers found that, when similar health care policies were attributed to Obama as opposed to Bill Clinton, racial resentment and stereotypes impacted negative support for reform. Eric Knowles and colleagues found unconscious anti-Black prejudice significantly associated with negative attitudes about Obama and diminishing support for his health reform plans. Lubin concludes:

> The use of specific terms by the media and political leaders can also trigger associations about certain groups and thus shape public opinion. For example, "government spending" is synonymous with welfare to the public and is associated with blacks, the poor, homeless and other vulnerable groups. The extent to which these groups are believed to be responsible for their circumstances (and not disadvantaged by structural or social barriers) influences one's opinion on whether the government should take steps to correct inequities in society.[40]

And here lies the rub. Regardless of the actual programs within the ACA (and almost all of Obama's more progressive undertakings), a large swath of white America has responded virulently against any policy that seemed to benefit the public good over an ephemeral and highly mythological hyper-individualism—"the public" itself has been racialized to be the enemy. As Amanda Marcotte wrote:

> Attitudes about race and about the ACA are tightly interwoven. … Research has found that white people with high racial resentment, regardless of their opinion on Obama, view health care reform as a giveaway to lazy black people. You can see why people don't say these things out loud in public, but the eyebrow-wriggling and hinting has been strong throughout this debate.[41]

In the end, too many people can't see past the dubious eyebrows and the knowing nudges. Americans' health and safety degrades and declines before our eyes, but the instinctive commitments to individualism and the bottom line make it hard to imagine what a different world might look like. So we get angry with each other, rationalize our inaction with an overarching sense of impotency, and let the historical DNA of American racism run its course while we eat junk food, consume junk science, and live junk freedom.

PART 4
The Life and Death of America's Economy and Government

overview: It's the Political Economy, Stupid

> "I give them all money and they do what I want. The system is broken ... but I will make you rich." (Donald Trump, Republican Presidential Debate, August 6, 2015)

> "It is profitable to let the world go to hell." (Jorgen Randers, *The Limits to Growth*)

> "It's the economy, stupid." (James Carville, Bill Clinton's Political Advisor in *The War Room*)[1]

James Carville's now-famous quote was never meant to expose his or Bill Clinton's dour economic determinism. The true meaning of the phrase rests on the ambiguous pronoun. What is the "it" that is "the economy?" We know Carville's campaign mantra (the one he spouted in D.A. Pennebaker's documentary *The War Room*):[2] "Don't complicate the simple." But perhaps the opposite is true—"It's the economy, stupid" simplifies something incredibly complicated and painfully raw. "It" represents a profoundly cynical sense of democracy and the structures and people that perversely control it. "It" stands for "what will convince the majority of poor, working- and middle-class Americans to vote for our candidates, despite the candidates themselves being bought and sold by wealthy oligarchs." "It" suggests a system subsidized by private interests that benefit from a democracy more about performance than policy making. Perhaps "it" mollifies fears of economic instability, or conjures false hopes of prosperity, or feeds hungry voters who think things could get better if they support the right candidate, even though things could never really get much better under our current system. None of these "its" seems very inspiring. But Bill Clinton won—twice.

The Republican Party has—certainly since Reagan, and really since Hoover—been the party of corporate America. During this same period, the Democratic Party represented a slightly wider net of capitalist interests, but espoused a more inclusive, classically liberal (*almost* European) style of social welfare capitalism. Thus, Roosevelt's attempt to create a welfare state to "save capitalism" from itself intensified a division within capital. On the one side were those who supported government as the primary source for creating and distributing a modicum of collective goods and services (such as education, health care, and housing).[3] On the other side were those who would strip these subsidies and use government primarily to protect private profits and economic expansion by managing discontent at home and deploying military power to control foreign markets. But even most Republicans in the first half of the 20th century supported a sense of economic and social stability at home: public education trained good, mostly obedient workers, built community solidarity and patriotism, and assimilated immigrant labor; federal housing policies and subsidized consumer goods secured working- and middle-class families; bridges, roads, and highways promised a feeling of mobility and wind-in-your-hair freedom, as well as subsidizing the movement of commodities, workers, and profits.[4]

But 1960s social movements upset what seemed like the great consensus after the Second World War. Civil Rights Movement activism challenged the white supremacy that had maintained a relatively obsequious poor, working-class white population in the South and union white workers in the North and Midwest. In fact, many New Deal reforms *never* reached non-white communities and persistent racial inequality had characterized the evolving welfare state.[5] As Lyndon B. Johnson once said, "If you can convince the lowest white man he's better than the best colored man, he won't notice you're picking his pocket. Hell, give him somebody to look down on, and he'll empty his pockets for you."[6] Such political stability was shattered by sit-ins and Freedom Rides in the South, as well as urban rebellions and Black, Latino, and Native American Power movements elsewhere in the U.S.

Meanwhile, Vietnam's successful anticolonial revolution (along with many similar upheavals in Africa, South and Central America, and—especially—the Middle East) ended the United States' almost unrestricted ability to conquer and extract resources anywhere it wanted. Nixon's demise and the ensuing oil crisis suggested that unbounded consumerism and the symbolic freedom of big cars and suburban homes might no longer assuage the ever frightened and declining white middle class.[7] Uncertainty at home and abroad suggested that the group C. Wright Mills called "the power elite" had to develop new ideological, political, and economic systems to maintain and enhance their wealth and power. What would be termed "foreign competition" in the evolving "global economy" symbolized the need for a fresh approach to corporate hegemony and American exceptionalism in what would become a meaner and more polarized political landscape.[8]

As I have argued throughout this book, what has taken hold of our national psyche is a "kill it to save it" cultural and political framework, which replaced debates within capital about *how much* public good should be supported with a political discourse committed to dismantling *any semblance* of the public good. Reagan's mythologies about unleashed and unburdened burly white guys competing in the rough-and-tumble world of global markets quickly devolved into the reality of most workers becoming weak, part-time, independent contractors. As temp agency ManpowerGroup rose to become one of America's largest employers in the 1990s, more workers became itinerant hands taking whatever jobs they could find for the longest hours and the lowest wages allowed by law.[9] By reducing taxes on the wealthy and outspending the Soviets into oblivion, Reagan restored a semblance of American domination over globalized production at the same time that he broke unions and reversed integration programs and gutted public education, health care, housing, and any environmental and financial regulation he could. He also allowed for the privatization of public lands and resources to the highest bidders, promising politics could deliver for the private sector that paid for his presidency.[10]

To talk about the monetization of democracy in the wake of Citizens United[11] would not shatter any illusions to the contrary—there are none anymore. Democracy—once the purview of patrician gentleman and liberal and conservative do-gooders—would eventually be usurped by experts, media pundits, and barely hidden large corporate interests. But now our government is almost completely owned and operated by blustery plutocrats. According to a recent series in *The New York Times*, 158 families and the companies they own dominated early 2016 campaign phases, donating over one quarter of all campaign money contributed to both parties through June 2015.[12] In the 2012 elections, casino billionaire Sheldon Adelson alone gave close to US$150 million to Mitt Romney and other GOP candidates.[13] The Koch brothers committed to spending almost US$1 billion on the 2016 elections.[14] In the end, these billionaires simply elected one of their own, Donald Trump, cutting out the middleman. But to understand how we got here is crucial. And to observe "kill it to save it" policy making's impact requires painting an accurate portrait of both capitalists' triumph over democracy and its daily effect on people struggling to survive within a system that barely needs them anymore.

Political parties heavily leveraged by corporations once required some mainstream legitimacy and popular rituals of solidarity. I grew up in the 1960s and 1970s watching Democratic and Republican conventions on television. They presented speeches, and entertainers, and lots of balloons—but they also included policy and platform debates. In 1964, the Mississippi Freedom Democratic Party (MFDP) shook up Democratic politics forever and broke down white supremacists' stranglehold over the "Solid South." For both parties, the 1968 and 1972 conventions were sites of massive protests that promised the last vestiges of backroom powerbrokers and an end to the war in Vietnam. Since Reagan, however, these events have devolved into perverse beauty pageants and pundit spin fests. Major networks don't even cover them and cable networks turn the selection process into reality TV. We have witnessed the full-fledged commodification of American democracy. In the end, Carville is just another carnival barker, and "it" just stands in for another sales slogan to convince us that the triumph of capitalism over democracy is good for us all—as Trump the icon both symbolizes and proclaims.[15]

In this chapter, I first identify some of the changes in political economy over the last three decades that have comprised and supported the rise of "kill it to save it." Then I look at some of the major political and corporate players who have essentially redesigned democracy and economics in the United States. Finally, I conclude with the ways in which austerity has become the key component for American economic common sense, presenting an easy and obvious explanation for why "kill it to save it" policies are in the public interest—despite the reality that they are *destroying* the public's interest.

EIGHT

Beyond Voodoo Economics: The Myth of Marco Rubio

> "We have never been a nation of haves and have-nots. We are a nation of haves and soon-to-haves, people who have made it and people who will make it. And that's who we need to remain." (Marco Rubio, Republican Senator from Florida, Floor Speech, December 16, 2011)[1]

It would be unfair to blame the entire state of our current economic and political demise on Marco Rubio. After all, he's 45 years old and has only been a U.S. Senator since 2010. But he represents and promotes so much of what is wrong with contemporary economics and politics that I think it's worthwhile examining one of his most popular speeches—one that many believe set him on a rapid trajectory towards competing for the White House. This speech not only suggests the blatant hypocrisy of Republican policy initiatives, but also encapsulates the new mythmaking underlying the Republicans' political and ideological success. I also want to use this speech as an opportunity to paint a statistical and political portrait about where we really are as Americans and how we got here.

On December 16, 2011, Rubio took to the Senate floor and (after a variety of obligatory gratitudes and platitudes) sang a brief ode to—of all things—Medicare. Rubio recognized the importance of Medicare because he represented Florida, a state in which many seniors receive its benefits. In particular, both his recently deceased father and then-ill mother counted on the program. He expressed concern, however, that Medicare had become unaffordable for a government already spending too much money on social benefits. His solution? In 2011, he suggested severe spending cuts or the privatization of other public programs in education, housing, and health care to save money for Medicare. More recently, Rubio advocated for Congressman (now Speaker of the House) Paul Ryan's budget plan to privatize Medicare, making it a voucher program "to save it."

Rubio then moved on to the major theme of his speech: what he perceived as an increasingly divisive narrative in political circles that "pits people against each other, convincing those doing poorly that the cause of their economic insecurity is others who are doing too well." "Some people are saying," he reported, "The reason why you've lost your job is because someone else is being too greedy … the reason why you're losing your home is because someone else owns too many homes. That the reason why you're making less money is because someone else is making too much money."[2] As in so many political speeches, who "these people" saying "these things" are, when they supposedly said it, and what specifically they did say is less important than Rubio's constructing the caricature of a "class war" instigator, lathering up the unfortunate masses to fight against the wealthy.[3]

But let's be clear about what *has* happened in the U.S. economy. Since the 1980s, smaller and smaller amounts of economic growth have gone to the bottom 90% of income earners (people earning under US$150,000 a year). Nowadays, in fact, it's more like none. Wages themselves have been relatively stagnant for the bottom 90% as well (about a 15% increase over 35 years), while they have skyrocketed for the rich (about 138% increase over that same period). Figure 8.1 depicts these changes. Figure 8.2, however, suggests that, while economic productivity continued to rise steadily over this same period, hourly compensation only rose conjointly from the late 1940s until 1973. From 1973 to 2013, U.S. productivity increased almost 75%, but average hourly wages rose only 9.2%. Thus, over the past 75 years, productivity has risen almost two and a half times more than wages—with hourly compensation remaining stagnant since the early 1970s. In

Figure 8.1: Cumulative change in real annual wages, by wage group, 1979-2013

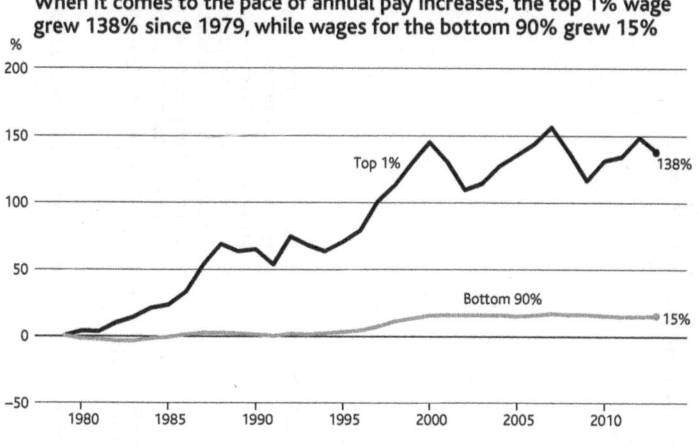

Source: EPI analysis of data from Kopczuk, Saez and Song (2010), and Social Security Administration wage statistics.
Reproduced from Figure F in *Raising America's Pay: Why It's Our Central Economic Policy Challenge,* with permission from the Economic Policy Institute.

other words, productivity has increased and significant economic growth continues, yet it went almost exclusively to the top 10%—and increasingly the top 5% (those earning over US$215,000 a year) and, of late, only the top 1% (over US$400,000). Some economists now argue that the largest shift in wealth has been to the top 0.1%—who held 7% of the nation's wealth in 1979 and almost one quarter of it in 2015.[4]

Add to this picture a staggering increase in the costs of housing, transportation, utilities, and even food over the last two decades and the day-to-day impact of such inequality percolates up into the imagination. In order to "make ends meet," most Americans not only labor longer hours and take on multiple jobs, but also accept what some economists call "strange work" (working weekends and late night/early morning shifts).[5] And to improve their marketability, Americans pursue more education (the cost of which has also skyrocketed), thus leaving them even further in debt while still having to compete with a now global surplus of labor for fewer jobs with decent wages to pay off debts and cover expenses. The lack of sleep and added stress, provoked by

Figure 8.2: Disconnect between productivity and typical worker's compensation, 1948–2013

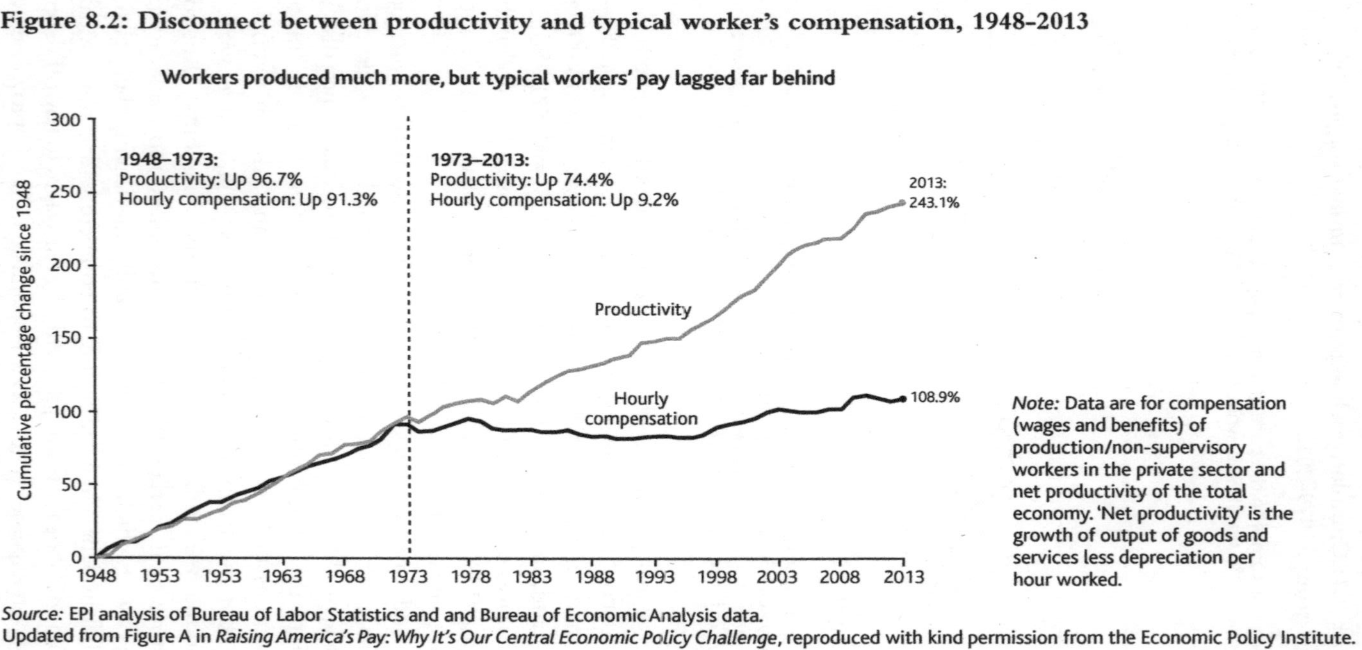

Note: Data are for compensation (wages and benefits) of production/non-supervisory workers in the private sector and net productivity of the total economy. 'Net productivity' is the growth of output of goods and services less depreciation per hour worked.

Source: EPI analysis of Bureau of Labor Statistics and and Bureau of Economic Analysis data.
Updated from Figure A in *Raising America's Pay: Why It's Our Central Economic Policy Challenge*, reproduced with kind permission from the Economic Policy Institute.

what researchers call the "precarity" of labor, shrouds Americans' daily rituals and most intimate relationships. Since 1980, the economy has been *very* good for a few people and devastating for most others.[6]

At the same time that wage differentials bifurcated dramatically, Reagan and ensuing administrations reduced Americans' tax burdens—primarily Americans in the top income earning groups. By the end of his second term in office, Reagan had reduced taxes on the highest income earners from 70% in 1980 to 28% in 1988. Reagan also reduced the number of tax brackets down to two, leaving those Americans making below US$30,000 with a 15% rate (actually raising taxes on the poorest Americans) and those making more than US$30,000 with a 28% rate (actually increasing taxes on many middle-income workers but reducing taxes on the wealthiest by almost half). Eventually, George Bush, Bill Clinton, and Barack Obama would raise taxes slightly on the wealthiest Americans—now close to 40% of their non-capital gains income. But by adding more tax brackets, they also reduced the percentage of earners in the highest categories.[7]

While the majority of income tax savings went to the highest income earners from 1980 to 2015, even more notable has been the reduction in capital gains taxes. Capital gains come primarily from the sale of stocks, bonds, precious metals, and property—not salary, tips, and wages. While this revenue may be considered "income," it is really about wealth (what people *own*, not what they *earn* from work), and historically wealth has been taxed at lower rates than wages. Reagan cut capital gains tax rates from 35% in 1980 to 20% in 1986. The rate went up and down a few points until George W. Bush reduced it to 15%, where it stands now (except for those earning over US$450,000, for whom Obama raised the capital gains tax rate back to 20%).[8]

The best way to understand the impact of capital gains tax cuts on the wealthy is to revisit the 2012 Democratic campaign advert that attacked Mitt Romney for paying a lower tax rate than most U.S. citizens, including his own housemaid. In 2010, Romney declared *no* regular income and therefore owed no payroll tax and no income tax at the 39.6% rate for which he would have been responsible. Yet, the bulk of the US$21 million dollars he *did* receive came from capital gains and was thus taxed at 15%. After myriad itemized deductions, Romney paid less than 14% income tax (while most citizens owed 25%—33% of their income in federal taxes), and after various deductions probably paid somewhere between 16% and 23%. Warren Buffet has famously written about paying a lower tax rate (17%) than his secretary (33%). In other words, while most tax cuts helped the rich a lot, some helped them even more.[9]

Of course, big tax cuts came about simultaneously with huge spending cuts. In part, Reagan argued that huge deficits *created* the need to cut spending. Some of the deficits arose from dramatic *increases* to military spending and corporate subsidies (what became known as "corporate welfare"). But most of the deficit was caused by huge tax cuts for the wealthy to begin with. In response to the burgeoning deficit, Reagan cut funding for education, public housing, and most other social welfare programs, not to mention the Environmental Protection Agency and Occupational Health and Safety Administration. Since Reagan, and even under Democratic presidents Clinton (who ended "welfare as we knew it") and Obama (does anyone remember the word "sequester"?), federal funding for public benefits from education to health and safety to daily infrastructure needs, such as water, sewers, roads, and bridges, have been reduced consistently and often drastically—the only significant exceptions being Obama's 2009 stimulus package and the 2010 Affordable Care Act. Wealthy people paid way less in taxes and many working- and middle-class people paid more taxes on less income. Simultaneously, working- and middle-class people had to work longer and harder to make less money to *spend more*—just to meet basic needs once covered or subsidized by the collective revenue raised by government through taxes and redistributed through social programs.[10]

In an excellent, underrated, and unfortunately all-too-prescient book on U.S. political economy from 1980 to the mid 2000s, economist Dean Baker explained that, before Reagan's election, the United States *seemed* to be nearing European nations in strengthening the country's welfare state. From the New Deal until the mid 1970s, public institutions provided increasingly equitable distributions of education, health care, and other social benefits and resources. While some claimed "the great U-turn" away from such policies resulted from western deindustrialization and the rise of a service economy, Baker suggests such forces had less impact than Reagan's policies in causing the *kinds* of changes experienced by most Americans. These policies included free trade and worker protection (for some); controlling immigration and labor supply; changing labor management and Federal Reserve Board (FRB) practices; bolstering deregulation; degrading the minimum wage, and tax transfer policies to benefit the wealthy.[11]

Baker contends that free trade policies—the North American Free Trade Agreement (NAFTA), the General Agreement on Tariffs and Trade (GATT), and the formation of the World Trade Organization (WTO)—led to "substantial reduction in U.S. manufacturing employment and a decline in relative wages for the remaining [American] workers in that sector." "Deindustrialization" itself was always a misnomer and actually represented only a respacialization of industrial production abroad, where production costs were cheaper and political and environmental regulations fewer. However, Baker notes that these trade agreements "did little or nothing to remove the professional and licensing barriers that protect *highly* [emphasis in original] paid professional workers," (p 202) such as doctors, dentists, and lawyers. He concludes: "While trade policy during this period was quite consciously designed to put manufacturing workers in direct competition with low-paid workers in the developing world, barriers that protected highly paid professionals from foreign competition remained largely untouched or … even increased."[12] The result: downward pressure on the wages of working- and middle-class citizens and upward pressure on wages for professional and highly paid workers.[13]

Changes in National Labor Relations Board (NLRB) enforcement and other labor-management policies resulted in major losses to union membership and the power of unions to protect jobs, wages, and benefits.[14] Ensuing deregulation in airlines, telecommunications, trucking, and so on also put downward pressure on wages and benefits. Similarly, Federal Reserve Board (FRB) policies attacked inflation at the cost of employment, and not only did unemployment rise to over 10% during Reagan's first term but such high rates also created significant downward pressure on the wages of those who still had jobs. Meanwhile, Reagan and Bush Sr initiated a minimum wage embargo, defeating all efforts to raise it. According to Baker, the minimum wage in 1980 equaled about 45% of average hourly wages for production and nonsupervisory workers—by 2005, it had dropped to 32%. Before 1980, minimum wage rates had kept pace with economic growth, but under Reagan and successors, inflation eroded its value by 40%. Baker concluded, "Had the minimum wage moved in step with average wage growth over this period [a period when average wage growth was *already* stifled by all of the other aforementioned policies] it would have been $7.30 in 2005, $2.15 higher than its actual level of $5.15."In 2016, the federal minimum wage is US$7.25 an hour.[15]

All of these policy changes, which resulted in the rich getting richer and everyone else getting poorer, overworked, and stressed out, were designed and decided upon by powerful corporations, wealthy individuals, the think tanks and foundations they fund, and the lobbyists and politicians they pay for. In other words—similarly to when the wealthy first lobbied for major tax cuts, resulting in resource-starved schools, then invested and promoted the privatization of education to profit from these schools' demise (see chapter three)—this creatively destructive dynamic has also taken place in health care, housing, and almost every other once-government-sponsored public program or policy focused on the collective good. These economic changes have degraded working- and middle-class lifestyles to the point where people working full-time-plus can't afford adequate housing, food, or other basic necessities.[16] And these changes were all planned for and promoted by rich people and the politicians they fund to increase their own wealth and power. Marco Rubio is right that "some people" talk about class warfare—but it's rarely the poor.[17] Class warfare has been discussed, strategized, and carried out over the past four decades as a blatant economic strategy of the wealthy against everyone else. But their political strategy sells such policies successfully because a "kill it to save it" framework suggests they benefit everyone.

To Rubio, however, "those people" who want to "correct" this reverse-Robin-Hood trend are only out to empower government itself. He explains:

> And I'm troubled by that rhetoric that pits people against each other. Because the second part of that argument … is: "Give the government more power … so [it] can step in and right this wrong, so we can take away from the people that have too much and give to those people that do not have enough."

Using government to further the wealth and power of a ruling class at the same time this class complains of too much government for others may be duplicitous, but it is nothing new. Reagan and his spin wizards made an art form out of running against government in order to take over government while blaming the poor and working class for economic outcomes they had no power to impact. For example, at the same time Reagan cut Housing and Urban Development (HUD) by over 50% and dismantled public housing, transportation, and other urban necessities, his political appointees and operatives used the agency's last crumbs to fund pet development projects, cater lavish affairs, and pay back major donors.[18]

Yet, to maintain Reaganesque narratives for a new generation, Rubio recreated and revised the mythology. "I'm troubled" by talk of class warfare, he said, "Because it is absolutely not the kind of country we have been for some two hundred odd years. It's not in our nature." And thus Rubio reconnects us with Reagan's myth of who we were to construct who we are now as Americans. He continues:

> Americans have never been a people to drive through a nice neighborhood and say, "Oh, I hate the people that live in these nice houses." Americans have been a people that drive through a nice neighborhood and say, "Congratulations on your nice house. Guess what? We will be joining you soon." We've never been people that go around and confront people that have been financially successful and say, "We

> hate you. We envy you because of how well you're doing." Americans have celebrated their success and say, "Guess what? We're going to be successful soon as well."[19]

I am not sure how Native Americans would respond to these first sentences; they had a pretty nice neighborhood stretching from New England to Northern California, but colonial America never celebrated *their* success. Nor does Rubio mention how the successful people in those nice houses did whatever they could, historically, to keep out newcomers—especially those who didn't look or sound like they did.

Yet the notion that people in our nation *never* confronted the wealthy and powerful for their greed is just plain wrong. Our nation's history is rich with stories of workers, farmers, veterans, and others challenging banks and railroads and politicians whose policies benefitted wealthy corporate owners at the cost of everyone else. From Shays' Rebellion (1786—when Revolutionary War veterans fought back against Massachusetts bankers and their militia, who foreclosed on farmers because of debts they accrued *while fighting in the Revolutionary War*)[20] to Coxey's Army (1894—unemployed workers primarily from the West and Midwest who marched on Washington, D.C. for jobs and more equitable monetary policies)[21] to the Bonus March (1932—tens of thousands of First World War veterans who came to collect veteran bonuses from President Hoover as unemployment neared 25% in the Great Depression),[22] working-class and poor people protested. As Tom Frank's quotation in the Introduction suggests, Americans almost always looked to the nation's economic and political elite (and their policies) as the *cause* of mass financial hardships. And they fought back.

Yet, Rubio's message is clear: upward redistributive economic policies and dwindling democracy are *not* to blame for working- and middle-class hardships—individuals have no one to blame but themselves. And the cure for their ills is to work harder, get more education, go to church, buy a gun, embrace others' prosperity, and celebrate our "American character." Rubio suggests it is this image of America that attracted immigrants from all over the world to these shores. Rubio's own parents came from Cuba to find the American Dream:

> My parents were working class folks. My dad was a bartender for most of his life. My mom was a maid, and a cashier, and a stock clerk at K-Mart. We were not people of financial means. … I didn't always have what I wanted, but I always had what I needed. My parents always provided that.[23]

Rubio's earlier narratives linked his parents to the hundreds of thousands of Cuban emigrants who left the island after Fidel Castro took power on January 1, 1959. Journalists eventually discovered that his parents had in fact emigrated almost three years *before* the revolution. His birth to supposedly Castro-fleeing émigrés gave him cultural and political capital and access to substantial financial support in South Florida—it just wasn't true. More notable, though, may be Rubio's seeming amnesia about what *did* make it possible for his working-class immigrant parents to provide "what he needed." They both worked in hotels in Las Vegas during the 1970s. Las Vegas was (and still is) a union town where most casinos and hotels are union shops and even those that aren't pay union wages with union benefits. Vegas, according to Harold Meyerson, was a place where "the power of the hotel workers' union transformed dead-end jobs into middle-class careers."[24] Rubio's dad was a member of the Culinary Union and went on strike to secure better wages, health care, and working conditions.

In Miami, his parents worked similar jobs but also benefitted from a strong union presence and a healthy network of public institutions and civic organizations. Union protections, good wages, and benefits made it possible for Rubio's parents and millions of other immigrants and non-immigrants to create and achieve "the American Dream." Like most Republicans these days, Rubio is anti-union and opposes almost every policy that gives workers rights to organize. He even suggests that the minimum wage law has "been a disaster" in the 21st century because, "If you raise the minimum wage, you're going to make people more expensive than machines."[25]

The inherent contradictions between Rubio's autobiography and his policy initiatives are even more apparent in the realm of education. Rubio benefitted from quality public schools from kindergarten through college. In elementary and then again high school, he attended Miami-Dade County Schools, known for the most innovative and comprehensive bilingual education programs in the nation.[26] Fully funded sports, music, and arts programs gave students well-rounded experiences, and Rubio himself won a football scholarship to Tarkio College in Missouri. Ironically, Tarkio closed after his first year in 1990, when federal audits exposed the College's Ponzi scheme that exploited inner-city youth and the federally guaranteed student loan system. According to a report in *The New York Times*, Tarkio hired a President, Dennis Spellman, with a reputation for *saving* struggling small colleges:

> [Spellman] abolished tenure and radically reduced the staff, sometimes replacing employees with members of his family. The college opened several extension sites … relying heavily on Federal loans and grants to recruit thousands of students, although many later turned out to be unqualified … The students were mostly poor city residents who in some cases had been swept off the streets and herded into nonacademic classes like truck driving. Private recruiters helped the students fill out loan forms [though] many of the students had no intention of continuing in class or repaying the loans. Tarkio closed after declaring a student loan default rate of almost 80 percent and owing the government over $22 million.[27]

Rubio returned to Florida to complete an associate degree at Santa Fe Community College in Gainesville, Florida, where tuition was just over US$500 a year in 1990. He then completed a bachelor's degree in Political Science at the University of Florida, Gainesville, where tuition was between US$1,220 and US$1,475 from 1990-1993. He subsequently graduated from The University of Miami School of Law in 1996. Since becoming a U.S. senator, Rubio seems to have supported primarily Republican legislation responsible for the continued degradation of public education—kindergarten through university. The lack of federal support and the culture wars against bilingual education have devastated programs for immigrant youth and resulted in heavily stratified funding for public education, based mostly on the socioeconomic status of local school districts. In Florida, the tuition at Sante Fe Community College is now over US$2,500 a year—almost five times more than Rubio paid in 1990. Tuition and fees at the University of Florida are now almost US$7,000—*over* five times as much as Rubio paid. The total cost estimated by the University of Florida financial aid office (including room and board, books and supplies, and so on) is over US$20,000 for on-campus students and just under US$12,000 for those who live at home.[28] And while most of Rubio's loans were federal government loans from Sallie Mae, recent higher education policies have resulted in increased interest rates and the growth of less flexible and more volatile private loans. Altogether, the same publically funded education that taught Rubio and resulted in his success has become less effective and way more expensive, due to the kinds of educational policies that he now supports.

Not that Rubio himself is the problem—I don't mean to paint him as some calculating and conniving politico with no memory, conscience, or consciousness. He may or may not be— but that is not my point. My contention is that he represents a "kill it to save it" policy-making framework, the instinctive deference of which to corporate interests and distaste for the public sector has him advocating "reforms" that would have destroyed his own career before it even got started. This irony is well articulated in his recent book, *American Dreams: Restoring Economic Opportunities for Everyone*, in which he writes extensively about the importance of higher education. Acknowledging the current crisis in student debt and the rising costs of college, Rubio takes no responsibility for the privatization and degradation of public higher education that caused these conditions to begin with.

Instead, he gives us a Reaganesque anecdote featuring a hero, Kristi, whose personal story exemplifies what Rubio thinks is wrong with higher education in America:

> While [Kristi] was at UCF [University of Central Florida] she landed an internship with one of the largest McDonalds franchises in Central Florida. She was responsible for the "point of purchase" advertising in the restaurants. This meant that if Barbie was being featured in the Happy Meals that month, she had to make sure that there was Barbie advertising in the store and at the drive-through window to entice customers to make last minute impulse purchases. She loved the job and she was good at it. It inspired in her a love of marketing that she pursued all the way through a degree in personal communications at UCF.
>
> Getting the degree took her four years. She had to quit her part-time job in order to take the classes required to graduate because they were offered only at certain times. Because she couldn't work, she had to take on $9,000 in debt. Did Kristi necessarily need her college to certify that she was credentialed in marketing? Why did she need to go into debt for degree when most of what she really needed to learn she could learn on the job? What about an apprenticeship option while she attended classes? And why weren't there more on-line options for the required classes so she could keep her job?[29]

Ah, where to begin? Rubio asks why there was no apprenticeship option, when Kristi's story actually *opens* with her getting an internship. Nowadays these are essentially the same things (although one hopes that internships link experience in the field with larger academic goals). Apprenticeships, traditionally, are hands-on, skill-based jobs that companies themselves offer without college credit and some still are. Colleges and universities have expanded their internship programs exponentially over the past two decades. Many of these corporate-based relationships are problematic, however, as private businesses get free labor subsidized by both colleges and (essentially) the students themselves, who pay for the opportunity through tuition. Students get credits, while businesses usually pay nothing.

Rubio's misunderstanding aside, he is clearly concerned for how hard Kristi's dilemma became. She had to quit her "part-time" job because required courses were only offered at certain times (apparently faculty were not available 24/7, nor have they been effectively replaced—yet—by machines that could be). Her taking these classes suggest that she "couldn't work," however; just not when the classes met. I'm sure having to actually attend classes is often considered an inconvenience by my own students, but I still consider it non-negotiable. Kristi may have had to give up a particular job to take a required course, but she did not have to give up working altogether.

Most of Rubio's argument, however, is implied by his questions. Why did she have to spend four years and go into debt for US$9,000 when she was getting *all* the experience and knowledge she needed "on the job?" Did she really "need her college to certify that she was credentialed in marketing?" Why can't colleges and universities be more consumer-friendly and just give students what they need to get their degree and get a real job? According to UCF Department of Communications materials,[30] the curriculum for Kristi's degree included core courses in composition, oral and technical presentations, basic math, statistics, and computer science; advanced core courses in research methods and interpersonal and human relationship communications; and then a host of concentration choices in fields such as business and marketing, health, technology, and so on. In other words, to get a college degree in Communications didn't just require courses to *annoy* Kristi with tedious tasks unrelated to her interests. Her degree program was designed to give both a breadth and depth in Communications so that she could master the field—not just get a job. Her work at McDonald's may have enhanced her academic work, but it could never have replaced it—especially if she hoped to move beyond marketing Barbie dolls at an Orlando drive-thru.

Most likely, however, Rubio wasn't criticizing the major degree requirements anyway. Instead— like so many conservative pundits, and even neoliberal democrats, who buy into education-as-job-training—the question of requirements has to do with distribution mandates in other areas such as the humanities, social sciences, and even hard sciences. Kristi was also required to take three courses in "cultural and historical foundations," two courses in "science foundations", two courses in "social foundations," and other elective courses totaling 36 credit hours or 12 courses *outside* of the major. Ironically, dozens and dozens of courses can be selected to fulfill these general distribution requirements, making the claim that fulfilling them forced significant scheduling difficulties for Kristi hard to imagine. Regardless, Rubio's concern is about why students in her major would have to take these courses to begin with when she was learning everything she needed on the job.

Yet the breadth of requirements is about students developing critical perspectives and citizenship skills—not only job skills. Perhaps a course in the humanities might have raised ethical questions about advertising that targeted children—especially when these impulse buys tend towards the unhealthiest products, such as cookies and candy. Perhaps a course in the sciences might have informed Kristi about the dangerous health impact of fast food and what it does to children's bodies, or how human evolution impacts the ways in which we become "addicted" to sugar and fat in our diets. And perhaps a course in history or sociology might have given Kristi a look at how the fast food industry itself grew to dominate food production, marketing, and policy making in the first place. Expecting McDonald's to offer Kristi "everything she needed to know" as a thinking and acting citizen in a democracy seems highly doubtful. But perhaps the McDonaldization of higher education takes these forms literally, not just figuratively.

Ultimately, what Rubio presents as "reforms" for higher education seem to be more of the same corporatization under the guise of individual, consumer-friendly packaging and "freedom of choice." These policies represent the point-of-purchase politics that comprise our commoditized democracy. Increasing online and distance learning to meet 24/7 consumer demand also decreases the number and power of tenured faculty, thus making campuses more likely to accept the corporatization of operations and curriculum. Creating subsidies for private education to compete with public institutions forces publics to seek more funding from private corporations and opens up public institutions to the vulture capitalism of private investment and profits. When Rubio claims the need for colleges and universities to be better equipped for training a 21st-century workforce, we understand that what he probably means is a workforce skilled to complete tasks but ill-equipped to question their outcomes; a workforce more beholden to a job and less likely to question the conditions of those jobs; and, ultimately, a workforce that performs similar to or better than any machine—only cheaper.

As Rubio concludes his speech by explaining that America's fundamental *principal* is prosperity itself, we see the dead corpse of Reagan's political alchemy reborn, dressed in its most cynical of swaddling clothes. Rubio asserts that prosperity will lead to more jobs, more taxpayers, and thus more revenue to "pay down our debt and do the things that government should do —like our national defense, like invest in infrastructure and in our people, like provide a safety net to help those who cannot help themselves."[31] Of course, aside from the military, these are all things that he and his party have terminated by depleting revenues through tax cuts and wars. The U.S. economy *has* created growth and prosperity—it just doesn't go to the middle and working classes anymore.

In the end, the real meaning of "voodoo economics"[32] is clear—it's a chant of old adages meant to conjure up the myth of the American dream, the image of which is increasingly blurred and fleeting. Rubio finishes by promising that we can recreate a "prosperous and growing America, where all things are possible:"

> Where anyone from anywhere can accomplish anything, or the son of a bartender and a maid can be a U.S. Senator. And where anyone watching, no matter where you start out in life, can accomplish anything and be anything you want to accomplish if you're willing to work hard, play by the rules, and have the ability to do it.[33]

In the end, even the old protestant work ethic platitudes aren't enough to convince Americans "it's the economy." It's not enough to just work hard to get ahead. Nor is it enough to "play by the rules." It's about having the "ability" to succeed—an ability increasingly defined by access, luck, and greed. It's about wealth, not hard work. It's about power and manipulating the rules, not abiding by them. It's about un-leveling the playing field and then lying about it.

Yet, the economic truths are clear: the majority of our nation's debt emanates from tax cuts to the rich and increased spending on corporate welfare, the military, and neoconservative nation-building to exploit resources in the Middle East and defeat China. Over three decades of our current economic policies transferred most income and wealth to the top 1% and devastated working- and middle-class families. These changes have created such powerful instability that most Americans don't know what prosperity would even look like—except for driving through "nice" neighborhoods during their spare time. What Rubio actually considers to be "prosperity" grew from public programs funded by a more equitable tax system that buttressed what we conceived of as a middle-class American dream. But the very nation Rubio claims he would like to recreate has been primarily destroyed by the policies that he promotes. *Kill it to save it.*

NINE

Shock Doctrines, Disaster Capitalism, and Smart ALECs

> "Katrina was the best thing that happened to the education system in New Orleans." (Arne Duncan, Secretary of Education for the Obama Administration)[1]

> "America leads the world in shocks. Unfortunately, America does not lead the world in deciphering the cause of shock." (Gil Scott-Heron, *We Beg Your Pardon (Pardon Our Analysis)*)[2]

If the social and economic stories our politicians tell are now myths built upon myths built upon myths, how can we understand the last thirty years of neoliberal capitalism and its wholesale consumption by Americans? How has what Bellah (1985) called "neocapitalism" been able to continually double down its critique of social welfare spending as responsible for economic woes when our nation has not supported social welfare spending to any significant degree in over thirty years? As I have argued throughout this book, most Americans now seem hardwired to accept privatization, severe inequality, and less access to public resources and political participation because these are packaged as creating prosperity and freedom—the toxic blend of corporate hegemony and hyper-individualism. But others, like Milton Friedman, have argued that only powerful moments of great upheaval allow for such fundamental transformations in economic policy and cultural hegemony to take place. People only accept the degradation of democracy and severe austerity when they are afraid of something worse.

In her artful and insightful book, *Shock Doctrine*, Naomi Klein argues that contemporary neoliberalism has three "trademark demands: privatization, government deregulation, and deep cuts to social spending."[3] Yet, she suggests, such requirements are too unpopular with most people as they invariably impact the programs that these people benefit from. Thus, she documents the ways in which various natural and manmade disasters (hurricanes and earthquakes, wars, financial meltdowns, terror attacks, and other major upheavals) create "shocks" that allow corporations and politicians to privatize, deregulate, and initiate austerity—all in the name of recovery and stability. The requisite "shock doctrine" echoes free market guru Milton Friedman's dictate that "only a crisis—actual or perceived—produces real change."[4]

After Hurricane Katrina destroyed much of New Orleans' public infrastructure—especially its schools—Friedman saw an opportunity to remake public education by bringing in private charters. In a 2005 editorial for the *Wall Street Journal*, Friedman explained: "New Orleans schools were failing for the same reason that schools are failing in other large cities, because the schools are owned and operated by the government." Instead, he proposed opening up the entire educational system to free markets by giving all students vouchers. He wrote:

> To make competition effective, Louisiana should provide a favorable climate for new entrants, whether they be parochial, non-profit or for-profit. More important, the vouchers would encourage private enterprise to provide schooling. Is there any doubt that the private market would provide schooling for children returning to New Orleans faster than the state? The state's objective would be better served by a competitive educational market than by a government monopoly. Producers of educational services would compete to attract students. Parents,

> empowered by the voucher, would have a wide range to choose from. As in other industries, such a competitive free market would lead to improvements in quality and reductions in cost.[5]

Thus began one of the biggest experiments in privatizing public education. New Orleans, Louisiana's (NOLA's) Recovery School District (RSD) was given complete authority and mega millions of public *and* private investment to rebuild the city's schools. Despite massive cash infusions, with annual spending between US$1000 and US$8000, more per charter-school student than public-school student, the experiment has had mixed results at best. Given what we learned about charters in chapter three, this outcome should come as no surprise. While some metrics do show progress in retention and graduation rates and some test scores, these advancements came primarily from comparisons with the dismally low numbers that existed pre-Katrina, when New Orleans was already one of the worst school districts in the U.S. Neither do the results account for the almost 30% of the city's poorest population who never returned to New Orleans.[6]

A recent report by the Network for Public Education compared charters in Louisiana—the majority of which are in New Orleans—to Louisiana public schools in general. Controlling for factors such as race, ethnicity, poverty, and special education, eighth-grade charter school students performed worse than their public school counterparts by enormous amounts. According to journalist Colleen Kimmett, "The researchers found that the gap between charter and public school performance in Louisiana was the largest of any state in the country. And Louisiana's overall scores were already the fourth-lowest in the nation."[7] As education scholar Diane Ravitch reports, experts noted that any actual gains "must be seen in terms of NOLA's shamefully low pre-Katrina starting point; post-Katrina demographic shifts; curriculum narrowing, a focus on test prep and remediation that doesn't prepare kids for college or life; and the nation's 3rd highest rate of young people out of school without a job."[8]

For some students, New Orleans charter schools have been a success. A rise in test scores, graduation rates, and college matriculation has certainly improved their future economic and social trajectories. But one third of the over 70 charter school principals reported "cherry-picking" students to improve test scores. By courting high-performing students and "counseling out" special-needs youth and students with behavioral or learning challenges, charter schools inflate their scores while negatively impacting public school numbers. Meanwhile, RSD schools have become less local and less democratic. Students now travel almost twice as far to school as they did before Katrina, averaging an extra 1.8 miles each way, with one in four students traveling over 5 miles to class every day. Teacher turnover has skyrocketed as many charters rely on Teach for America and other similar programs that bring in primarily young, inexperienced white students from around the country for one- or two-year stints, resulting in few if any neighborhood commitments or long-term relationships between teachers and communities. This dynamic has added to the racialization of school leadership, as students of color are now taught by white teachers in schools that are run by an unelected white majority, not democratically elected by the predominantly non-white community.[9]

But the product of education as a public good—community-based institutions that provide good education, resources, local leadership, and social capital—is never really the primary goal when it comes to the focus of education as an industry and the impact of shock therapy. The mission of shock therapy is to change the ideological framework and policy commitments of institutions from public sector to private, from service provision to profitmaking. As I described in chapter three, Lehman Brothers' strategy making the once-public sector ripe for private investment and enterprise—converting public dollars into corporate profits. And, paraphrasing Milton Friedman (see endnote 5), if people are reeling and stressed out from devastation, confused and fearful about the future, they are more likely to accept the plans of those whose wealth and power promises stability and order. Americans can embrace a "new common sense," no matter how flawed or counterproductive to their own interests, because it "feels" right—echoing, again, the kind of "truthiness" that Stephen Colbert said came "from the gut," not fancy books or messy facts. The federal government has poured billions of dollars into the New Orleans RSD in order to make charters work, hoping that certain measurements, data indicators, and so on, all *prove* their success. But the numbers are inflated, the samples manipulated, and the formulas tailored to favor a racialized, neoliberal project—despite its negative impact on a large swath of the city's population. Klein calls Friedman's goal of dismantling the boundaries between Big Government and Big Business "corporatist capitalism." She explains:

> Its main characteristics are huge transfers of public wealth to private hands often accompanied by exploding debt, an ever-widening chasm between the dazzling rich and the disposable poor, and an aggressive nationalism that justifies bottomless spending on security. For those on the inside of the bubble of extreme wealth created by such an arrangement, there can be no more profitable way to organize society. But because of the obvious drawbacks for the vast majority of the population left outside the bubble, other features of the corporatist state tend to include aggressive surveillance (once again with government and large corporations trading favors and contracts), mass incarceration, shrinking civil liberties and often, though not always, torture.[10]

Klein seems adamant that, given "normal" conditions, people would resist; therefore, "aggressive surveillance" and policing are necessary (p. 18). It is within this context that we should place the growing controversies around school-to-prison pipelines, increased police shootings of young minority males, and the general police state that now exists in many poor, urban neighborhoods across the country. This shift may explain in part how Wilson and Kelling's "broken windows" became Rudolph Giuliani's "zero tolerance" became Michael Bloomberg's "stop and frisk" became a national siege resulting in more and more infamous police murders of unarmed, young men and women of color.

Still, Klein's analysis suggests that even corporatist economies and state policies must ultimately create a kind of "disaster" capitalism that relies on perpetual instability. Antony Lowenstein claims that a "war on terrorism" creates the kind of constant fear that allows for an even greater private exploitation of public transfers of wealth and power to corporate entities. The key element is that the private sector no longer waits to profit from instability because that would be too unpredictable. Instead, Lowenstein writes:

> my definition of "disaster" has deepened to include companies that *entrench* a crisis and then sell themselves as the only ones who can resolve it. Resources and detention centers are just the latest in a long line of assets and institutions that have been made the instruments of unaccountable private power.[11]

Private corporations not only lobby to establish policies good for business; they also *create* the actual disasters necessary to then sell their wares—think the controversy over Halliburton and the Gulf Wars. Or take for example, Enron's infamous energy scandal in California.

After exploiting the state's deregulation of energy industries to take control of California's power grid, Enron withheld electricity from cities throughout the state until rolling blackouts were necessary to regulate what resources were left in San Francisco, San Diego, and L.A. Enron literally turned off California's power to *create* a crisis and only restored the juice when the state agreed to pay exorbitant rates for energy from other Enron providers. Enron's "smartest guys in the room" found they could manipulate supply to drive up rates, causing public emergencies that allowed the company to "legally" blackmail the state. Despite the company's ultimate failure, many of Enron's most controversial accounting and investment strategies created models and frameworks that large investment banks would use throughout the 2000s.[12] And despite the massive failure of these financial strategies, few banks and their CEOs have ever been held accountable. Instead, most CEOs got huge bonuses and the deregulation and investment practices that brought us the financial crisis of 2007 and 2008 remain today—enriching hundreds and impoverishing millions.

The idea that companies could not only take advantage of social upheavals but also cause, promote, maintain, and legislate them for the sake of economic profit is an extremely frightening one, but all too real. We live in a state of perpetual shock, and thus support policies that promise to create prosperity and liberate us from fear, regardless of their actual impact—which is usually to prosper the wealthy and leave the rest of us more vulnerable. Yet, as the economic and social conditions get worse, school shootings, terrorist attacks and Donald Trump's latest assault on what's left of America's tact and intelligence take media center stage. Our political discourse and policy making are dominated by those who engineer the biggest threats to our health and safety as they design and promote "kill it to save it" policies. The best example of this dynamic is the group known as ALEC.

The American Legislative Exchange Council (ALEC) was cofounded in 1973 from the shell of a nonprofit organization called the Conservative Caucus of State Legislators. Right-wing titans including Paul Weyrich (founder of the Heritage Foundation) and Lou Barnett (Political Director of Ronald Reagan's PAC) saw the possibility of creating what historian Rick Pearlstein called a "nonpolitical Trojan horse" for conservative political activity.[13] Essentially, from the late 1970s until the late 2000s, ALEC brought together Republican legislators (mainly state senators and representatives), conservative think tanks, and increasingly large corporations and trade groups to develop legislation fulfilling the organization's mission of "limited government, free markets and federalism"[14]—the things that "kill it to save it" policy making is all about.As I suggested in chapter one, the 1970s marked a period of instability for American identity as a whole. While progressive and radical movements had resulted in significant institutional and social changes, many conservative (and even some liberal) standard bearers wanted to restore what they perceived of as order and normalcy. Whether it was Treasury Secretary William Simon's concern about capitalism's reputation or soon-to-be Supreme Court Justice, Lewis Powell, fearing attacks on the American Free Enterprise System, the moment seemed ripe for a conservative corporate counterinsurgency movement. Powell, a top tobacco industry attorney, wrote a famous memo to the U.S. Chamber of Commerce calling on corporations to be more aggressive in writing and passing legislation. Weyrich realized that ALEC could be a mechanism for such a strategy, bringing conservative businesses, legislators, and think tanks together under a "non-partisan, non-political" guise, the primary motive of which was to undertake partisan political work as a pro-corporate "bill mill." By acting primarily on a state level, ALEC's impact often remained under the radar of media criticism and public awareness. But for over three decades, the group passed thousands of laws in states and counties across the country that turned public institutions and public funding into private profits.

In the area of corrections, two of the largest for-profit prison corporations, GEO Group (formerly Wackenhut) and the Corrections Corporation of America, are longtime ALEC members who have contributed millions of dollars in fees and donations. In return, ALEC has designed and helped pass a variety of "Truth in sentencing" (TIS) laws that increased the length of prison terms in 35 states—especially sentences related to drug crimes. Other laws most favorable to keeping private prison populations huge and profitable include the Private Correctional Facilities Act (allowing states to contract out to private prisons), various mandatory minimum sentencing acts (expanding prison sentences for drug and other offenses), and the Habitual Juvenile Offender Act (which sentences juveniles like adults).[15] Meanwhile, ALEC also designed and helped pass the Prison Industries Act (now in over 30 states), allowing inmates to work for private companies and have their "fair market wages" paid directly to prisons. In Florida, prisons run the largest printing shops in the state (undercutting small local businesses), and in Wisconsin (where former ALEC member, Governor Scott Walker, dismantled collective bargaining), the city of Racine now uses inmates for landscaping, painting, and other maintenance work once tasked to unionized public employees. Ironically, as crime rates (especially violent crime rates) decreased dramatically during the last twenty-five years, ALEC has achieved remarkable success in designing and passing laws to *expand* the prison industrial complex and its fortunes. By manufacturing a state of fear over increased threats of crime—despite the actual *decrease* in crime rates—ALEC and the politicians they nurture are able to win elections and pass legislation that contributes to a state of panic as well as to job loss and unemployment.[16]

It seems ALEC found that immigration issues could create fear and panic, too—especially racial and ethnic paranoia—at the same time that it created a new pool of predeported people who would need monitored and protective shelter. The group teamed up with numerous state officials across the country to pass strict immigration enforcement legislation. The most famous and controversial bill was Arizona's Senate Bill 1070, which *required* that police "determine the immigration status of someone arrested or detained when there is 'reasonable suspicion' they are not in the U.S. legally." If not carrying appropriate I.D., people could be immediately arrested and sent to jail. Eight states (including Georgia, Alabama, Indiana, Utah, and South Carolina) quickly followed suit, and now dozens have passed or considered such legislation. While these efforts initially targeted states addressing immigration issues, I would argue that the most interested market for such legislation has been the private prison industry. In fact, almost a quarter of the Corrections Corporation of America's US$1.7 billion profits in 2013 came from incarcerating non-citizens, many of whom had been arrested for being undocumented.[17]

As Americans wonder why it is so hard to pass immigration reform, consider Texas Senator John Cornyn's adamant focus on "enforcement and security" instead of citizenship or amnesty. According to *The Nation's* Lee Fang:

> Cornyn's idea of "robust" border security was made clear in an amendment he offered during debate over a supplemental spending bill three years ago. Cornyn's amendment called for $3 billion to be spent on a mix of drones, border security guards and funding for 3,300 beds for immigrant detention over two years, as well as 500 additional detention officers. In 2005, Cornyn's immigration reform legislation called for 10,000 new ICE detention beds.[18]

At about US$164 per day, each bed is worth almost US$60,000 annually.[19] Ironically, immigration reform would not only decriminalize many currently undocumented people, but would also undoubtedly reduce the constant flow of undocumented workers from Mexico, Central America, and elsewhere. In other words, ALEC and its members lose money if effective legislation on immigration is *ever* passed. More instability, more upheaval, and more paranoia are all more profitable.

Another example of tapping America's bulging vein of fear to *reverse* what proved to be effective public policy can be seen in ALEC's work in the bail bonds industry. Historically, most non-violent arrests resulted in accused citizens being released on their own recognizance (ROR). However, legislation created by ALEC in the mid 1990s expanded the list of crimes where bail *must* be assigned and posted for everything from murder and manslaughter to "burglary," "desecrating religious or sectarian premises," and any "drug related crimes." Passed in various forms in dozens of states, this Act makes it harder for low-income people to avoid bail bondsman fees and left those unable to pay bail or secure bonds in jail until their trial date—sometimes a year or more behind bars before their right to due process kicked in.[20]

Over the past decade, counties across the nation created "pretrial release programs" to counter the damage and cost of long pretrial incarceration. These practices allowed non-violent arrestees to accept some form of electronic monitoring, make a pledge to return for trial, and then go back home. In county after county, state after state, accused people stayed out of jail, kept their families and jobs intact, and then returned for trial at the same rate or higher than those using private bail bonds—all while saving tax payers millions of dollars (between US$80 and US$100 per prisoner per day in most states).[21]

As an example of good public policy, pretrial release programs blossomed around the country— only to be ultimately defeated in many places by huge campaign contributions from the American Bail Coalition (ABC), whose stated mission is "to educate local government on the benefits of commercial bail bonding and to advance the interests of the member companies' many retail agents." In other words, ABC educates by fear mongering and supporting candidates who vow to rid counties and states of pretrial release programs. As a premier member of ALEC's Corporate Board, ABC helped ALEC compose the Uniform Bail Act and the Citizens Right to Know: Pretrial Release Act, both of which have stymied pretrial release programs throughout the United States.[22]

National Public Radio (NPR) reporter Laura Sullivan documented an example in Broward County, Florida in which pretrial release programs reduced overcrowded jails to such a degree that county commissioners avoided spending US$70 million on a new jail and saved taxpayers almost US$20 million more to boot. But bail bonds companies lost money and responded by hiring a lobbyist who spread "campaign" contributions around just before the council voted on an ALEC-modeled bill to gut pretrial release programs. The bill passed, allowing local bail bondsman Wayne Spath to enforce his "principled" position that: "People should not just be released from jail and get a free ride. I mean, this is the way the system's got to work."[23] Presumed innocence suggests that serving extensive prison time *before* being found guilty of a non-violent offense is itself a sign that the system doesn't work. But private interests, manipulating the confluence of money and politics, beat back public policy that worked for citizens but not bail bondsmen—all in the name of reforming a system wasn't broken. *Kill it to save it.*

As if pretrial bail interference wasn't enough, ALEC is now supporting legislation that ABC Executive Director, Nicholas Wachinski, called the "sexy side of bail."[24] States across the nation are now looking to Mississippi's experiment with "post-conviction" bail. It works like this: if a person is convicted of a crime and can't pay the adjudicated fine, they now have an option to purchase bail from private bail bondsmen instead of serving prison time. Bail companies charge 10—20% of the fine and give offenders a few months to pay it back—plus interest—to bail bonds companies. If convicted borrowers can't remit full payment, bail agents track down scofflaws to collect. Other states, like South Dakota and Michigan, have adopted ALEC's model legislation and dozens of others are debating the bill mill's work in this area. In the past, Mississippi state courts would have worked with offenders on a payment plan and then pursued those who violated agreements. But states like Mississippi no longer have the revenues from local, state, and federal tax dollars to staff such operations. ALEC's legislation manipulates the state's permanent financial crisis to privatize services and profit from criminal justice system convictions and offenders' poverty. The fact that these laws result in *more* unpaid bonds and scofflaws snatched by bounty hunters only to be sent back to prison just makes even larger pools of profit for ALEC members. Only those convicted of misdemeanors and petty crimes (and the rest of Mississippi tax payers) are worse off.[25]

But maybe we are *all* worse off. ALEC has not only turned public policy-making into private profit-making, its chipped away at what little of our democracy is left. Take, for example, the almost comical number of times state legislators have gotten caught trying to "ram through" ALEC-generated laws in their own government houses. In Missouri, Governor Jay Nixon vetoed a bill that would have created significant impediments for health care "navigators" to enroll people into the Affordable Care Act. The bill passed both House and Senate—despite reportedly incorrect references to a federal law that had nothing to do with the bill. Apparently, ALEC's "model" legislation carried the initial mistake and legislators never bothered to correct it when they filed it with the state. Kansas legislators made the same oversight. In Florida, it seems state representative Rachel Burgin forgot to remove ALEC's mission statement from a bill she introduced. In Minnesota, poor Rep. Steve Gottwalt reportedly got caught vehemently claiming his own authorship of another ALEC health care bill at the same time that a colleague noted ALEC's logo on the legislation's handout. Apparently lawmakers don't even use the bill mill's cheat sheets as guides for writing new laws; they turn in the cheat sheets themselves.[26]

Luckily, in one of democracy's last vestiges, Americans still have the opportunity to vote these people out. Voting in local, state, and federal elections is the signature act in a democratic republic and all citizens have the right to participate in this nation's governmental process. However, ALEC is all over this aspect of democracy, too. Aside from modeling bills opposing public campaign financing, opposing campaign contribution disclosure requirements, and opposing "false statement" laws that might regulate misleading "third party" campaign ads, ALEC has been instrumental in dozens of states passing "voter fraud" laws.[27] After Obama's first election resulted in millions of new voters—primarily young people and people of color—it seems ALEC step up its strategies to create laws that could legally disenfranchise large portions of this new electorate.

In 2012, the Brennan Center for Justice reported on the impact of voter fraud laws in the first ten states to pass them: Alabama; Georgia; Indiana; Kansas; Mississippi; Pennsylvania; South Carolina; Tennessee; Texas, and Wisconsin. The Center concluded that 11% of *currently eligible* voters did not presently have the I.D. necessary to vote. They continued:

> The 11 percent of eligible voters who lack the required photo ID must travel to a designated government office to obtain one. Yet many citizens will have trouble making this trip. In the 10 states with restrictive voter ID laws:
>
> - Nearly 500,000 eligible voters do not have access to a vehicle and live more than 10 miles from the nearest state ID-issuing office open more than two days a week. Many of them live in rural areas with dwindling public transportation options.
> - More than 10 million eligible voters live more than 10 miles from their nearest state ID-issuing office open more than two days a week.
> - 1.2 million eligible black voters and 500,000 eligible Hispanic voters live more than 10 miles from their nearest ID-issuing office open more than two days a week. People of color are more likely to be disenfranchised by these laws since they are less likely to have photo ID than the general population.
> - Many ID-issuing offices maintain limited business hours. For example, the office in Sauk City, Wisconsin is open only on the fifth Wednesday of any month. But only four months in 2012 — February, May, August, and October—have five

> Wednesdays. In other states—Alabama, Georgia, Mississippi, and Texas—many part-time ID-issuing offices are in the rural regions with the highest concentrations of people of color and people in poverty.
>
> More than 1 million eligible voters in these states fall below the federal poverty line and live more than 10 miles from their nearest ID-issuing office open more than two days a week. These voters may be particularly affected by the significant costs of the documentation required to obtain a photo ID. Birth certificates can cost between $8 and $25. Marriage licenses, required for married women whose birth certificates include a maiden name, can cost between $8 and $20. By comparison, the notorious poll tax that disenfranchised millions of African American voters pre-1964—eventually outlawed by civil rights legislation—cost $10.64 in current dollars.[28]

In other words, millions of eligible voters (maybe tens of millions; 37 states now have some form of ALEC's bill) won't even be able to use their right to vote to throw out the very same bums who took those rights away. All this without *any* evidence that voter fraud in general, and fraud specifically linked to false identities, has been a problem *anywhere* in the United States since the 19th century. These laws' only intent is to stop people voting.

The triumph of capitalism over democracy is not just a theoretical platitude from progressive politicos or lefty professors. The real degradation of political discourse and debate, the media's infantilizing of its audiences, and the purposeful dismantling of our rights to be an informed, active electorate (one that actually gets to vote) no longer threaten our democracy—our democracy has been defeated. And nowhere is our inability to act politically and democratically more obvious than in the ways in which our nation creates its economic policies. As the U.S. increasingly entrenches austerity as the framework for all economic policy making, the inability to debate or challenge the "kill it to save it" paradigm becomes ever more debilitating.

TEN

The Myth of Common Sense Austerity and the Slow Death of America's Economy

> *Johnny Carson*: How *do* you balance the budget—you don't spend more than you take in?
>
> *Ronald Reagan*: It's like protecting your virtue—you have to learn to say "no." (Governor Reagan guest appearance on *The Tonight Show*, March 13, 1975)

Social scientists generally define an economy as the way a society manages the production and distribution of raw materials and resources needed to survive and thrive. A *political* economy recognizes that the management of these resources will be characterized by relations of power, political systems, class conflicts, and the overall ways in which a society makes decisions about *how* to run its economy. In most of the world's industrialized nations (including the post-New-Deal United States), domestic political economies developed around the goal of producing enough economic resources to meet the basic food, shelter, education, safety, and health care needs of its people while still remaining committed to a capitalist economy and profit-driven growth. The role of government then was in part—if not primarily—the protection and welfare, as well as prosperity, of its people. Those goals included not only public institutions—schools, hospitals, fire, police, military, public transportation, clean water and sewerage, and so on,—but also policies on housing, wages, due process, and the taxation policy needed to redistribute resources enough to pay for all of these things. This framework came to be known as the "social welfare state."[1]

Since Ronald Reagan, the great U-turn in America has resulted in the growing conviction (or, as I have argued, a new social and cultural "hardwiring") that government should *not* be in the business of such things. The "nanny state" might try to provide some semblance of resources to protect the health, education, and safety of its citizens—but it shouldn't. Such attempts only stifle the free market and individual entrepreneurship. For Reagan, government had thus become "the problem." And so the United States broke with most other industrialized nations as our government reduced both its financial and political commitments to public institutions and public consumption. Instead, the government would privatize and deregulate in order to turn everything public into private enterprise.

The economic premise of these decisions promised that increased wealth would trickle down to all citizens and then unfettered individuals would be able to take care of their own health care, their own safety, and their own education. Just as the World Bank and International Monetary Fund (IMF) encouraged structural adjustment programs (SAPs) on developing nations (arguably to liberate their markets for greater exploitation by the world's wealthiest nations), Reagan would force similar changes on his own nation to free up public institutions and resources for private profiteering. Called "voodoo economics" by its critics, (see Krugman 2014 and chapter eight of this book) it became a common sense way of economic management, which remains the underpinning of contemporary "job creator" narratives. Deregulate business, cut taxes, open up markets, and wealthy people will create jobs so that everyone has the prosperity to care for themselves and their families. It hasn't and doesn't work this way. In fact, it's made it harder for the majority of Americans to do these things. But we continue to believe in it.

With huge tax cuts on the rich and increased military spending to intensify global market domination, debt in the U.S. continued to rise. Globally, structural adjustment programs [SAPs] had forced drastic cuts in public services on the governments of poorer countries in order to prioritize paying back IMF and World Bank loans. Now, Reagan's America would do the same at home, and the public sector began its steep decline as our own government tried to balance its budget on the backs of America's poor, working and middle classes. Of course, most social spending was never that big a portion of the debt to begin with, so the economic policy of cutting public funding to lower the debt didn't work. Meanwhile, unemployment and personal debt rose dramatically under Reagan and the first George Bush. Public schools crumbled, public housing disappeared, and health indicators plummeted.[2]

The economic recovery under Clinton had some positive impact for many Americans: more jobs, less poverty, and relatively strong economic growth. But more jobs did not mean *good* jobs: income inequality skyrocketed and extreme poverty rates rose significantly. New service sector work and increased "independent contractors" did not have union protections, good health plans, retirement, or the kinds of benefits and stability that helped full-time workers take care of their families. Disappearing were the very foundations on which a working- and middle-class American dream had been built. By the time George W. Bush came along, even Clinton's "economic miracle" had faded; Bush just blew the whole thing up.[3]

With the 2000—2001 economy already in decline, Bush wasted what was left of Clinton's surplus on US$300—US$600 tax rebates for working- and middle-class citizens while reducing income tax rates, capital gains tax rates, and even inheritance tax rates for the very wealthy. But tax cuts had little impact on increasing economic growth and the debt continued to rise even before 9/11. Post-9/11, the neoconservative foreign policy goals of destabilizing the Middle East to control oil intensified debt exponentially.[4] And by not including war expenditures in the budget, Bush hid the actual size of the debt from Americans for years. Meanwhile, the privatization frenzy continued, especially spending hundreds of billions on a Gulf War that was increasingly outsourced to companies like Halliburton and Blackwater. The public debt grew larger while private sector profits skyrocketed.[5]

But little, if any, of America's continued economic growth went to the bottom 90% of the nation's income earners (see Figures 8.1 and 8.2 in chapter eight). One might have expected more intense protest and unrest among the growing number of economically dispossessed workers—especially middle-class professionals, who increasingly couldn't afford to live in the cities where they worked.[6] But 9/11 in particular, and terrorism in general, promoted the kind of disaster capitalism neoconservatives, and now neoliberals, desired. By the time the financial crisis of 2008 brought economic tremors to a critical mass, the country had already been shocked, frightened, stressed, and beaten down to the max. Like farmers under the thumb of Monsanto and poultry growers indentured to "Big Chicken," the American public was so far under financial water and paralyzed by perpetual war and color-coded paranoia that the global destruction of the economy barely registered.[7]

Sure, politicians made a big deal about the bailout. The unrestrained world of finance and investment capital had created such a complicated morass of financial bets leveraged against other bets that few people could even calculate, let alone imagine, what kind of economic implosion lay imminent. The world economy fell so big so fast that governments saw no alternative but to buy into the largest banks' and their political representatives' proclamations that they were indeed "too big to fail." Despite budget hawks on the Right who did not want the government to spend money on the bailout, and progressives on the Left who after years of spending cuts thought this outright "socialism for the rich" went too far, most eventually got on board with the bailout. In a perverse moment of capitalist jujitsu, former Goldman Sachs CEO and Bush Treasury Secretary, Henry Paulson, fell to bended knee and begged House Speaker, Nancy Pelosi, not to "blow up" the bailout. She replied, "It's not me blowing this up, it's the Republicans." They both chuckled. Predictably, without much of a popular movement against it, the bailout passed.[8]

The ultimate irony of the bailout was that government proved again that not only did it have a role in economic recovery, but also could even clean up a global mess almost entirely caused by private (not public) sector collapse. And despite all of the right-wing squawking about the Obama stimulus, the program actually had serious impact on preventing what would surely have been an even worse recession and almost certain Depression following the bailout. But the most important element left behind by thirty-five years of deregulation and privatization, of ravaging the public sector for corporate profiteering, of constant economic and political upheaval and paranoia, has been the overwhelming victory of *austerity* as a way of life. In times of economic crisis and debt, in times of political paralysis and global uncertainty, austerity now seems obvious—its necessity is just common sense. And, like so much common sense, it's wrong.[9]

What is austerity? For an individual or small business, austerity means cutting back on expenditures during period of debt, until debts can be repaid. This, of course, seems like economic common sense. For a national economy, however, austerity means a "reduction in the 'structural deficit' of the government," regardless of any economic cycles that might cause surpluses or deficits.[10] In other words, a kind of perpetual cutting of certain types of public spending—usually on collective services like education, health care, and civil services—while maintaining military and cutting taxes to encourage growth. Economist Marc Blythe defines austerity as "the 'common sense' on how to pay for the massive increase in public debt caused by the financial crisis, mostly through the slashing of government services."[11] For whatever the *causes* of debt, austerity has been pushed by most government, financial, and corporate leaders around the world as the obvious way to reduce it. As I suggested earlier, such austerity has influenced U.S. economic policy for decades; "kill it to save it" common sense suggests that governments stop the business of public spending and focus only on tax cuts and the military. Thus, even before the financial crisis of 2008, U.S. policies portrayed slashing public spending as crucial to sound economic policies.

Usually, such policies are sold as common sense by using the family or personal budget as a comparison. In April 2013, Speaker John Boehner asked for deep cuts to public spending because: "Every family has to balance its budget, Washington should as well."[12] Earlier that year, Paul Ryan argued: "The government should only spend what it takes in. This is how every family tries to live—in good times and in bad. Your government should do the same."[13] These comparisons are nothing new—they go back at least as far Regan and Bush I—but, as with most common-sense analogies, they are fallacies. First off, most American families *never* balance their budget—nor could they if they own a home, need a car, send a child to college, and so on. In fact, the U.S. economy depends on some household debt and most economists suggest that home purchases and higher education are important investments—as long as you avoid McMansions and bloated private college tuitions.[14] But, more significantly, national governments are *not* small families. Families don't print their own money, they can't control inflation rates, and they can't lend themselves money. More importantly, families have little control over how much they get paid—and here lies the rub.

So much of the government debt pre-2008 came from massive tax cuts on the wealthiest 5%—10% of Americans that the only way to really understand the majority of U.S. debt is to identify it as planned obsolescence. In other words, the very purposeful policies from Reagan through Obama continued to reduce revenue, thus creating the need to cut spending. Austerity became the economic narrative that allowed, legitimized, and even popularized redistributing money to the rich and dismantling the public sector that had made social mobility possible for so many working- and middle-class citizens like Marco Rubio. Blyth calls austerity, in essence, an "offensive canard" that obscures the current cause of inequality and ensures a future owned and controlled by an oligarchy.[15]

Blyth's book, *Austerity: The History of a Dangerous Idea,* is not only a poignant analysis of austerity's devastating impact on global economies; therein, his own story also becomes powerfully illustrative.

Born to a working-class family in Scotland, Blyth's mother died when he was young; his grandmother primarily raised him in relative poverty. He writes: "My upbringing was, in the original sense of the word, quite austere. Household income was a government check, namely a state retirement pension, plus occasional handouts from my manual worker father. I am a welfare kid. I am also proud of that fact."[16] Now an Ivy League Economics Professor, Blyth continues:

> I am as an extreme example of intra-generational social mobility as you can find anywhere. What made it possible for me to become the man I am today is the very thing now blamed for creating the crisis itself: the state, more specifically the so-called runaway, bloated, paternalist, out-of-control, welfare state. But the claim doesn't pass the sniff test ... [because of austerity, though,] the social mobility that societies such as the United Kingdom and the United States took for granted from the 1950s through the 1980s that made me and others like me possible has effectively ground to a halt.[17]

Austerity has *not* brought economic growth; nor is it responsible for creating good jobs, and it certainly has not staved the surge of inequality. It has helped increase the wealth and power of the already rich and powerful. And as they embrace greater political power over policy making, they see austerity as the perpetual crisis necessary to discipline citizens' economic expectations under the guise of fixing a nation's economy—systems they were responsible for breaking to begin with.

Just like bad food, health, and gun policies, bad economic policies like austerity also need their intellectual apologists. Aside from the always available free-market purists like Friedmanites and libertarians like Ron Paul, the work of economists Kenneth Rogoff and Carmen Reinhart (R&R) seemed to prove austerity hawks right: serious debt reduction was the best remedy for governments after the 2008 financial crisis. Their now infamous paper, *Growth in a Time of Debt*, delivered at the 2010 American Economic Association conference, "found conclusive empirical evidence that gross debt (meaning all debt that a government owes, including debt held in government trust funds) exceeding 90% of the economy has a significant negative effect on economic growth."[18] Although the paper was not peer reviewed, it became the research underpinning everyone from Paul Ryan and Rand Paul to European Union Commissioner Olli Rehn and British

Chancellor of the Exchequer George Osborne. Everyone seemed to jump on the R&R bandwagon. Everyone except a University of Massachusetts (UMass) graduate student, who couldn't seem to make the numbers in R&R's study add up. Thomas Herndon had been assigned to take a recent economics publication and reproduce the results—but he couldn't figure out how R&R had reached their conclusions. With the help of his UMass professors, he finally realized R&R had made some very significant mistakes. The Harvard professors had accidentally only included 15 of the 20 countries under analysis in their key calculation (of average GDP growth in countries with high public debt). Not including countries like Canada, Australia, and New Zealand made a significant difference in the findings. The UMass group also thought R&R erred when they averaged small and large samplings together, distorting the weight of influence on the final calculations. While Herndon and his faculty found there *could* be correlations between large debt and slower growth, they contend the evidence is much more nuanced and other variables can easily have equal or greater influence on large economies.[19] But maybe this was all just intellectual posturing and a tempest in a teapot?

According to economist Daniel Hamermesh of the University of London: "I don't think jobs were destroyed because of [R&R's mistake] but it provides an intellectual rationalisation for things that affect how people think about the world ... And how people think about the world, especially politicians, eventually affects how the world works."[20] But U.S. economist Paul Krugman has gone further, suggesting that austerity critics "underestimated just how destructive" it would be, not only imposing short-term problems but also crippling long-term growth. Even countries who have *mostly* recovered, like the United States, are "far poorer than pre-crisis projections suggested they would be at this point." Citing a paper by Lawrence Summers and Antonio Fatás, Krugman explains: "in addition to supporting other economists' conclusion that the crisis seems to have done enormous long-run damage, [the authors] show that the downgrading of nations' long-run prospects is strongly correlated with the *amount* of austerity they imposed."[21] Krugman concludes:

> What this suggests is that the turn to austerity had truly catastrophic effects, going far beyond the jobs and income lost in the first few years. In fact, the long-run damage suggested by the Fatás—Summers estimates is easily big enough to make austerity a self-defeating policy even in purely fiscal terms: Governments that slashed spending in the face of depression hurt their economies, and hence their future tax receipts, so much that even their debt will end up higher than it would have been without the cuts. And the bitter irony of the story is that this catastrophic policy was undertaken in the name of long-run responsibility, that those who protested against the wrong turn were dismissed as feckless.[22]

In essence, those who pushed austerity—not just post-2008 crisis, but really from the 1980s onward—did so either based on bad analyses and bad ideas, or knowing full well that continued financial crises would benefit those who controlled financial markets and political power, but not the majority of its citizens. The perpetual economic disaster for middle- and working-class families meant incredible profit for the top 1%, who were not beyond killing the very economy they controlled in order to create even more for themselves.

Austerity, then, does have its victims—most of us, actually. But some have faced the dangers wrought by austerity more severely than others. Take, for example, the results of major tax cuts on state services. With fewer dollars coming from the federal government, and states unable to make up for less revenue—especially after the financial crisis of 2008—more and more municipalities instituted fee-for-service plans. Garbage collection, after school programs, you name it. But in Obion County, Tennessee, a US$75 fee for fire protection stood between families and fire safety. On September 29, 2010, the Cranick family reportedly watched their home, possessions, and pets burn while firefighters refused services because they hadn't paid the fee. According to South Fulton Mayor, David Crocker, "if the city's firefighters responded to people who didn't pay there would be no incentive for anyone to subscribe. There's no way to go to every fire and keep up the manpower, the equipment, and just the funding for the fire department [without the fee]."[23] On December 5 the following year, another Obion County family witnessed their trailer home burn, again while firefighters watched. In nearby Blount County, firefighters will work to extinguish a blaze even if resident haven't prepaid for subscriptions—but they are charged US$2,200 for the first two hours and $1,000 for each subsequent hour that it takes to put out the fire.

Fee-for-public-services predate the fiscal crisis; some of the earliest urban firefighters were gangs, often jostling to control turf where they could extort fees from local businesses and landlords for putting out fires of mysterious origins. But since the 1970s and Reagan-era property tax movements, water and sewer fees have skyrocketed and more and more municipalities are initiating "pay for accidents" or "first responder fees" for fire, Emergency Medical Technicians (EMTs) and even police services.[24] Geographer Jamie Peck calls these trends "austerity urbanism," suggesting that, "Due to the spatial concentration of unionized labor, communities of color, poor people, and liberal constituencies, cities are favored – and particularly vulnerable – targets of austerity measures." These new policies feature local governments that "cut social services and the wages of public sector workers (increasingly denying these workers the right to bargain collectively), slash school budgets, and eliminate affordable housing units—all while privatizing core city functions and subsidizing private investors."[25] Once again, the day-to-day lives of poor, working-class and middle-class citizens become increasingly precarious, decreasingly safe, and "served" by governments they have decreasing power to influence and hold accountable. And nowhere has this become truer than in the state of Michigan.

As I close out this book, I note that Hillary Clinton raised the trials and tribulations of Flint during her campaign, Senator Bernie Sanders called for Michigan's Governor, Rick Snyder, to resign, and the Democratic National Committee held one of the Presidential debates in Flint.[26] Michael Moore called for Snyder's arrest.[27] While much of the current disaster in Flint can be traced back to the impact of austerity budgets on poor cities, especially in Michigan, the perfect storm of "kill it to save it" policy making brought together neoliberal economic forces, financial austerity planning, and the anti-democratic Emergency Manager Law in Michigan, with the result being the state poisoning its own people. Here's how the storm surged.[28]

In 1988, Michigan passed Public Act 101, which allowed a Local Emergency Financial Assistance Loan Board to review a city's failure to pay debts and salaries, requests by local residents or officials, and—if deemed appropriate—appoint an emergency financial manager (EM). In 1990, Public Act 72 broadened the EM's powers to handle all matters of municipal finances, as well as providing a statute applicable to school districts. However, between 1988 and 2000, only two cities had asked for such help: Hamtramck in 1988 and Highland Park in 2000. In 2002, Flint had an EM selected, but had its own local government restored to power in 2004. Following the financial crisis of 2008, however, municipalities in Michigan began to crumble. In many ways, few Michigan cities steeped in the old auto industry's rise and fall had been able to rebound from forty years of deindustrialization and white flight. But the crash may have been the final straw.[29]

Between 2009 and 2010, Democratic Governor Jennifer Granholm responded to local requests and placed the cities of Benton Harbor, Ecorse, and Pontiac, and the Detroit public school system under Emergency Managers. But following the election of Republican Rick Snyder in 2010, EMs have been imposed not only on Detroit and (again) Flint, but also on the school districts of Muskogean Heights and Highland Park. More notable, though, was the passage of Public Acts 4 (2011) and 436 (2012), which expanded both the reach of the state in declaring emergencies and the powers of the EMs once selected. Regardless of each city's particulars, the first major impact removes democratic control and accountability over local decisions. Local elections can be held—but, under the most recent incantations of the EM statutes, they have little to no power.[30]

What have EMs done without democratic oversight? Mostly, they have imposed severe austerity budgets and sold off as much public land, buildings, and resources as possible for private investment and debt reduction. In Benton Harbor, the Whirlpool Company reportedly used land giveaways and huge tax breaks to turn public property into a privately owned and operated Jack Nicklaus PGA Tour golf course. It seems the Harbor Shores development company also used mostly public land to build large, luxury condos and a marina. Intense gentrification is now displacing a majority-Black community and has resulted in one African American activist being convicted by an all-white jury and sentenced to three to ten years for voter fraud. After almost a year in jail, the Reverend Edward Pinkney had his conviction overturned by an appeals court and has returned to continue his struggle against unelected officials and the corporation whose bidding they do. Upon leaving prison, Pinkney explained: "Here, Whirlpool controls not only Benton Harbor and the residents, but also the court system itself. They will do anything to crush you if you stand up to them."[31]

In Pontiac, the EM began by selling off the Silver Dome, former home to the Detroit Lions, for half a million dollars—US$55 million less than it cost to build in the 1970s, and US$29 million less than its current owners asked for when they put it up for sale again in 2015. But the fire sale continued throughout the early 2010s. According to *The New York Times*:

> unfettered by normal checks, balances and the pressures of getting re-elected, emergency managers here have overhauled labor contracts, sold off city assets and privatized nearly every service Pontiac once provided to citizens. Its police force has been outsourced to the county. Its Fire Department belongs to a nearby township. The city's payroll, once numbering more than 600 workers, now amounts to about 50 public employees. Even parking meters have been sold. All this, and more cuts may be coming, all on the way to balancing the books.[32]

Now back under local control, elected officials are trying to maintain the sustainability and integrity of its population while having to cater to new investors and their plans for gentrification and redevelopment. But it was Flint, Michigan featured in the news throughout early 2016. In a rush to save US$5 million by terminating its water supply relationship with the City of Detroit, Flint's EM failed to conduct a proper study on the water quality of its interim water source, the Flint River. For almost two years, Flint took its water from the river with devastating effects. Within hours of the switch, residents recognized a difference in the smell, appearance, and taste of their tap water. From March through the summer of 2014, problems continued and complaints increased. Water testing started showing signs of E. coli and officials finally issued a boiled water advisory in September 2014.[33]

To address E. coli, water management officials began treating the river with chlorine. However, the chlorine combined with naturally occurring organic compounds such as dead leaves, grasses, and plants to create a new problem. Researchers found high levels of the carcinogenic trihalomethanes (TTHM) in Flint's water supply throughout late 2014 and 2015. Despite its potential hazards, the EM instructed city officials to claim the water was still safe, usable, and drinkable. The water quality got so bad that General Motors stopped using it at their one remaining auto plant because its corrosive effects were ruining car parts. Soon, however, TTHM's threats took a back seat when Virginia Tech researchers found shocking levels of lead poisoning in the water supply.[34]

Flint's water system had been built with lead pipes and lead soldering—as were many of its homes. But the corrosiveness of Flint River water, especially after being treated with chlorine to address E. coli, leached lead from pipes and brought it directly into people's homes and kitchen taps. Schools, companies, office buildings, and hospitals also had high levels of lead enter their water supply. According to local physicians and health researchers, almost 27,000 local children now have elevated levels of lead up to three times more than might be normally permissible. Lead poisoning is one of the most dangerous neurotoxins known to humans; it can be especially damaging to children, causing anemia, stunted growth, and various brain damage and cognitive difficulties.[35]

Despite information about the potential dangers in the drinking water, officials from the EM's office all the way to the Governor's office denied the threats to children and families. For over a year, the city did *nothing* to stop citizens from drinking, bathing, and cooking with contaminated water—despite having information about lead leaching into its supply.[36] In fact, on numerous occasions the Department of Environmental Quality debunked the level of contamination. According to Evan Osnos from *The New Yorker*:

> A memo from the U.S. Environmental Protection Agency warned that the city's use of a new water source was exposing the public to unsafe levels of lead, but Brad Wurfel, the [DEQ's] lead spokesperson, told a reporter, "Let me start here—anyone who is concerned about lead in the drinking water in Flint can relax." Even after a group of Virginia Tech researchers found unsafe levels of lead, Wurfel disputed the importance of the findings because, he wrote, the group "specializes in looking for high lead problems. They pull that rabbit out of that hat everywhere they go." He added that "dire public health advice based on some quick testing could be seen as fanning political flames irresponsibly. Residents of Flint concerned about the health of their community don't need more of that."[37]

Eventually a local physician, Dr. Mona Hanna-Attisha, had collected enough data on lead levels in young children's blood tests to declare a serious emergency was brewing. Still, state officials called her irresponsible and her results a matter of "slicing and dicing" data. Hanna-Attisha released her research in a press conference after state officials refused to act. Months later, she published her data in the peer reviewed *American Journal of Public Health*.[38] About the same time, state doctors and scientists corroborated her data with their own, admitting they missed an opportunity to intervene earlier. In December of 2015, a newly elected Flint Mayor declared a state of emergency. One month later, Governor Snyder declared a state emergency, just days before President Obama would declare a national emergency and release additional resources and support from both the Federal

Emergency Management Authority (FEMA) and Homeland Security. But such actions were too late for many.

Mark Edwards, Virginia Tech professor and water quality expert, had predicted early in their work in Flint that high levels of Legionella—the cause of Legionnaires Disease—had been found in large buildings in the city. On January 13, 2016, Snyder released information that 87 cases of Legionnaires had been reported between June 2014 and November 2015, resulting in ten known deaths. Numerous public officials knew of these cases and had discussed possible links to Flint's water contamination, but no information was released to the public and no formal action taken to protect citizens. Because of researchers, numerous citizen protests, Freedom of Information Act requests by local journalists, and increased media attention on a national level, the story of Flint, Michigan's poisoning of its own people is now widely known and the impact of such governmental pathology is yet to unfold completely. Tens of thousands of children have been contaminated and the impact of such poison will only appear over time.[39]

And as sociologist Robert Newby reminds us, most of those impacted by the Flint debacle are African Americans. Despite Black and Latino people making up just over 19% of the state's entire population, over half of the people under EM managers in Michigan are Black or Latino.[40] Along with Michigan's voter suppression laws requiring photo I.D.'s and other discriminatory qualifications, Newby suggests that a "New Jim Crow" may be in effect:

> Jim Crow was more than segregation, it was a system of degradation, but first and foremost it was a denial of citizenship rights for a whole segment of the population based upon their so-called "race" and race alone ... Much like the old Jim Crow in which blacks were denied the right to vote, when it comes to local government, Gov. Snyder has invalidated the power of a majority of Michigan's black voters and the meaning of that vote with his emergency manager policy ... The citizens of Flint, many of whom are black, have been denied their representative

> democracy. All decisions for city services, including switching to the poisonous water directly were made by the governor's emergency managers. Instead of democracy, there was an arrogance that usurped the right of these citizens to govern themselves.[41]

Once again, race is central to the effective dismantling of public systems and the rationalization of these policies by a "kill it to save it" narrative. Only instead of requiring a shock or disaster to demolish public infrastructures, these explanations need only a sense of economic austerity and a racialized "other" whose children don't count.

By the time the body count left behind by austerity budgets, privatization, the degradation of democracy, and prioritizing corporate profits over people's health and safety—especially people of color—is known, it may be too late to reverse the logical irrationality of "kill it to save it" policy making. As the toxic blend of corporate hegemony and hyper-individualism oozes through the pipes and arteries of American life, we may not find the opportunity to stop the serial killing of our long-gone citizens. In the end, "kill it to save it" may save no one and kill us all.

EPILOGUE

Innocents Abroad, Trouble at Home: Kill it to Save it Goes Global

We saw rude piles of stones standing near the roadside, at intervals, and recognized the custom of marking boundaries which obtained in Jacob's time. There were no walls, no fences, no hedges—nothing to secure a man's possessions but these random heaps of stones. The Israelites held them sacred in the old patriarchal times, and these other Arabs, their lineal descendants, do so likewise. An American, of ordinary intelligence, would soon widely extend his property, at an outlay of mere manual labor, performed at night, under so loose a system of fencing as this. (Mark Twain, *Innocents Abroad*[1])

As I went walking, I saw a sign there
  And on the sign it said, "No Trespassing"
  But on the other side, it didn't say nothing
  That side was made for you and me.
(Woody Guthrie, "This Land is Your Land"[2])

Kill it to Save it: Czech Republic

In the late 1990s, Czech Republic officials discussed the possibility of steep new taxes on cigarettes. Inspired by studies that showed the exorbitant cost of smoking-related illnesses on their universal public health care system, the debate soon turned to those who advocated an outright ban on smoking. To influence the policy discussion, Philip Morris, the world's largest tobacco manufacturer at that time, made illegal contributions to the Czech's Civic Democratic Alliance (CDA) Party. The donations were discovered; the country's Environmental Minister—a CDA member—was forced to resign and policy makers moved closer to an outright ban in an effort to save billions of dollars on health care expenditures, as well as improve its citizens' overall wellbeing. Saving lives and effectively managing public resources are things we might expect from good government.[3]

But Philip Morris decided that if they couldn't interfere with a foreign government's political process by pocketing high-level officials, perhaps they could produce a scientific and economic argument to counter the *premise* of saving money and increasing health outcomes.[4] To accomplish this goal, the tobacco company commissioned Arthur D. Little International to study smoking's actual cost to the country's public coffers.[5] The accounting firm's findings? They concluded that, "Based on up-to-date reliable data and consideration of all relevant contributing factors, the effect of smoking on the public finance balance in the Czech Republic in 1999 was *positive*,estimated at +5,815 million CZK [Czech Koruna], or just over $300,000,000 a year." The study continued:

> Public finance saved between 943 mil. CZK and 1,193 mil. CZK from reduced health-care costs, savings on pensions and housing costs for the elderly—all related to the early mortality of smokers. Among the positive effects, excise tax, VAT [Value Added Tax] and health care cost savings due to early mortality are the most important.[6]

In other words ... well, you don't need other words. "Early mortality" saves money. It seems that Philip Morris—along with their "objective," corporate, cost-benefit researchers from Arthur D. Little—could argue effectively that it was in the economic best interests of the Czech Republic to not only lift its ban on smoking, but, by logical extrapolation, encourage *more* people to smoke *more* cigarettes. The government's budget difficulties could be solved by eliminating a huge chunk of its people. *Kill it to save it.*

While the Philip Morris—Arthur D. Little study was roundly denounced by anti-tobacco activists and public officials on both sides of the Atlantic,[7] the premise of the logic was not so easily dismissed. In fact, the belief that government or corporate bottom lines should drive public policies has been at the heart of domestic policy strategies around the globe for decades now, and at the heart of my argument throughout this book.

In many respects, the United States and other industrialized nations have been destroying the world in search of economic gain for centuries. Initially, colonialism and imperialism extrapolated valuable resources (including people) and built what we now call "western civilization" on the backs and blood of bodies strewn from East Africa and East Asia to the West Indies and Western Plains of the United States. While some Christian apologists suggested a missionary zeal in "saving" souls at the point of the sword, few could rationally argue that slavery and savagery was a public reform strategy.

As democracy gained stable, if limited, footholds in America and elsewhere, social movements and welfare states in Europe and even in the U.S. called into question brutality and exploitation abroad. And as postcolonial governments used independence to acquire authority over their own resources, western powers required new ways of maintaining control and profiting from an increasingly "global" economy. By lending money and imposing conditions such as structural adjustment programs, "First World" nations conspired to ensure that "modernizing" and "industrializing" countries would be "hooked" on unaffordable and unsustainable debt at the same time that they allowed western corporations to dominate the domestic marketplaces of developing nations. But for every few million people in poorer countries who couldn't pay school fees or access potable water or tend their native lands, columnists such as Thomas Friedman or David Brooks would wax poetically in *The New York Times* about level playing fields and the internet's magical elixir for inequality: free enterprise.[8] And when world commerce and trading policies couldn't do the trick; when global inequality intensified instead of diminished; when postcolonial uprisings challenged the power of western finance and political hegemony, or when we suddenly had to compete with China for valuable resources like oil in the Middle East, we enforced control the old fashioned way—we "bombed them back into the stone age." *Kill it to save it.*

But this book is about the ways in which exploitation and greed have been rationalized here at home to carry out the most effective and efficient extraction of profit possible in the United States. To achieve such goals, new political and cultural strategies were necessary to manufacture the consent[9] of the very people whose lives would be destroyed by such policies. It's not simply that a huge swath of poor and middle-class whites were diverted by white supremacy (although that's part of it); or that similar groups of former "middle American" populists now gather in the fundamentalist flocks of pro-life, pro-death penalty, anti-death tax, anti-evolutionist *Hannity*—Huckabee fanatics (although that's part of it, too). More effective has been the invidious recasting of American core *instincts* that now identify personal character and virtue—our individualism and our freedom—with free-flowing capital for the wealthy and austerity for the rest of us. Junk freedom for all.

Kill it to Save it: Africa

But we in the United States are no longer alone in this trend. In East and South Africa, government and business leaders are supporting Monsanto's practices by inviting the company to spread its genetically modified (GM) "drought resistant" seed. With huge grants from the Gates Foundation, Monsanto is planting its stake on the continent—despite resistance from many regional scientists, nongovernmental organizations

(NGOs) and activists. Although ecologically sound and proven alternatives to address the drought exist, government officials have embraced Monsanto's program *without* standard approval processes; they simply trust Monsanto and Gates to do the right thing. Meanwhile, Gates has purchased over US$23 million in Monsanto stock as the company makes permanent inroads into the region's agricultural markets by offering seeds without charging royalties. But the company maintains patent rights and can retract free royalties at any time. Once the seeds are planted, however, there will be no turning back from Monsanto's progeny. Current laws thus give Monsanto control over agricultural markets for generations to come.[10]

While Monsanto, Gates, and their African supporters proclaim the possibility of a Second Green Revolution, African scientists suggest such a "revolution" may result in disaster.[11] Studies of the long-term effects of the *first* Green Revolution in the 1950s and 1960s show strong evidence that, despite increasing overall crop yields, the expensive "technology packages" (fertilizers, pesticides, and irrigation technology) "deepened the divide between large farmers and small ones as the latter could not afford the technology."[12] To address this disparity, governments in India, Mexico, and South Africa subsidized technology packages, thus increasing the region's saturation of pesticides and fertilizers, often with serious health, environment, and economic consequences.[13] Even more devastating was the long-term effect on the land itself as high yielding seeds were also high-feeding seeds. Their implementation depleted the fragile tropical and hillside soils of their natural fertility, thus requiring more and more applications of less and less effective fertilizers, ultimately intensifying soil erosion.[14] As corporations and their supporters claimed miracle yields, mostly for export, the sustainability of small farmers and the land itself dramatically declined.

In East Africa, the pressure to lift the ban on genetically modified organisms (GMOs) intensifies as the impact of colonialism, the first Green Revolution, and climate change make agricultural subsistence increasingly challenging. In a classic "kill it to save it" moment, it appears Monsanto is not only promoting drought-resistant seeds, but is also pushing the same failed seeds that screwed up South Africa and East African farmers. When Monsanto designed its Bacillus thuringiensis (Bt) corn seeds with pesticide-infused DNA, they "got the science all wrong." According to the African Centre for Biosafety (ACB) Director, Miriam Mayet:

> Independent biosafety scientists have discovered that the inheritance of resistance in African stem borers is a dominant, not recessive, trait as erroneously assumed [by Monsanto scientists] ... hence the insect resistance management strategies that Monsanto developed, and [that were] accepted by our regulators based on these erroneous assumptions, were utterly ineffective.

It seems Monsanto and Gates are now dumping these seeds on drought-challenged countries like Mozambique, Uganda, Tanzania, and Kenya.[15]

Time after time, scientific research demonstrates that GMO quick fixes are often long-term disasters for the people who must live with them, despite being short-term gold mines for the people who propagate them. The emphasis on increasing *yield* for international trade and the resulting industrialization of food production not only threatens environmental and agricultural degradation (similar to what has occurred in North America) but also devastates traditional farming communities. African scientists and farmers believe smaller-scale efforts focused on biodiversity and other alternatives are not only possible, but may be the only sustainable hope to reverse "kill it to save it" agricultural policies on the African continent. According to sociologist Cornelia Butler Flora, technology and industrialization destroys traditional agricultural practices and systems, leaving African nations beholden to Monsanto and other GMO companies. Instead, she suggests, "A systems approach that focuses on sustainability of the local ecosystem, social and cultural relationships and economic security can be as, or more, productive than industrial agriculture, and have a much better opportunity to increase food security in developing countries." She continues:

> Such a systems-based shift in practices … have potential of addressing household livelihood strategies and production issues in a sustainable, farmer-based way. Resource-conserving agriculture has been shown to increase yields in developing countries. Priority should be given to developing technologies that follow the systems principles of sustainable agriculture, integrating biological and ecological processes (such as nutrient cycling, nitrogen fixation, soil regeneration and biodiversity) into the production processes; minimizing use of non-renewable inputs that cause harm to the environment or to the health of farmers and consumers; and making productive use of the knowledge and skills of farmers and their collective capacities to work together to solve common problems. A variety of models are on the ground in Africa, and there is political will in the African Union to increase investment in agriculture.[16]

But the political will can be overrun by the money and power Monsanto, Gates, and other GMO multinationals wield.

Meanwhile, far from the agricultural wheat fields of east and South Africa, another form of kill it to save it suggests a different way for corporate sponsors and commercial dollars to expand the continent's economy. One of the purest examples of "kill it to save it" came to light recently when Minnesota dentist, Walter Palmer, drew international consternation for shooting and killing a beloved lion (Cecil) just outside of Hwange National Park in Zimbabwe. Palmer claims that he paid US$55,000 to a safari operator and a professional hunter orchestrated the kill. The controversy gave rise to global debates about the legal big-game hunting industry and the growing practice of auctioning off "hunting rights" for big game in order to (of course) raise money to protect rare big game animals.

For example, in Namibia, officials auction off black rhino hunting permits to save the black rhino. Implemented in 2003, Namibia's Black Rhino Conservation Strategy authorized an annual harvest of up to five male black rhinos. According to officials, studies demonstrated the removal of "limited numbers" of males reduced fighting, shortened calving intervals, reduced juvenile mortality, and ultimately stimulated population growth. In 2014, the Dallas Safari Club (DSC) auctioned off a "killing license" for US$350,000; just over a year later, club member Corey Knowlton shot and killed a black rhino. Afterwards, Knowlton reflected: "I felt like from day one it was something benefiting the black rhino … Being on this hunt, with the amount of criticism it brought and the amount of praise it brought from both sides, I don't think it could have brought more awareness to the black rhino."[17]

Of course, critics suggest that there are other ways to address the endangerment of black rhinos—such as land and habitat conservation, better security and enforcement against poaching, and banning the international market for rhino horns. As Jeff Flocken, North American Regional Director for the International Fund for Animal Welfare, blogged:

> the idea of creating a bidding war for the opportunity to gun down one of the last of a species ostensibly in the name of conservation is perverse and dangerous to buy into. … If an animal like the rare black rhinoceros is worth the most with a price on its head, what possible incentive does this provide range countries and local people to move the species toward recovery when the biggest buck can be made short-term by selling permits to kill them to the highest bidders?

But the DSC's participation has not only resulted in almost US$500,000 for conservation efforts; it has also helped reaffirm the idea that trickle-down economics could make the black rhino prosperous, too.[18]

Kill it to Save it: India

Monsanto's work in India has already demonstrated the devastating impact of failed GMO policies on small farmers. Not only did copious amounts of increasingly ineffective pesticides damage environment and human health, but Green Revolution technology packages also required heavy irrigation. The Indian Government subsidized digging more than 20 million tube wells, which, over the past decade, resulted in drying up water tables and forcing vast areas to return to traditional dryland farming or give up farming altogether. As Holt-Gimenez and his colleagues write: "In the Punjab—home of the Green Revolution—nearly 80% of groundwater is now 'overexploited or critical'". The water shortage may be irreversible. And, as most grain crops are exported, "the hydrological result of the Green Revolution packages is the sacrifice of India's ancient aquifers to the voracity of international trade, a situation surely to become more critical given predicted climate change."[19]

Loss of fertile soil, sufficient water supplies, and traditional agricultural practices and social customs has had massive impact on farmers throughout the nation. Over 300,000 Indian farmers have committed suicide over the past two decades. Debate continues over the extent to which Monsanto seeds *caused* this spate of suicides. But the most recent and in-depth examinations explain that, while particular GMO seeds may not be an exclusive trigger for suicide, "India's shift to industrial farming techniques starting in the 1960s [and intensifying in the 1980s and 1990s] left the majority of the nation's cotton farmers increasingly reliant on loans to purchase pricey fertilizers, pesticides, and hybrid seeds." GM seeds and buying the technologies to grow them made farmers more "vulnerable to bankruptcy when the vagaries of rain and global cotton markets turned against them."[20] Insecurity, fear, indignity, poverty, embarrassment, and shame have led to a suicide epidemic. Like the profit from industrialized agribusiness in the U.S., financial fortunes divide unequally and with increasing severity—in a nation of 1.2 billion people, India's top 100 richest people own assets equivalent to one quarter of the country's gross domestic product (GDP). Yields increase initially, but more and more people die.

Along with other GMO companies, reports suggest Coca-Cola has had a hugely negative impact on many regions of India. In March 2000, Coca-Cola opened a bottling plant at Plachimada in the southern state of Kerala. According to journalist Rohan D. Mathews, within six months local residents complained that their water had turned milky-white and brackish. Others complained of unusual stomachaches and farmers reported their wells were emptying unusually fast and crop yields decreasing. Regional NGOs found high levels of calcium and magnesium in the water, caused by Coca-Cola's excessive water extraction. Mathews explained:

> The bottle washing taking place at the plant involved chemicals, and the resulting sludge was taken out of the plant ... and sold as fertilizer to unsuspecting farmers, following which it was given free, and with increasing resentment among villagers, it was merely dumped on the roadside ... more than 1000 families in the surrounding villages had been affected.[21]

Similar situations occurred in other regions as Coca-Cola continued its production at the expense of local communities, agricultural livelihoods, and growing numbers of illnesses and poverty.

Throughout India, government officials and business leaders have advocated for increased industrialization and reaped major profits while the majority of small farmers and laborers have borne the brunt of poverty, sickness, and death. As Arundhati Roy writes:

> In India the 300 million of us who belong to the new, post-International Monetary Fund (IMF) reforms middle-class—the market—live side by side with spirits of the netherworld, the poltergeists of dead rivers, dry wells, bald mountains, and denuded forests; the ghosts of 250,000 debt-ridden farmers who have killed themselves, and of 800 million who have been impoverished and dispossessed to make way for us. And [they] survive on twenty Indian rupees a day (30 cents US).[22]

Businessmen and politicians sing the praises of economic growth and the globalization of India's thriving markets while the majority of its people suffer. "Kill it to save it."

Kill it to Save it: The U.K.

Even in Western Europe, "kill it to save it" policy making has been advancing—with all of the predictably negative impacts it has had elsewhere. England, Ireland, Scotland and Wales have all been facing the onset of an obesity epidemic since the early 2000s. Researchers suggest that the two most notable causes are the increase in sedentary lifestyles and the growth of fast food, processed foods, and industrialized food production. Fast food restaurants, in particular, seem to conglomerate in low-income urban communities, where Europeans are showing the greatest rates of rising obesity. But early evidence suggests that countries willing to establish "fat taxes" (imposing monetary premiums on fast and processed foods), as well as nations prepared to incentivize *healthy* food production while penalizing heavily industrialized methods, could reverse trends significantly. Historically, Western European countries would have seemed like places to accomplish these kinds of regulatory public policies. But the advent of austerity suggests that increasing taxes and restricting markets may not be on the cards for anyone.[23]

Austerity is, in many ways, the pinnacle of today's global "kill it to save it" policy making. With the United States and Europe leading the way, austerity now comprises the language, the religion, and the very culture of contemporary society, born out of a global fiscal crisis not unlike America's own post-Vietnam postcolonial crisis. Of course, the 2008 financial crisis predominantly emanated from the ways in which private U.S. banks operate in the global system—much in the way old imperialism did. As Michael Lewis explains in *Boomerang*:

> The global financial system may exist to bring borrowers and lenders together, but over the past few decades, it has become something else, too: a tool for maximizing the number of encounters between the strong and the weak, so that one might exploit the other. Extremely smart traders inside Wall Street investment banks devise deeply unfair, diabolically complicated bets, and then send their sales forces out

> to scour the world for some idiot who will take the other side of those bets.[24]

Such a system not only allowed Wall Street to ravage national banks across the globe, it also allowed other very smart people to do the same to their own countries' banking systems. As Lewis chronicles, Ireland and Iceland in particular allowed their investment bankers to go crazy with credit, debt, and a variety of high-risk bets and loans that ultimately crippled their national economies.

But the result of a global financial crisis caused primarily by private banks and financial companies was immediately made a public debacle by nation after nation coming to the aid of banks, portrayed as "too big to fail." (One exception was Iceland, where banks were allowed to fail and where the economic recovery has ironically been faster and fuller than anywhere else.) Essentially, financial and government leaders in the United States "democratized" the private failings of financial institutions, resulting in massive domestic spending on bank bailouts. For decades now, American "kill it to save it" policies have generated socialism for the rich and laissez-faire for everyone else. But even throughout Europe (and especially in the U.K.), U.S.-generated "private" debt was "rechristened as a sovereign debt crisis of profligate European states," according to Mark Blyth. He concludes, "The argument that austerity was necessary and that the crisis was the fault of state spending was constructed by an assortment of business leaders, bankers and paradoxically European politicians."[25]

The result of austerity in places like Flint, Michigan may now live infamously in U.S. history. Still, the impact of austerity in the U.K. has had similarly devastating effects. It began with a coalition of bankers, politicians, and corporate tycoons developing well-crafted and often repeated stories rationalizing austerity as the only alternative. According to Afoko and Vokins from the New Economics Foundation:

> The coalition has an economic narrative that is the textbook definition of a powerful political story. They have developed a clear plot, with heroes and

> villains, and use simple, emotional language to make their point clear. Repeated with remarkable discipline over several years, their austerity story has gained real traction with the British public. The government has successfully framed all economic debates on its own terms, but what is most powerful about their narrative is how resilient it is to different circumstances. If the economy is strong the medicine is working; if the economy is weak, we need more medicine.[26]

Rumblings Abroad and Trouble at Home

The power of austerity common sense is that, like the neocapitalist take on U.S. political economy, it is impervious to critique. "Kill it to save it" policy makers stand naked at the castle door and if any young children were to ask about their apparent lack of clothing, they would simply roll up their pretend sleeves and adjust their pretend ties.

But, as I discussed in the last chapter, austerity as a theory was wrong. Some would say as wrong as the International Monetary Fund (IMF) and World Bank imposing structural adjustment programs (SAPs) in poor and developing nations—so wrong, in fact, that the IMF has begun to "reconsider" SAPs. And despite austerity's global popularity—even official gospel—movements to stop the surge have been growing for over a decade.[27] I had the honor of working with South African poet and activist, Dennis Brutus, on the Jubilee Africa campaign for almost a decade before he died in 2009. Brutus traveled the world with his call for the IMF and World Bank to cancel all debt on poor and developing nations. He explained:

> We want the cancellation of the debt which is a burden on the [poorer] countries of the South—it's strangling their economies and preventing them from building schools and hospitals and housing because they have to give priority to paying debt before they can provide services to people not serve the banks.[28]

Jubilee 2000 eventually morphed into many smaller campaigns, and also fueled the Make Poverty History organization, which is part of the Global Call to Action Against Poverty campaign. Even before the financial crisis of 2008, millions of people around the world had gone to the streets demanding the cancellation of debt and protesting austerity measures enforced by international financial organizations.[29]

These movements did have some impact in changing the dialogue and moving global inequality to the forefront of economic discussions—most notably in the United Nations Millennium Project in 2002. But even massive demonstrations and multiple international campaigns faced powerful opposition and little structural transformation occurred. Eventually, though, reality caught up with austerity as it came home to roost in Western Europe and the United States after 2008. Throughout Europe—most notably in Greece, but also Ireland, Spain, and the U.K., to name a few countries—deregulation, privatization, and cuts in social spending resulted in grand swaths of people and communities bottoming out. National economies were ruined and, as governments struggled to infuse cash into paying off bank debts, gone were the basic safety nets that might have caught the expanding population of abject poor. In the wake of the global financial meltdown, the world hosts a growing number of now superfluous people. Ironically and perversely—as journalist Mary O'Hara offers—overstretched, professional, and informal servers, as well as thousands of small voluntary and community organizations, had for years unintentionally helped a coalition of neoliberal and corporate leaders by "obscuring the full force of cuts on the ground." In fact, "in the initial phase [of austerity] they endeavored to keep providing vital services as austerity was blowing the lives of people in their communities to smithereens." But people in the U.K. (as elsewhere) have fought back. O'Hara concludes her chronicle of austerity's savagery by writing: "if there was one overriding message from the journey I made around Austerity UK it was this: people were only prepared to take so much." She quotes one activist: "If Mr. Cameron thinks he's getting away with this, he has another thing coming. It may take people to hit rock-bottom, but we'll fight him."[30] It is partially correct to see the British exit ("Brexit") from the European Union as a nativist response to a rapid influx of political and economic non-white refugees, but it would be a mistake to completely ignore that some progressive and socialist citizens saw "Brexit" as a challenge to neoliberalism in general and Cameron's austerity policies in particular.[31]

Here at home, Occupy Wall Street (OWS) stopped more than just traffic on the Brooklyn Bridge. OWS put "the 1%" and "the 99%" into our everyday lingo. It elicited a 2012 State of the Union that discussed economic inequality over a dozen times. But Obama had barely left the stage when the "class warfare" attack from Republicans began. One could argue, however, that so much of the Marco Rubio's appeal for unity in the face of class warfare is a sign of OWS success—OWS was the "they" of which he was speaking. Anti-austerity movements have influenced even Janet Yellin—current Federal Reserve Chair—to announce that "income inequality" may be the primary economic challenge of the next decade. She explained:

> It is no secret that the past few decades of widening inequality can be summed up as significant income and wealth gains for those at the very top and stagnant living standards for the majority. I think it is appropriate to ask whether this trend is compatible with values rooted in our nation's history, among them the high value Americans have traditionally placed on equality of opportunity.[32]

But she also proclaimed: "research about the causes and implications of inequality is ongoing." Like climate change, I would suggest the research is in. The numbers are clear. Our current income inequality is a direct result of austerity for the poor and socialism for the rich. It is a direct result of "kill it to save it" policy making that has convinced a large enough chunk or middle- and working-class people to support austerity despite its absolute failure. It has, however, been a huge success for the top 1%.

But, of course, so much of the "income inequality" narrative misses the point. Instead of shaking off the language of individualism, the neoliberal story of inequality embraces it.

The Federal Reserve, the Democratic Party, and the non-profit management industry all promote the argument: help individual people improve earning potential with better job training and education. They adopt the language of workforce development. As if lazy, ignorant, working-class sloths had been behind the financial crisis, its declining labor markets, and the continued below-poverty-level minimum wage. And, while Republicans want to dismantle the public sphere, the best Democrats can offer is more programs to bolster the individual's ability to compete in the private sector—*à* la Janet Yellin. Even the Democrats seem to have lost their welfare state muster.

Into this morass stepped Bernie Sanders. His campaign rhetoric was sometimes inspiring and, as you could probably tell from the tone of this book, I was not turned off by his curmudgeonly delivery. He has been the first major, national political figure in the United States to claim that federal financial challenges don't require spending cuts—they require increased revenues. They don't require belt tightening—they require infrastructure building and replacing economies built on poisoning and imprisoning our people with economic development that improves people's lives. But even more inspiring is the fever created by his campaign among younger voters, who appear to be embracing the idea that serious fundamental change is possible with collective action—a paradigm anathema to "kill it to save it."

Of course, we saw this fervor with Obama's election, but he quickly brought in a cohort of traditional moderate-to-conservative Democrats beholden to the moderate wing of capital and willing to triangulate and compromise at every turn. He brought in Wall Street leaders to run the economy and, eventually, agreed that austerity would rule the day. In other areas, education in particular, Obama has relied on "kill it to save" measures to create programs like Race to the Top and the Common Core, as well as massive support for private charter schools and high-stakes testing. The excitement of the campaign got lost in the wealth and power of those who own the means of political production. And the grassroots fervor withered at the door of the Oval Office.

But perhaps the most exciting mass social movement that brings hope to the possibility of terminating our "kill it to save it" hegemony in the U.S. is Black Lives Matter (BLM). With all of its idiosyncrasies and internal tensions, the movement has risen from the cracks of what Michelle Alexander calls the "New Jim Crow" to claim that the torture end of Klein's shock doctrine cannot be tolerated by human society. BLM has linked successful movements to ban solitary confinement in jails and zero-tolerance disciplinary procedures in schools with calls for demilitarizing police forces and restoring basic democratic principles to communities like Flint, Michigan. In so doing, BLM has inspired "All Lives Matter."

While All Lives Matter [ALM] remains mostly a narrative strategy for racists, it's also become a defensive posture for an even larger group of whites and even moderate non-whites who want to be color blind (an aging canard for maintaining white supremacy).[33] ALM as a proposition or hashtag is *prima facie* absurd—white people are not facing disproportionate imprisonment, prejudiced policing, or unarmed shootings by police officers. But the underlying premise that all lives matter in the face of increasingly democratic exploitation may eventually drive a wedge through "kill it to save it." In a "kill it to save it world" (validated by Trump's victory) anything that advocates people's lives over say profit and fascism, can be seen as having radical possibilities. ALM may in fact suggest that neoliberalism is criminal at its roots and there may be a coalition from which to build resistance to "kill it to save it." Or, perhaps Donald Trump will persuade the white supremacist wing of ALM that Mexicans, refugees, Muslim refugees, and anyone else he decides to "shoot on Fifth Avenue" are to blame for the degradation of American democracy and prosperity.

Trump's victory (although defeat in the popular vote) has suggested to many that we live at a time of great division in America. More than ever before in the nation's history, people are divided by ideology, political party, identity, culture and class. But I want to argue that such an analysis ignores the great similarity between Trump and Sanders' following and the possibility of an alternative vision that might unite people around issues of class and democracy instead of separating them by race and gender.

Trump successfully tapped into the violent racism that streams through our nation's historical soul, thus galvanizing his followers' passionate commitment to his bigotry. But this same population could be open to more effective arguments suggesting solutions will come not from fearing and hating and blaming others, but from rebuilding public institutions along the lines of equality and democracy, not privatization and profiteering. And embracing the language of BLM may be a crucial first step.

BLM remains very articulate in its messages about linking contemporary police killings, the prison industrial complex and racist laws (such as "Stand Your Ground," which empowered George Zimmerman's murder of Trayvon Martin in 2012 and racist governing like Michigan's Emergency Management laws). But leaders have continued to reach outwards, linking antiracist work at the grass roots with organizing around economic exploitation and a variety of "kill it to save it" policies. Civil Rights historian and long-time activist, Barbara Ransby, recently wrote about BLM:

> Black Lives Matter, which includes nearly a dozen black-led organizations, is as much an example of a U.S.-based class struggle as Occupy Wall Street was. To focus on the black poor is not to ignore others who also endure economic inequality. In speech after speech, the leading voices of this movement have insisted that if we liberate the black poor, or if the black poor liberate themselves, we will uplift everybody else who's been kept down. In other words, any serious analysis of racial capitalism must recognize that to seek liberation for black people is also to destabilize inequality in the United States at large, and to create new possibilities for all who live here.[34]

BLM is about the refusal to allow what has become status quo and accepted policy making to continue. The impact of these policies has been devastating to working-class, poor, and now middle-class people of all races and ethnicities—but disproportionately worse for disenfranchised people of color. Our current economic and political system—welded together by "kill it to save it" narratives into a seamless story rationalizing, justifying, and moralizing the status quo—can no longer adequately apologize for the death and destruction it has caused. The neoliberal, corporate, and political coalition can't get away with it anymore.

In the United States—from the streets of Flint, Chicago, and Orlando, outward across America—people are organizing and acting collectively to publicize the effects of "kill it to save it" in their neighborhoods, their communities, their regions. It may just be that hundreds and thousands and tens of thousands of people in the United States *are* awakening from their slumber. Strategic and political unity *can* be forged to rattle the ideological chains of "kill it to save it" and exorcise ourselves from false idols, our mythological heroes, and our acceptance of junk freedom. That it may not be too late to save our planet and ourselves has inspired me to write this book. We will undoubtedly have to take risks, push ourselves into uncomfortable places, and wrestle with uncomfortable ideas. We may have to risk everything, even our own lives, in this struggle. But as "kill it to save it" would sell our genes, poison our children, and destroy our planet, what choice is there?

Notes

Introduction

[1] K. Eagan, E.B. Stolzenberg, A.K. Bates, M. Aragon, M.C. Suchard, and C.R. Rios-Aguilar. 2015. The American Freshman: National Norms Fall. Retrieved at http://heri.ucla.edu/monographs/TheAmericanFreshman2015.pdf.

[2] Institute for Education Sciences. 2015. Indicators of School Crime and Safety. Retrieved at www.air.org/resource/college-hate-crimes-compared-category-bias.

[3] T. Frank. 2004. *What's the Matter with Kansas?* New York: Henry Holt & Company.

[4] M. Apple. 1990. "Ideology, Equality, and the New Right." *Phenomenology + Pedagogy*, 8: 298.

[5] R. Perlstein. 2009. *Before the Storm: Barry Goldwater and the Unmaking of the American Consensus*. New York: Nation Books; A. Dillard. 2002. *Guess Who's Coming to Dinner Now? Multicultural Conservatism in America*. New York: NYU Press; C. Robin. 2013. *The Reactionary Mind: Conservatism from Edmund Burke to Sarah Palin*. New York: Oxford University Press.

[6] James w. Russell. 2014. *Social Insecurity: 401(k)s and the Retirement Crisis*. Boston: Beacon Press.

[7] D. Baker and M. Weisbrot. 1999. *Social Security: The Phony Crisis*. University of Chicago Press.

[8] The actual quote from Calvin Coolidge was "The chief business of the American people is business." But the mainstream historical consciousness of most Americans have popularized it as "what's good for business, is good for America."

[9] Destroying Communism justified the mass murder of tens of thousands (millions if you include the Cambodian genocide). Similar sentiments would be echoed by Boston University President John Silber a few years later when he suggested that the United States could not consider humanitarian aid and challenging right wing death squads in central America until Communism and Socialism were defeated in the region.

[10] Antonio Gramsci. 1971. *Selections From The Prison Notebooks*. Edited by Quentin Hoare and Geoffrey Smith. New York: International Publishers Co.

[11] http://www.cc.com/video-clips/63ite2/the-colbert-report-the-word---truthiness

[12] Emile Durkheim. 1982. *The Rules of Sociological Method, 2nd Printing Edition.* New York: Free Press.

[13] Gramsci. 1971. *Selections From The Prison Notebooks.*

Part One: Overview

[1] Thomas Mann. 1927. *The Magic Mountain.* London: Secker & Warburg.

[2] B. Wearne. 2001. "Elias and Parsons: Two transformations of the problem of historical method." In A.J. Treviño (Ed.). *Talcott Parsons Today: His theory and legacy in contemporary sociology*. Boulder, CO: Rowman & Littlefield, pp 67-79.

[3] Todd Gitlin. 1993. *The Sixties: Years of Hope, Days of Rage.* New York: Bantam Books.

[4] N. Chomsky. 2014. *Hegemony or Survival: America's Quest for Global Dominance* (Reprint Edition). New York: Holt Paperbacks.

Chapter One

[1] C. Durang. 1976. *The Vietnamization of New Jersey: An American Tragedy*. New York: Dramatists Play Service, Inc.

[2] W. Kaminer. 2000. *Sleeping With Extra-Terrestrials: The Rise of Irrationalism and Perils of Piety*. New York: Vintage Press.

[3] J. Lembcke. 2003. *CNN's Tailwind Tale: Inside Vietnam's Last Great Myth.* Oxford: Rowman & Littlefield.

[4] P. Arnett. 1968. "Major Describes Move." *The New York Times*. 8 February.

[5] W.T. Allison. 2012. *My Lai: An American Atrocity in the Vietnam War*. Baltimore: Johns Hopkins University Press.

[6] R. Boyle. 1972. *The Flower of the Dragon: The Breakdown of the U.S. Army in Vietnam*. New York: Ramparts Press.

[7] S. Karnow. 1983. *Vietnam: A History.* New York: Viking Press; W. Shawcross. 1979. *Sideshow: Kissinger, Nixon, and the Destruction of Cambodia*. New York: Simon & Schuster; G. Herring. 2001. *America's Longest War: The United States and Vietnam, 1950—1975* (4th Edition). New York: McGraw Hill.

[8] W. Churchill and J.V. Wall. 1988. *Agents of Repression: The FBI's Secret War against the Black Panther Party and the American Indian Movement*. Boston: South End Press; R. Jacobs. 1997. *The Way the Wind Blew: A History of the Weather Underground*. London: Verso. In an August 25, 1967 letter to 23 field offices, FBI officials explained COINTELPRO's mission: "to expose, disrupt, misdirect, discredit, or otherwise neutralize the activities of black nationalist, hate-type organizations and their groupings, their leadership, spokesmen, membership and supporters, and to counter their propensity for violence and civil disorder." Targets included the Student Nonviolent Coordinating Committee, Southern Christian Leadership Conference, Congress of Racial Equality, the Nation of Islam, and the Black Panther Party. COINTELPRO expanded to 41 field offices in 1968. For more, see files at ww2.arhive.org,

especially https://archive.org/details/FBI-COINTELPRO-BLACK and https://archive.org/details/FBI-COINTELPRO-NewLeft.

[9] Quote from Ted Gold in T. Gitlin. 1987. *The Sixties: Years of Hope, Days of Rage*. New York: Bantam Books.

[10] Kenneth Keniston and Michael Lerner. 1971. "Campus Characteristics and Campus Unrest," *The Annals of the American Academy of Political and Social Science*. Vol. 395, Students Protest (May) pp. 39-53; Keniston and Lerner. 1971. *New York Times Magazine*, November 18.

[11] J. Varon. 2004. *Bringing the War Home: The Weather Underground, the Red Army Faction, and Revolutionary Violence in the Sixties and Seventies*. Berkeley: University of California Press; K. Sale. 1973. *SDS*. New York: Random House; H. Jacobs. 1970. *Weatherman*. New York: Ramparts Press; D. Caute. 1988. *The Year of the Barricades: A Journey through 1968*. New York: Harper & Row; W. Ayres. 2008. *Fugitive Days: Memoirs of an Antiwar Activist*. Boston: Beacon Press; M. Small. 2002. *Antiwarriors: The Vietnam War and the Battle for America's Hearts and Minds*. New York: Rowman & Littlefield.

[12] Bobby Allyn. 2009. 1969, "A Year of Bombings." *New York Times*. August 27.

[13] F. Bardacke and J. Weinberg, as quoted in the film *Berkeley in the Sixties*, directed by M. Kirchelle. For more on revolutionary visions of the time, see S. Hall. 2005. *Peace and Freedom: The Civil Rights and Antiwar Movements in the 1960s*. Philadelphia: University of Pennsylvania.

[14] H. Zinn. 2005. *A People's History of the United States*. New York: Harper Perennial Modern Classics; B. Schulman. 2004. *The Seventies: The Great Shift in American Culture, Society, and Politics*. New York: The Free Press; R. Perlstein. 2008. *Nixonland: The Rise of a President and the Fracturing of America*. New York: Scribner; L. Kalmen. 2010. "Gerald Ford, the Nixon Pardon, and the Rise of the Right." *Cleveland State University Law Review*, 58:349-368.

[15] Zinn, p. 546.

[16] Zinn, p. 546.

[17] Zinn, p. 406.

[18] D. Horowitz. 2004. *Jimmy Carter and the Energy Crisis of the 1970s: The "Crisis of Confidence" Speech of July 15, 1979*. New York: Bedford/St Martin's Press.

[19] R.A. Strong. 1986. "Recapturing Leadership: The Carter Administration and the Crisis of Confidence." *Presidential Studies Quarterly*, 16, 4: 636-650.

[20] Strong, p. 25; Horowitz, p. 189; E. Hargrove. 1988. *Jimmy Carter as President: Leadership and the Politics of the Public Good*. Baton Rouge: Louisiana State University Press. Full transcript of the speech available at http://millercenter.org/president/speeches/speech-3402.

[21] Jimmy Carter. 1979. "Crisis of Confidence Speech". Retrieved at http://www.pbs.org/wgbh/americanexperience/features/primary-resources/carter-crisis/.

[22] Jimmy Carter. 1979. "Crisis of Confidence Speech."

[23] Jimmy Carter. 1979. "Crisis of Confidence Speech."

[24] Jimmy Carter. 1979. "Crisis of Confidence Speech."

[25] Jimmy Carter. 1979. "Crisis of Confidence Speech."

26 K. McQuaid. 1989. *The Anxious Years: America in the Vietnam—Watergate Era.* New York: Basic Books.

27 R. Reagan. 1981. "First inaugural Address." Retrieved at https://reaganlibrary.archives.gov/archives/speeches/1981/12081a.htm.

28 M. Rogin. 1988. *Ronald Reagan: The Movie and Other Episodes in Political Demonology*. Berkeley, C.A.: University of California Press; H. Johnson. 2003. *Sleepwalking Through History: America in the Reagan Years.* New York: W.W. Norton & Co.; G. Wills, 2000. *Reagan's America: Innocents at Home.* New York: Penguin Books.

29 R. Reagan. 1989. "Farewell Speech". Retrieved at http://www.pbs.org/wgbh/americanexperience/features/primary-resources/reagan-farewell/.

30 Paul Pierson. 1995. *Dismantling the Welfare State?: Reagan, Thatcher and the Politics of Retrenchment.* Cambridge: Cambridge University Press; Frances Fox Piven and Richard A. Cloward. 1982. *The New Class War: Reagan's Attack on the Welfare State and its Consequences*. New York: Pantheon.

31 L.M. Heilbronn. 1994. "Yellow Ribbons and Remembrance: Mythic Symbols of the Gulf War." *Sociological Inquiry*, 64, 4: 151—78; G. Mariscal. 1991. "In the Wake of the Gulf War: Untying the Yellow Ribbon." *Cultural Critique*, 19: 97—117.

32 J. Lembcke. 2000. *The Spitting Image: Myth, Memory, and the Legacy of Vietnam.* New York: New York University Press; T. Tuleja, 1994. "Closing the Circle: Yellow Ribbons and the Redemption of the Past." *Journal of American Culture*, 17, 1: 23-30.

33 C. Cahill. 2008. *Fighting the Vietnam Syndrome: The Construction of a Conservative Veterans Politics, 1966—1984.* Chicago: Northwestern University Press.

34 J. Kohler-Hausmann. 2007. "The Crime of Survival:" Fraud Prosecutions, Community Surveillance and the Original 'Welfare Queen.'" *Journal of Social History*, 41, 2: 329-354; T. Edsall and M. Edsall. 1997. *Chain Reaction: The Impact of Race, Rights, and Taxes on American Politics.* New York: W. W. Norton & Company.

35 P. Nadasen. 2004. *Welfare Warriors: The Welfare Rights Movement in the United States*. New York: Routledge; T. Funiciello. 1994. *Tyranny of Kindness: Dismantling the Welfare System to End Poverty in America.* New York: Atlantic Monthly Press; S. Schram. 2000. *After Welfare: The Culture of Post-Industrial Social Policy*. New York: New York University Press.

36 K. Moody. 1988. *An Injury to All: The Decline of American Unionism*. London: Verso Press; S. Aronowitz and W. DiFazio. 1994. *The Jobless Future: Sci-Tech and the Dogma of Work*. Minneapolis: University of Minnesota Press; B. Bluestone and B. Harrison 1988. *The Great U-Turn: Corporate Restructuring and the Polarizing of America*. New York: Basic Books; D. Clawson and M.A. Clawson, 1999. "What Has Happened to the US Labor Movement? Union Decline and Renewal." *Annual Review of Sociology*, 25: 95-119.

37 N. Zaretsky. 2007. *No Direction Home: The American Family and the Fear of National Decline, 1968—1980.* Chapel Hill: University of North Carolina Press.

[38] M. Rogin. 1987. *Ronald Reagan, The Movie*. Berkeley: University of California Press, pp. 30—44.
[39] R. Reagan. 1981. First Inaugural Address. January 20.
[40] A. de Tocqueville. 1900. *Democracy in America*, Vol. II. New York: The Colonial Press.
[41] A. de Tocqueville. 1900. *Democracy in America*.
[42] A. de Tocqueville. 1900. *Democracy in America*.
[43] R. Barthes. 1972. *Mythologies*. New York: Farrar, Straus and Giroux.
[44] J. Lembcke. 2000. *The Spitting Image: Myth, Memory, and the Legacy of Vietnam*. New York: NYU Press.
[45] H. Johnson. *Sleepwalking Through History*, p. 11.
[46] R. Bellah, et. al. 1985. *Habits of the Heart: Individualism and Commitment in American Life*. Berkeley: University of California Press.
[47] J. Hector St. John de Crèvecœur. 2012. *Letters from an American Farmer and Other Essays*. Ed. D. Moore. Cambridge: Belknap Press; A. Taylor. 2013. "The American Beginning: The dark side of Crèvecœur's "Letters from an American Farmer." *The New Republic*. July 18. Retrieved at https://newrepublic.com/article/113571/crevecoeurs-letters-american-farmer-dark-side.
[48] Hector St. John de Crèvecœur. 2012. *Letters from an American Farmer*. Of course, current data suggests that unlike European countries such as England, Germany, and France—where the ratio between CEO and average worker pay ranges from 11:1 to 22:1—the ratio in the U.S. is 475:1. Haughty indeed.
[49] Although one of Crèvecœur's letters concerning a fictional visit to Charlestown did in fact recognize some of these conditions; Alan Taylor depicts the author's observation that, "Lacking sensibility and true sociability, [Southern plantation masters] could "neither see, hear, nor feel for the woes of their poor slaves, from whose painful labours all their wealth proceeds." On their rice and indigo plantations, masters worked slaves to death and denied them the uplift of education and the consolations of Christianity.
[50] T. Skocpol. 2000. *The Missing Middle: Working Families and the Future of American Social Policy*. New York: Norton Co.; E. Humes. 2014. *Over Here: How the G.I. Bill Transformed the American Dream*. New York City: Diversion Books.

Chapter Two

[1] G. Troy. 2005. *Morning in America: How Ronald Reagan Invented the 1980s*. Princeton: Princeton University Press.
[2] R. Bellah, et al. 1996. *Habits of the Heart: Individualism and Commitment in American Life* (2nd edition). Berkeley: University of California Press; updated sub edition.
[3] R. Reich. 2016. *Saving Capitalism: For the Many, Not the Few*. New York: Vintage Books.
[4] Economic Policy Institute. 2012. *The State of Working Class America: 12th Edition*. Retrieved at http://stateofworkingamerica.org/.

[5] G. Andres. 1995. "Pork Barrel Spending—On the Wane?" *Political Science & Politics*, 28, 2: 207-11.

[6] D. Baker. 2007. *The United States Since 1980*. Cambridge: Cambridge University Press.

[7] D. Baker. 2007. *The United States Since 1980*; Larry Bartels. 2012. *Unequal Democracy: The Political Economy of the New Gilded Age*. Princeton: Princeton University Press.

[8] P. Rucker. 2011. "Mitt Romney says 'corporations are people'." *Washington Post*. 11 August.

[9] R. Reich. 2008. *Supercapitalism: The transformation of business, democracy, and everyday life*. New York: Vintage Books USA; J. Hickel and A. Khan. 2012. "The culture of capitalism and the crisis of critique." *Anthropological Quarterly*, 85, 1: 203-27.

[10] The rates for the highest income earners were slightly increased during Clinton's administration, and those did ultimately contribute to lower levels of inequality and higher levels of surplus for a brief amount of time. See R. Reich. 2012. *Beyond Outrage: What Has Gone Wrong with Our Economy and Our Democracy, and How to Fix It*. New York: Vintage Books.

[11] The International Consortium for Investigative Journalists. 2016. *The Panama Papers: Politicians, Criminals and the Rogue Industry That Hides Their Cash*. Retrieved at https://panamapapers.icij.org/.

[12] Jason Kelly. 2012. *The New Tycoons: Inside the Trillion Dollar Private Equity Industry That Owns Everything*. New York: Bloomberg Press; Matt Taibbi. "Greed and debt: The true story of Mitt Romney and Bain Capital." *Rolling Stone*; Tom Hamburger. 2012. "Romney's Bain Capital invested in companies that moved jobs overseas." *The Washington Post*. Retrieved at https://www.washingtonpost.com/business/economy/romneys-bain-capital-invested-in-companies-that-moved-jobs-overseas/2012/06/21/gJQAsD9ptV_story.html?utm_term=.ba97b8b2f463; David G. Levasseur and Lisa M. Gring-Pemble. 2015. "Not All Capitalist Stories Are Created Equal: Mitt Romney's Bain Capital Narrative and the Deep Divide in American Economic Rhetoric." *Rhetoric & Public Affairs*, 18,1: 1-37; M. Maremont. 2012. "Romney at Bain: Big gains, some busts." *Wall Street Journal*. Retrieved from http://online.wsj.com/article/SB10001424052970204331304577140850713493694.html; Joshua Holland. 2012. "How the Corporate Media Obscure the Truth About Mitt Romney's 'Vulture Capitalism' at Bain" AlterNet. Retrieved at http://www.alternet.org/story/155689/how_the_corporate_media_obscure_the_truth_about_mitt_romney's_'vulture_capitalism'_at_bain.

[13] R. Paul. 2011. *Liberty Defined*. New York: Grand Central Publishing; R. Paul, 2011. "Plan to Restore America." Retrieved at http://c3244172.r72.cf0.rackcdn.com/wp-content/uploads/2011/10/RestoreAmericaPlan.pdf.

[14] G. Lardner, Jr. 1997. *Washington Post*, September 7, p A01.

[15] A. Santo. 2015. "When Freedom Isn't Free the Bail Industry Wants to be Your Jailer." The Marshall project. Retrieved at www.themarshallproject.org/2015/02/23/buying-time#.fDVXUCrd2.

[16] E. Reeve. 2012. "Why the NRA Is Still Winning the War on Guns." *The Atlantic*. December 12. Retrieved at www.theatlantic.com/national/archive/2012/12/nra-guns-2012/320461/.

[17] P. Krugman. 2009. "Socialsecuritymedicareandmedicaid." *New York Times*. October 11. Retrieved at http://krugman.blogs.nytimes.com/2007/10/11/socialsecuritymedicareandmedicaid/?_r=0.

[18] Quoted in L. Beinhart. 2005. *Fog Facts: Searching for Truth in the Land of Spin*. New York: Nation Books, p 122.

[19] Kenneth Saltman. 2005. *The Edison Schools: Corporate Schooling and the Assault on Public Education*. New York: Routledge; V. Straus. 2015. "Ohio Supreme Court sides with for-profit company over charter schools." *Washington Post*. September 16.

[20] Federal Bureau of Investigation. 2012. "Threats Against Members of Congress, 2000-2010." *FBI Vault*. Washington, DC. Retrieved at https://vault.fbi.gov/threats-against-members-of-congress.

[21] I don't include San Bernardino here (14 dead, 17 injured) because for that incident, the issue of terrorism seemed more salient than that of mental illness (although both may have played a role). Ironically, though, being on terrorist lists also does not preclude one from purchasing a gun in the United States.

[22] The federal budget sequestration was the result of the 2011 budget agreement between the congressional Republicans and Democrats. It mandated severe cuts in spending in almost all federal areas, ranging from military to health care. S. Abramsky. 2013. "The Government Shutdown was a War against the Poor." *The Nation*. October 16. Retrieved at https://www.thenation.com/article/government-shutdown-was-war-against-poor.

[23] S. Abramsky. 2013. "The Government Shutdown was a War against the Poor."

[24] Personal Interview with Horace Small, 13 December, 2013.

[25] G. Simmel, "The Metropolis and Mental Life," adapted by D. Weinstein from Kurt Wolff (Trans.) *The Sociology of Georg Simmel*. New York: Free Press, 1950, pp 409-24.

[26] G. Scott Heron. 2000. "We beg Your Pardon America" in *Now and Then: The Poems of Gil Scott Heron*. Edinburgh: Payback Press, p 86.

[27] G. Rizer. 1993. *The McDonaldization of Society*. Thousand Oaks, CA: Sage Publications.

[28] Spoken by Gordon Gecko in the film, *Wall Street* (1987), directed by Oliver Stone, Twentieth Century Fox Film Corporation and American Entertainment Partners L.P.

Part Two: Overview

[1] Quoted in L.J. Kamin, R.C. Lewontin, and S. Rose. 1984. *Not in our Genes: Biology, Ideology, and Human Nature*. New York: Pantheon Press.

[2] Quoted in W. Fleming and C. Juneau. 2006. "Myths and Stereotypes About Native Americans." *Phi Delta Kappan*, 88, 3(Nov): 213-17.

[3] Lehman Brothers Education Group. 1996. *Investment Opportunity in the Education Industry*. New York: Lehman Brothers, February 9.

[4] Kenneth J. Saltman. 2005. *The Edison Schools: Corporate Schooling and the Assault on Public Education*. Psychology Press; Stephen J. Ball and Deborah Youdell. 2008. *Hidden Privatisation in Public Education*. Brussels: Education International; Barbara Miner. 2012. "Business goes to school: The for-profit corporate drive to run public schools (Privatization: Rip - Offs and Resistance)." *Multinational Monitor,* p. 13; Alex Molnar, David Garcia, Carolyn Sullivan et al. 2005. "Profiles of For Profit Educational Management Organizations: 2004-2005." Education Policy Studies Laboratory at Arizona State University. Retrieved at www.edpolicylab.org; Kenneth J. Saltman. 2006. "The right-wing attack on critical and public education in the United States: from neoliberalism to neoconservativism." *Cultural Politics*, 2, 3: 339; Howard Nelson and Nancy Van Meter. 2003. "Student Achievement in Schools Managed by Mosaica Education, Inc". Washington: American Federation of Teachers; Monica Eva Pini. 2001. "Moving Public Schools toward For-Profit Management: Privatizing the Public Sphere." Paper presented at the Annual Meeting of the American Educational Research Association.

[5] E. Durkheim. 1956. *Education and Sociology*. New York: The Free Press; P. Bourdieu and J.-C. Passeron. 1990. *Reproduction in Education, Society and Culture*. Thousand Oaks, CA: Sage Publications; R. Collins. 1979. *The Credential Society: An Historical Sociology of Education and Stratification*. New York: John Wiley; E.C. Lagemann. "Contested Terrain: A History of Education Research in the United States, 1890—1990," *Educational Researcher*, 26, 9: 5—17.

[6] R. Hofstadter. 1955. *The Age of Reform*. New York: Vintage Press.

[7] R.H. Taylor. 1925. "Humanizing the Slave Code Of North Carolina." *The North Carolina Historical Review*, 2, 3: 323—31; H.A. Bullock. 1967. *A History of Negro Education in the South: 1619 to the Present*. Cambridge: Harvard University Press; A.L. Higginbotham. 1978. *In the Matter of Color: Race and the American Legal Process: The Colonial Period*. New York: Oxford University Press; H. Williams. 2009. *Self-Taught: African American Education in Slavery and Freedom*. Chapel Hill: University of North Carolina Press.

[8] A. Saxton. 1990. *The Rise and Fall of the White Republic: Class Politics and Mass Culture in Nineteenth Century America*. London: Verso Press; I. Haney-López. 2006. *White by Law: The Legal Construction of Race*. New York: NYU Press; T.J. Guess. 2006. "The Social Construction of Whiteness: Racism by Intent, Racism by Consequence." *Critical Sociology*, 32, 1: 649-673; E. Baptist, 2014. *The Half Has Never Been Told: Slavery and the Making of American Capitalism*. New York: Basic Books.

[9] D.W. Adams. 1995. *Education for Extinction: American Indians and the Boarding School Experience, 1875—1928*. Lawrence, K.S.: University Press of Kansas; W. Churchill. 2004. *Kill the Indian, Save the Man: The Genocidal Impact of American Indian Residential Schools*. San Francisco: City Lights Books.

[10] G. Sanchez. 1994. "Go After the Women: Americanization and the Mexican Immigrant Woman, 1915—1929." In V. Ruiz and E.C. Dubois (Eds.). *Unequal Sisters: A Multi-Cultural Reader in U.S. Women's History*. New York: Routledge; S.L. Camp. 2012. "Reform to Repatriation: Gendering an Americanization Movement in Early Twentieth-Century California." In S.M. Spencer-Wood (Ed.). *Historical and Archaeological Perspectives on Gender Transformations Contributions to Global Historical Archaeology*. New York: Springer.

[11] Y. Pai and S. Adler. 1997. *Cultural Foundations of Educations*. Saddle River, N.J.: Prentice Hall.

[12] R. Daniels. 2002. *Coming to America: A History of Immigration and Ethnicity in American Life*. New York: Harper Perennial; C. Ziegler-McPherson. 2010. *Americanization in the States: Immigrant Social Welfare Policy, Citizenship, and National Identity in the United States, 1908—1929*. Gainesville: University of Florida Press.

[13] P. Faler. 1974. "Cultural Aspects of the Industrial Revolution: Lynn, Massachusetts, Shoemakers and Industrial Morality, 1826—1860." *Labor History*, 15, 3: 367-394; H. Gutman. 1977. *Work, Culture and Society in Industrial America*. New York: Vintage Books.

[14] M. Katz. 1989. *Reconstructing American Education*. Cambridge: Harvard University Press. While sociologists of education would come to call this the "hidden curriculum," it was hardly obfuscated by early educational reformers, who made it front and center in their pitches to political leaders and citizens alike.

[15] M. Katz. *1968. The Irony of Early School Reform*. Cambridge: Harvard University Press; M. Katz. 1995. *Improving Poor People: The Welfare State, The Underclass, and Urban Schools as History*. Princeton: Princeton University Press.

[16] S. Bowles and H. Gintis. 1976. *Schooling in Capitalist America: Educational Reform and the Contradictions of Economic Life*. New York: Basic Books.

[17] H. Braverman. 1974. *Labor and Monopoly Capital: The Degradation of Work in the Twentieth Century*. New York: Monthly Review Press; G. Gerstle. 2002. *Working-Class Americanism: The Politics of Labor in a Textile City, 1914—1960*. Princeton: Princeton University Press.

[18] Bowles and Gintis, p. 170; D. Boyles. 2000. *American Education and Corporations: The Free Market Goes to School*. New York: Routledge.

[19] J.M. Rice. 1913. *Scientific Management in Education*. New York: Hynes, Noble & Eldridge. W. Au. 2011. "Teaching under the New Taylorism: High-Stakes Testing and the Standardization of the 21st Century Curriculum." *Journal of Curriculum Studies*, 43, 1: 25—45.

[20] R. Lynd and H. Lynd. 1928. *Middletown: A Study in Modern American Culture*. New York: Harcourt, Brace and World.

[21] N. Chomsky, L. Nader, I. Wallerstein; R. Lewontin and R. Ohmann. 1998. *The Cold War and the University: Toward an Intellectual History of the Postwar Years*. New York: New Press.

[22] C. Kerr. 2001. *The Uses of the University* (5th Edition). Cambridge: Harvard University Press; R. Geiger. 2004. *Research and Relevant Knowledge: American Research Universities Since World War II.* New Brunswick, N.L.: Transaction Publishers.

[23] E. Schrecker. 1986. *No Ivory Tower: McCarthyism and the Universities.* Oxford: Oxford University Press; B. Blauner, 2009. *Resisting McCarthyism: To Sign or Not to Sign California's Loyalty Oath.* Stanford: Stanford University Press.

[24] D. Bell. 1960. *The End of ideology: On the Exhaustion of Political Ideas in the Fifties.* Cambridge: Harvard University Press.

[25] C.W. Mills. 1951. *White Collar Man: The American Middle Classes.* Oxford: Oxford University Press.

[26] D. Riesman. 1950. *The Lonely Crowd: A Study of the Changing American Character.* New Haven: Yale University Press; W.H. Whyte. 1956. *The Organization Man.* New York: Simon & Shuster; V. Packard. 1957. *The Hidden Persuaders.* New York: Random House.

[27] J.K. Galbraith, 1958. *The Affluent Society.* New York: Houghton Mifflin, Harcourt.

[28] M. Savio. 1964. "On the Operation of the Machine." *YouTube.* Retrieved at www.youtube.com/watch?v=PhFvZRT7Ds0; R. Allison. 2014. *Bodies on the Line: Performance and the Sixties Poetry Reading.* Iowa City: University of Iowa Press.

[29] T. Gitlin. 1987. *The Sixties: Years of Hope; Days of Rage.* New York: Bantam Books; M. Adler. 1997. *Heretic's Heart: A Journey Through Spirit and Revolution.* Boston, M.A.: Beacon Press.

[30] S. Adickes. 2005. *A Legacy of a Freedom School.* New York: Palgrave Macmillan; C. Payne and C.S. Strickland. 2009. *Teach Freedom: Education for Liberation in the African American Tradition,* New York: Teachers College; A. Nelson. 2011. *Body and Soul: The Black Panther Party and the Fight Against Medical Discrimination.* Minneapolis: University of Minnesota Press.

[31] The passage of the Adult Education Act in 1966 (as part of the War on Poverty) also led to a boom in adult education centers around the country, suggesting that progressive education policies might be cradle-to-grave.

[32] E. Rose. 2010. *The Promise of Pre-School: From Head Start to Universal Pre-Kindergarten.* Oxford: Oxford University Press; J. Ellsworth and L. Ames. 1998. *Critical Perspectives on Project Head Start: Re-visioning the Hope and Challenge.* Albany, N.Y.: SUNY Press; P. Greenberg. 1990. *The Devil Has Slippery Shoes: A Biased Biography of the Child Development Group of Mississippi (CDGM), A Story of Maximum Feasible Poor Parent Participation.* Los Angeles, C.A.: Youth Policy Institute.

Chapter Three

[1] D. Ravitch. 2014. *Reign of Error: The Hoax of the Privatization Movement and the Danger to America's Public Schools.* New York: Vintage Books.

[2] M. Fabricant and M. Fine. 2012. *Charter Schools and the Corporate Makeover of Public Education.* New York: Teachers College Press; K. Saltman. 2009.

"Putting the Public Back in Public Schooling: Public Schools Beyond the Corporate Model." *DePaul Journal for Social Justice*, 3:9; H. Nelson and N. Van Meter. 2003. *Student Achievement in Schools Managed by Mosaica Education, Inc.* Washington, D.C.: American Federation of Teachers.

3 M. Raymond. 2013. *National Charter School Study.* Stanford, C.A.: Center for Research on Education Outcomes, Stanford University. Retrieved at http://credo.stanford.edu/documents/NCSS%202013%20Final%20 Draftpdf; Ron Zimmer, Brian Gill, Kevin Booker, Stephane Lavertu, Tim R. Sass, John Witte. 2009. "Are Charter Schools Making a Difference? A Study of Student Outcomes in Eight States." Retrieved at http://www.rand.org/pubs/research_briefs/RB9433.html; Wayne Au. 2015. *Mapping Corporate Education Reform: Power and Policy Networks in the Neoliberal State.* New York: Routledge. A historical irony similar to Head Start also tugs at the charter school movement. Many of the original backers of "public" charter schools were progressive educators and union officials; they saw the possibility of innovative schools led by creative teachers, whose autonomy and control would allow them to focus on underperforming students with various learning challenges. Like Head Start, the original intentions were hijacked.

4 R. Sobel. 1988. *Essays, Papers & Addresses Coolidge and American Business.* Retrieved at https://coolidgefoundation.org/resources/essays-papers-addresses-35/.

5 B. Barber. 2012. "Can We Teach Civic Education and Service-Learning in a World of Privatization, Inequality, and Interdependence?" *Journal of College and Character*, 13, 1; N.Z. Keith. 2005. "Community Service Learning in the Face of Globalization: Rethinking Theory and Practice." *Michigan Journal of Community Service Learning*, 11, 2.

6 S. Coutts. 2011. "Charter Schools Outsource Education to Management Firms With Mixed Results." *Pro Publica.* Retrieved at www.propublica.org/article/charter-schools-outsource-education-to-management-firms-with-mixed-results; C. Howley and C. Haeley. 2015. "Farming the Poor: Cultivating Profit at the Schoolhouse Door." In *Neoliberalizing Educational Reform: America's Quest for Profitable Market-Colonies and the Undoing of Public Good.* Edited by Keith M. Sturges. Boston: Sense Publishers, pp.23-52; G. Miron, J.L. Urschel, W.J. Mathis and E. Tornquist. 2010. *Schools without Diversity: Education Management Organizations, Charter Schools and the Demographic Stratification of the American School System.* Boulder: University of Colorado. Retrieved at http://files.eric.ed.gov/fulltext/ED509329.pdf; A. Molnar. 2001. "Benefits and Costs of For-Profit Public Education." *Education Policy Analysis Archives*, 9, p.15.

7 J. Mason and M. Bottari. 2014. "White Hat's Magic Trick: Transforming Public Schools into Private Assets." Retrieved at www.prwatch.org/news/2014/10/12624/white-hat%E2%80%99s-magic-trick-transforming-public-schools-private-assets#sthash.KshadMv3.dpuf.

8 See also D. Ravitch. 2013. *Reign of Error: The Hoax of the Privatization Movement and the Danger to America's Public Schools.* New York: Vintage

Press; J. Underwood, and J.F. Mead. 2012. "A smart ALEC threatens public education." *Phi Delta Kappan*, 93, 6, 51—55. More on ALEC in chapter five and nine.

[9] Fabricant and Fine. 2012. p. 43; E.P. Bettinger. 2005. "The effect of charter schools on charter students and public schools." *Economics of Education Review*, 24, 2: 133-147. Emphasis in original.

[10] J. Underwood and J.F. Mead. 2012. "A smart ALEC threatens public education."

[11] J. Anyon. 2014. *Radical possibilities: Public policy, urban education, and a new social movement*. New York: Routledge; P. Pierson and T. Skocpol. 2007. *The Transformation of American Politics: Activist Government and the Rise of Conservatism*. Princeton: Princeton University Press; C. Collins. 2012. *99 to 1: How Wealth Inequality is Wrecking the World and What We Can Do About It*. Williston, VT: Berrett-Koehler Publishers.

[12] Lehman Brothers Education Group. 1996. *Investment Opportunity in the Education Industry*, p. 18.

[13] J. Fouts, D. Baker, C. Brown, and S. Riley. 2006. *Leading the Conversion Process: Lessons Learned and Recommendations for Converting to Small Learning Communities*. Retrieved at https://docs.gatesfoundation.org/Documents/leadingtheconversionprocess.pdf.

[14] J. Barkan. 2011. "Got Dough? How Billionaires Rule Our Schools." *Dissent*, Winter. Retrieved at https://www.dissentmagazine.org/article/got-dough-how-billionaires-rule-our-schools. See also P. Kovacs. 2011. *The Gates Foundation and the Future of US "Public" Schools*. New York: Routledge; H. Giroux. 2011. *Education and the Crisis of Public Values: Challenging the Assault on Teachers, Students, and Public Education*. New York: Peter Lang Publishing.

[15] J. Barkan. 2011. "Got Dough?"; M. Pini. 2001. "Moving Public Schools Toward For-Profit Management: Privatizing the Public Sphere." Presentation at AERA Annual Meeting, Seattle, Washington; K. Saltman. 2009. "The Rise of Venture Philanthropy and the Ongoing Neoliberal Assault on Public Education: The Eli and Edythe Broad Foundation." *Workplace: A Journal for Academic Labor*, 16.

[16] C. Darwin. 2012. *The Voyage of the Beagle*. New York: Modern Library Press.

[17] Lehman Brothers Education Group. 1996. *Investment Opportunity in the Education Industry*.

[18] J.V. Heilig. 2011. "As Good as Advertised? Tracking Urban Student Progress through High School in an Environment of Accountability." *American Secondary Education*, 39, 3:17.

[19] S. Jay Gould. 1981. *The Mismeasure of Man*. New York: W.W. Norton Company.

[20] S.J. Gould. 1996. *The Mismeasure of Man: Revised and Expanded*. New York: W.W. Norton Company; N. Lehmann. 2000. *The Big Test*. New York: Farrar, Straus and Giroux; D.L. Arthur. 1983. "Educational Testing and Measurement: A Brief History." CSE Report 216. Center for the Study of Evaluation, University of California, Los Angeles.

[21] N. Segool, JS Carlson, AN Goforth. 2013. "Heightened Test Anxiety among Young Children: Elementary School Students' Anxious Responses to High-Stakes Testing." *Psychology in the Schools*, 50, 5:489-499; M.S. Mosesand M.J. Nanna. 2007. "The Testing Culture and the Persistence of High Stakes Testing Reforms." *Education and Culture*, 23, 1: 55-72.

[22] S.L. Nichols, G.V. Glass, D.C. Berliner. 2005. "High-Stakes Testing and Student Achievement: Problems for the No Child Left Behind Act."Tempe, A.Z.: Education Policy Research Unit, Arizona State University. Retrieved at http://files.eric.ed.gov/fulltext/ED531537.pdf; Keith Gayler and Nancy Kobel. 2004. "The Hidden Costs of High School Exit Exams." In *Pay Now or Pay Later: The Hidden Costs of High School Exit Exams*. Washington, DC: Center on Education Policy; Cathy O'Neil. 2016. *Weapons of Math Destruction: How Big Data Increases Inequality and Threatens Democracy*. New York: Crown Publishers.

[23] W. Au. 2007. "High-Stakes Testing and Curricular Control: A Qualitative Metasynthesis." *Educational Researcher*, 36, 5: 258—67; D.C. Berliner and L. Nichols. 2005. "Test Results Untrustworthy." Tempe, A.Z.: Education Policy Research Unit, Arizona State University.

[24] M. DeCesare. 2015. "Shut Up in Measureless Content: Confronting the Measurement Problem in Sociology." In L. Zake and M. DeCesare. *New Directions in Sociology: Essays in Theory and Methodology*. Jefferson, NC: McFarland & Co.

[25] T. Farley. 2009. *Making the Grades: My Misadventures in the Standardized Testing Industry*. San Francisco: Barrett-Koehler Publishers.

[26] D. DiMaggio. 2012. "The Loneliness of the Long-Distance Test Scorer." In W. Au and M. Tempel. *Pencils Down: Rethinking High Stakes Testing and Accountability in Schools*. Milwaukee, W.I.: Rethinking Schools.

[27] DiMaggio. 2012, p. 198; T. Farley, 2012. "Lies, Damn Lies, and Statistics, or What's Really up with Automated Essay Scoring." *Huffington Post*. June 8. Retrieved at http://www.huffingtonpost.com/todd-farley/lies-damn-lies-and-statis_b_1574711.html.

[28] W. Bennett. 1995. *The De-Valuing of America: The Fight for Our Culture and Our Children*. New York: Simon & Schuster, p. 79.

[29] R. Hofstadter. 1963. *Anti-intellectualism in American Life*. New York: Vintage Press, pp. 301—6. For more on Joe Clark, see D. Karp. 1989. "Education: The Movie." *Mother Jones*, January: 36-45; I.A. Hyman. 1989. "The Make-Believe World of *Lean on Me* (Movie about High School Principal Joe Clark)." *Education Digest*, 55, 3: 20

[30] R. Hofstadter. 1944. *Social Darwinism In American Thought 1860–1915*. Philadelphia: University of Pennsylvania Press.

[31] Galaviz, Brian, Jesus Palafox, Erica R. Meiners, and Therese Quinn. 2011. "The militarization and the privatization of public schools." *Berkeley Review of Education*, 2, 1: 12-29.

[32] B. Douglas, C. Lewis, A. Douglas, M.E Scott, & D. Garrison-Wade. 2008. "The Impact of White Teachers on the Academic Achievement of Black Students: An Exploratory Qualitative Analysis." *Educational Foundations*,

Winter—Spring: 47-62; C.W. Cooper. 2003. "The Detrimental Impact of Teacher Bias: Lessons Learned from the Standpoint of African American Mothers." *Teacher Education Quarterly*, 30, 2: 101-116; P.B. Baker. 2005. "The Impact of Cultural Biases on African American Students' Education: A Review of Research Literature Regarding Race Based Schooling." *Education and Urban Society*, 37, 3:

[33] E. Rios and J. Lurie. 2016. "Black Kids Are 4 Times More Likely to Be Suspended Than White Kids and other infuriating statistics about the racial gap in public schools." *Mother Jones*. June 8. Retrieved at www.motherjones.com/politics/2016/06/department-education-rights-data-inequality-suspension-preschool.

[34] J. Wald and D. Losen. 2003. "Defining and Redirecting A School-to-Prison Pipeline." *New Directions for Youth Development*, 2003, 99; C. McClellan. 2011. "Teacher/Police: How Inner-City Students Perceive the Connection Between the Education System and the Criminal Justice System." *Yale Journal of Sociology*, 8: 53-84.

[35] D. Figlio. 2006. "Testing Crime and Punishment." *Journal of Public Economics*, 90, 4/5: 837-851; J. Thomas. 2013. "Mass Incarceration of Minority Males: A Critical Look at its Historical Roots and How Educational Policies Encourage its Existence." *Race, Gender & Class*, 20, 1/2:177.

[36] W. Ayers. 2009. "A Teacher Ain't Nothin' But a Hero." In P. Joseph and G. Burnaford (Eds.). *Images of School Teachers in America*. Mahwah, N.J.: Lawrence Erlbaum Publishers.

[37] M. Visser. 2016. "Donald Trump relies on a simple phrase: 'Believe me'." *Boston Globe*. May 24; L. Mascoro. 2016. "'Believe me': People say Trump's language is affecting political discourse 'bigly'," *Los Angeles Times*. September 16.

Chapter Four

[1] J. Trumpbour. 1989. *How Harvard Rules: Reason in the Service of Empire*. Boston: South End Press.

[2] R. Geiger. 2004. *To Advance Knowledge: The Growth of American Research Universities, 1900—1940*. New Brunswick: Transaction Publishers; D. Noble. 1979. *America by Design: Science, Technology, and the Rise of Corporate Capitalism*. Oxford: Oxford University Press; Atomic Energy Commission. 2014. *Atoms for Peace and War 1953—1961: Eisenhower and the Atomic Energy Commission*. Washington, D.C.: Progressive Management Publishers.

[3] S. Aronowitz. 2001. *The Knowledge Factory: Dismantling the Corporate University and Creating True Higher Learning*. Boston: Beacon Press; T. Veblen. 1918. *The Higher Learning In America: A Memorandum On the Conduct of Universities By Business Men*. Retrieved at www.elegant-technology.com/resource/HI_LEARN.PDF; R. Lynd. 1939. *Knowledge for What?: The Place of Social Science in American Culture*. Middletown, CT: Wesleyan University Press.

[4] C. Kerr. 1963. *The Uses of the University*. Cambridge: Harvard University Press; N. Chomsky, L. Nader, I. Wallerstein; R. Lewontin and R. Ohmann.1998. *The Cold War and the University:Toward an Intellectual History of the Postwar Years*. New York: New Press; S. Leslie. 1993. *The Cold War and American Science: The Military-Industrial Complex at MIT and Stanford*. New York: Columbia University Press.

[5] C. Newfield. 2008. *Unmaking the Public University: The Forty-Year Assault on the Middle Class.* Cambridge, M.A.: Harvard University Press; J. Washburn. 2005. *University, Inc.: The Corporate Corruption of American Higher Education.* New York: Basic Books; C. Dolgon, 1999. "Soulless Cities: Ann Arbor, the Cutting Edge of Discipline: Postfordism, Postmodernism, and the New Bourgeoisie." *Antipode*, 31, 2: 129-162.

[6] D.L. Scott. 2012. "How the American University was Killed, in Five Easy Steps." *The Homeless Adjunct.* August 12. Retrieved at https://junctrebellion.wordpress.com/2012/08/12/how-the-american-university-was-killed-in-five-easy-steps/.

[7] B. Readings. 1996. *The University in Ruins*. Cambridge: Harvard University Press, pp. 13—31.

[8] B. Ginsburg. 2011. *The Fall of Faculty: The Rise of the All-Administrative University and Why it Matters*. Oxford: Oxford University Press.

[9] N. Chomsky. 2014. "How America's Great University System Is Being Destroyed." *Counter Punch*. February. Retrieved at http://www.alternet.org/corporate-accountability-and-workplace/chomsky-how-americas-great-university-system-getting.

[10] D. Noble. 1998. "Digital Diploma Mills: The Automation of Higher Education." *First Monday,* 3, 1. Retrieved at http://journals.uic.edu/ojs/index.php/fm/article/view/569/490. Republished in 2003. *Digital Diploma Mills: The Automation of Higher Education.* New York: Monthly Review Press.

[11] Jonathan Knight. 2014. "The AAUP's Censure List." Retrieved at https://www.aaup.org/aaups-censure-list.

[12] C. Koeber. 2012. "Self-Service in the Labor Process: Control and Consent in the Performance of "Consumptive Labor."" *Humanity & Society*, 36, 1: 6—29; R. Naidoo and I. Jameison. 2005. "Empowering Participants or Corroding Learning? Towards a Research Agenda on the Impact of Student Consumerism in Higher Education." *Journal of Education Policy*, 20, 3:267-281; M. Delucchi and W.L. Smith. 1997. "Satisfied Customers versus Pedagogic Responsibility: Further Thoughts on Student Consumerism". *Teaching Sociology*, 25, 4: 336.

[13] John H. Pryor, Linda DeAngelo, Laura Palucki Blake, Sylvia Hurtado, Serge Tran. 2012. *The American Freshman: National Norms for Fall 2011.* Los Angeles, C.A.: Higher Education Research Institute.

[14] A. Ross. 2014. *Creditocracy: And the Case for Debt Refusal*. New York: OR Books.

[15] D. Leigh Scott. 2012. "How the American University was Killed, in 5 Easy Steps." Retrieved at www.opednews.com/articles/How-The-American-Universit-by-Debra-Leigh-Scott-120819-373.html.

[16] D. Leigh Scott. 2012. "How the American University was Killed, in 5 Easy Steps."
[17] C. Dolgon. 1998. "Rising From the Ashes: The Michigan—Memorial Phoenix Project and the Corporatization of University Research." *Educational Studies*, 23, 1: 7.
[18] C. Dolgon. 1998. "Rising From the Ashes: The Michigan—Memorial Phoenix Project and the Corporatization of University Research."
[19] C. Dolgon. 1998. "Rising From the Ashes: The Michigan—Memorial Phoenix Project and the Corporatization of University Research.".
[20] C. Dolgon. 1998. "Rising From the Ashes: The Michigan—Memorial Phoenix Project and the Corporatization of University Research."
[21] C. Dolgon. 1998. "Rising From the Ashes: The Michigan—Memorial Phoenix Project and the Corporatization of University Research."
[22] J.-J. Simard. 1990. "White Ghosts, Red Shadows: The Reduction of North-American Natives." In J. Clifton (Ed.). *The Invented Indian: Cultural Fictions and Government Policies*. New Brunswick, N.J.: Transaction Publishers.
[23] C. Dolgon. 1998. "Rising From the Ashes: The Michigan—Memorial Phoenix Project and the Corporatization of University Research."
[24] E. Tyler May. 2008. *Homeward Bound: American Families in the Cold War Era*. New York: Basic Books.
[25] C. Dolgon. 1998. "Rising From the Ashes: The Michigan—Memorial Phoenix Project and the Corporatization of University Research.".
[26] C. Dolgon. 1998. "Rising From the Ashes: The Michigan—Memorial Phoenix Project and the Corporatization of University Research."

Part Three: Overview

[1] A. Camus. 1991. *The Plague*. New York: Vintage Books, p 229.
[2] J.S. Feinstein. 1993. "The Relationship between Socioeconomic Status and Health: A Review of the Literature. *The Milbank Quarterly*, 71: 279-322; K.M. Fitzpatrick. 2013. *Poverty and Health: A Crisis among America's Most Vulnerable*. New York: Praeger.
[3] N. Finzsch. 2008. "Extirpate or Remove that Vermine": Genocide, Biological Warfare, and Settler Imperialism in the Eighteenth and Early Nineteenth Century." *Journal of Genocide Research*, 10, 2: 215—32; E.A. Fenn. 2002. *Pox Americana: The Great Smallpox Epidemic of 1775—82*. New York: Hill and Wang.
[4] A. Lichtenstein. 1996. *Twice the Work of Free Labor: The Political Economy of Convict Labor in the New South*. New York: Verso Press; M.C. Fierce. 1994. *Slavery Revisited: Blacks and the Southern Convict Lease System 1865—1993*. Brooklyn, N.Y.: Africana Studies Center.
[5] H.A. Washington. 2008. *Medical Apartheid: The Dark History of Medical Experimentation on Black Americans from Colonial Times to the Present*. New York: Knopf Doubleday Publishing; J.H. Jones. 1993. *Bad Blood: The Tuskegee Syphilis Experiment* (New and Expanded Edition). New York: Free Press; K. Reiter. 2009. "Experimentation on Prisoners: Persistent Dilemmas in Rights and Regulations." *California Law Review*, 97, 2:501-566.

[6] M. Hane. 2009. "Wartime Internment." *The Journal of American History*, 77, 2: 46-73; W. Ng. 2001. *Japanese American Internment During World War II: A History and Reference Guide*. Westport, C.T.: Greenwood Press.

[7] J. Vickery and L.M. Hunter. 2014. "Native Americans: Where in Environmental Justice Theory and Research?" Working Paper. Boulder, C.O.: Institute of Behavioral Science; R.D. Bullard. 2001. "Environmental Justice in the 21st Century: Race Still Matters." *Phylon*, 49:151-171; A. Gedicks. 1993. *The New Resource Wars: Native and Environmental Struggles Against Multinational Corporations*. Boston, M.A.: South End Press.

[8] M. Alexander. 2010. *The New Jim Crow: Mass Incarceration in the Age of Colorblindness*. New York: The New Press; C. Parenti. 2000. *Lockdown America: Police and Prisons in the Age of Crisis*. New York: Verso.

[9] G. Rizer. 2007. *The McDonaldization of Society* (2nd Edition). Thousand Oaks, C.A.: Sage Publications.

[10] M.E. Fissell. 2008. "Introduction: Women, Health, and Healing in Early Modern Europe." *Bulletin of the History of Medicine*, 82, 1: 1-17; M. Alic. 1986. *Hypatia's Heritage: A History of Women in Science from Antiquity through the Nineteenth Century*. Boston: Beacon Press; H.A. Cahill. 2008. "Male Appropriation and Medicalization of Childbirth: An Historical Analysis." *Journal of Advanced Nursing*, 33, 3: 334-342.

[11] M. Sandler. 2015. "Music Physicianers: Blues Lyric Form and the Patent Medicine Show." *Journal of American Studies*, 50, 01: 125-142; B. McNamara. 1971. "The Indian Medicine Show." *Educational Theatre Journal*, 23, 4: 431-454.

[12] P. Starr. 1982. *The Social Transformation of American Medicine*. New York: Basic Books; J. Leavitt and R. Numbers. 1997. *Sickness and Health in America: Readings in the History of Medicine and Public Health*. Madison: University of Wisconsin Press; M. Thomasson. 2008. "From Home to Hospital: The Evolution of Childbirth in the United States, 1928—1940." *Explorations in Economic History*, 45: 76-99.

[13] R. Wertz and D. Wertz. 1977. *Lying-In: A History of Childbirth in America*. New York: The Free Press; J. Demos. 1982. *Entertaining Satan: Witchcraft and the Culture of Early New England*. New York: Oxford University Press; R.J. Tannenbaum. 2000. *The Healer's Calling: Women and Medicine in Early New England*. Ithaca, N.Y.: Cornell University Press.

[14] P.F. Radosh. 1986. "Midwives in the United States: Past and Present." *Population Research and Policy Review*, 5, 2: 130.

[15] B. Ehrenreich and D. English. 2010. *Witches, Midwives & NursesLA History of Women Healers* (2nd Edition). New York: Feminist Press; P.F. Radosh. 1986. "Midwives in the United States: Past and Present," pp 129-146.

[16] F. Korbin. 1966. "The American Midwife Controversy: A Crisis of Professionalization." *Bulletin of the History of Medicine*, 40: 350-363; R. Apple. 1990. *Women Health and Medicine in America: A Historical Handbook*. New York: Garland Press; P. Brodsky. 2008. *The Control of Childbirth: Women Versus Medicine Through the Ages*. New York: McFarland & Company.

[17] J.B. DeLee. "The Prophylactic Forceps Operation." *American Journal of Obstetrics & Gynecology*, 1, 1: 34—44.

[18] P.L. Brodsky. 2008. "Where Have All the Midwives Gone?" *Journal of Prenatal Education*, 17, 4: 48-51; E.R. Van Teijlingen, G.W. Lowis, and P. McCaffery. 2011. *Midwifery and the Medicalization of Childbirth: Comparative Perspectives*. Happaugue, N.Y.: Nova Science Publishers; Adrian E. Feldhusen. 2000. "The history of midwifery and childbirth in America: A time line." *Midwifery Today*, 27.

[19] P.V. Fishback and S.E. Kantor. 2000. *A Prelude to the Welfare State: The Origins of Workers' Compensation*. Chicago: University of Chicago Press; J.E. Murray. 2007. *Origins of American Health Insurance: A History of Industrial Sickness Funds*. New Haven, CT: Yale University Press.

[20] F.D. Roosevelt. 1944. "State of the Union Address." Retrieved at www.presidency.ucsb.edu/ws/?pid=16518; J. Kooijman. 1999. "Soon or Later On: Franklin D. Roosevelt and National Health Insurance, 1933—1945." *Presidential Studies Quarterly*, 29, 2: 336-350.

[21] John Murray. 2007. *Origins of American Health Insurance: A History of Industrial Sickness Funds*. New Haven: Yale University Press.

[22] L. Shi and D.A. Singh. 2014. *Delivering Health Care In America: A Systems Approach*. Burlington, M.A.: Jones & Bartlett Learning; T. Skocpol. 1996. *Boomerang: Clinton's Health Security Effort and the Turn Against Government in U.S. Politics*. New York: Norton & Company; K.J. Mueller. 1993. *Health Care Policy in the United States*. Lincoln, N.E.: University of Nebraska Press.

[23] N. Freudenberg. 2012. "The Manufacture of Lifestyle: The Role of Corporations in Unhealthy Living." *Journal of Public Health Policy*, 33, 2: 244-256; American Psychological Association. 2012. *Stress in America: Our Health at Risk*. Washington, D.C.: American Psychological Association; Guenter Risse, Ronald L. Numbers, and Judith Walzer Leavitt, eds. 1977. *Medicine without doctors: Home health care in American history*. Science History Publications/USA.

Chapter Five

[1] M. Pollan. 2007. *The Omnivore's Dilemma: A Natural History of Four Meals*. New York: Penguin Books.

[2] E. Green. 2001. "The Bug That Ate The Burger: E. coli's Twisted Tale of Science in the Courtroom and Politics in the Lab." *Los Angeles Times*. June 6. Retrieved at http://articles.latimes.com/2001/jun/06/f-od/fo-6863; J. Benedict. 2011. *Poisoned: The True Story of the Deadly E. coli Outbreak that Changed the Way Americans Eat*. Buena Vista, V.A.: Inspire Books; C. Wilson and E. Schlosser. 2006. *Chew On This: Everything You Don't Want to Know About Fast Food*. New York: Houghton Mifflin Harcourt.

[3] Stacy M. Crim, Patricia M. Griffin, Robert Tauxe, Ellyn P. Marder, Debra Gilliss, Alicia B. Cronquist, Matthew Cartter, Melissa Tobin-D'Angelo, David Blythe, Kirk Smith, Sarah Lathrop, Shelley Zansky, Paul R. Cieslak, John Dunn, Kristin G. Holt, Beverly Wolpert, Olga L. Henao. "Preliminary Incidence and Trends of Infection with Pathogens Transmitted Commonly

Through Food—Foodborne Diseases Active Surveillance Network, 10 U.S. Sites, 2006—2014." *Morbidity and Mortality Weekly Report (MMWR): Center for Disease Control*, 64, 18: J. Andrews. 2014. "CDC Shares Data on E. Coli and Salmonella in Beef." *Food Safety News*. October 29. Retrieved at http://www.foodsafetynews.com/2014/10/cdc-shares-mass-of-data-on-e-coli-and-salmonella-in-beef/#.WAkioYWcGuU.

4 J. Johnston, A. Biro, N. MacKendrick. 2009. "Lost in the Supermarket: The Corporate-Organic Foodscape and the Struggle for Food Democracy." *Antipode*, 41, 3: 509–32.

5 C.L. Ogden, M.D. Carroll, B.K. Kit, and K.M. Flegal. 2014. "Prevalence of Childhood and Adult Obesity in the United States, 2011—2012." *Journal of the American Medical Association*, 311, 8: 806-814; Y. Wang and M. Beydoun. 2007. "The Obesity Epidemic in the United States—Gender, Age, Socioeconomic, Racial/Ethnic, and Geographic Characteristics: A Systematic Review and Meta-Regression Analysis." *Epidemiologic Review*, 29, 1: 6-28.

6 A. May, D. Freedman, B. Sherry, H.M. Blanck. 2013. "Obesity—United States, 1999–2010." *Morbidity and Mortality Weekly Report (MMWR) Supplements*. 22 November, 62, 3:120-28; National Institute of Diabetes and Digestive and Kidney Disease. "Overweight and Obesity Statistics." Retrieved at https://www.niddk.nih.gov/health-information/health-statistics/Pages/overweight-obesity-statistics.aspx; J. Levi, L. Segal, J. Rayburn, A. Martin. 2016. *State of Obesity: 2015. Better Policies for a Healthier America*. Washington, D.C.: Robert Wood Johnson Foundation. Retrieved at http://stateofobesity.org/files/stateofobesity2015.pdf.

7 M. Pollan. 2007. *The Omnivore's Dilemma: A Natural History of Four Meals*.

8 U. Sinclair. 1906. *The Jungle*. New York: Dover Publications; Unabridged edition (9 November, 2001).

9 V. Smil. 2004. *Enriching the Earth: Fritz Haber, Carl Bosch, and the Transformation of World Food Production*. Cambridge, M.A.: MIT Press.

10 R. Carson. 1962. *Silent Spring*. New York: Houghton-Mifflin; F.M. Lappe. 1965. *Diet for a Small Planet*. New York: Ballantine Books; W. Berry. 1977. *The Unsettling of America: Culture and Agriculture*. Washington, D.C.: Sierra Club; B. Commoner. 1971. *The Closing Circle: Nature, Man, and Technology*. New York: Random House.

11 M. Pollan. 2010. "The Food Movement, Rising." *The New York Review of Books*. June 10. Retrieved at http://www.nybooks.com/articles/2010/06/10/food-movement-rising/; M. Pollan. 2007. *The Omnivore's Dilemma: A Natural History of Four Meals.*

12 A. McKnight. 2010. "Supersizing Farms: The McDonaldization of Agriculture." In G. Rizer (Ed.). *McDonaldization: The Reader*. Thousand Oaks, C.A.: Pine Forge Press, pp. 192-105; H. Ulrich. 1989. *Losing Ground: Agricultural Policy and the Decline of the American Farm*. Chicago: Chicago Review Press.

13 Pew Commission on Industrial Farm Animal Production. 2014. *Putting Meat on the Table: Industrial Farm Animal Production in America*. Washington,

D.C.: Pew Charitable Trusts; A. Nihart. 2013. "Corporate Consolidation and Power in the Food System: An Interview with Dr. Mary Hendrickson." *UVM Food Feed: Sustainable Food Systems and the University of Vermont*. Burlington, V.T.: University of Vermont. Retrieved at https://learn.uvm.edu/foodsystemsblog/2013/06/21/corporate-consolidation-and-power-in-the-food-system-an-interview-with-dr-mary-hendrickson/.

[14] Interview with Bill Haw. 2002. "Modern Meat." *Frontline*. Retrieved at http://www.pbs.org/wgbh/pages/frontline/shows/meat/interviews/haw.html.

[15] D. Gurian-Sherman. 2008. *CAFOs Uncovered: The Untold Costs of Confined Animal Feeding Operations*. Cambridge, M.A.: Union of Concerned Scientists; J. Silver. 2012. *The Poisoning of Americans: A Tale of Congress, the FDA, the Agricultural Department, and Chemical and Pharmaceutical Companies and How They Work*. Bloomington, I.N.: iUniverse Publications; D. Imhoff. 2010. *The CAFO Reader: The Tragedy of Industrial Animal Factories (Contemporary Issues)*. Roxbury, M.A.: Watershed Media.

[16] D. Hamilton. 2002. *Modern Meat*. PBS Frontline Episode; M. Pollan. 2002. "Power Steer." *New York Times Magazine*. March 31; R. Albin. "How Feces Get Into the Food Supply." *News 21*. Retrieved at http://foodsafety.news21.com/2011/safety/inspection/feces/#sthash.yMQzMtnw.dpuf.

[17] Scott Ratzan. 1998. *Mad Cow Crisis: Health and the Public Good*. New York: Routledge; E. Haapapuro, N.D. Barnard, and M. Simon. 1997. "Review—Animal Waste Used as Livestock Feed: Dangers to Human Health." *Preventive Medicine*, 26, 5: 599-602; C. Leonard. 2015. *The Meat Racket: The Secret Takeover of America's Food Business*. New York: Simon and Schuster.

[18] A. Rock. 2015. "How Safe Is Your Ground Beef?" *Consumer Reports*. October 10, http://www.consumerreports.org/cro/food/how-safe-is-your-ground-beef ; USDA Agricultural Research Service. 2000. "Study Urges Pre-Processed Beef Test for E. coli," Health Letter on the CDC, March 13; Thomas Pawlick. 2012. *The End of Food: How the Food Industry Is Destroying Our Food Supply and What You Can Do About It*. Vancouver: Greystone Books; E. Schlosser. 2001. *Fast Food Nation*. New York: Harper Perennial.

[19] Interview with Tom Grumbly. 2014. "The trouble with Anti-Biotics." *Frontline*. October.

[20] M. Specter. 2003. "The Extremist: The Woman Behind the Most Successful Radical Group in America." *The New Yorker*. April 4. Retrieved at http://www.michaelspecter.com/2003/04/the-extremist/.

[21] P. Webster. 2009. "Playing Chicken with Antibiotic Resistance." *Pacific Standard Magazine*, August. Retrieved at https://psmag.com/playing-chicken-with-antibiotic-resistance-f005306869de#.g2voh54qo; K. Pal. 2015. *Diseases of Poultry*. Oxford: Oxford Book Company; B.M. Marshall and S.B. Levy. 2011. "Food Animals and Antimicrobials: Impacts on Human Health." *Clinical Microbiology Reviews*, 24, 4: 718-733. Emphasis in original.

[22] Center for Disease Control. "Get Smart: Know When Anti-Biotics Work." Retrieved at www.cdc.gov/getsmart/community/index.html; C.L. Ventola.

2015. "The Antibiotic Resistance Crisis: Part 1: Causes and Threats." *Pharmacy and Therapeutics*, 40, 4: 277-83.

[23] A. Fleming. 1945. "Nobel Lecture: Penicillin." December 11. *Nobelprize.org*. Retrieed at www.nobelprize.org/nobel_prizes/medicine/laureates/1945/fleming-lecture.html.

[24] A. Rock. 2015. "How Safe Is Your Ground Beef?" p. 17.

[25] S. Levy, 2014. "Reduced Antibiotic Use in Livestock: How Denmark Tackled Resistance." *Environmental Health Perspectives*, 122, 6. Retrieved at http://ehp.niehs.nih.gov/122-a160/.

[26] Levy. 2014. "Reduced Antibiotic Use in Livestock," p. 163.

[27] D. Sarathchandra, T.T. Eyck, and A. Toby. 2013. "Tell the Truth Food." *Culture & Society*, 16, 1; S. Rampton and J. Stauber. 2002. *Trust Us We're Experts: How Industry Manipulates Science and Gambles with Your Future*. New York: Tarcher Publishing.

[28] A. McKnight. 2010. "Supersizing Farms: The McDonaldization of Agriculture." In G. Rizer (Ed.). *McDonaldization: The Reader*. Thousand Oaks, C.A.: Pine Forge Press, pp. 192-105; H. Ulrich. 1989. *Losing Ground: Agricultural Policy and the Decline of the American Farm*. Chicago: Chicago Review Press.

[29] T. Jefferson. 1785. "Notes on the State of Virginia." *William and Mary Quarterly*, 35, 1 (1978): 88.

[30] P. Schmeiser, quoted in *David vs. Monsanto*, directed by Bertram Verhaag.

[31] S.A. Schwartz. 2013. "The Transformation of the American Food System, and its Effects on Wellness." *EXPLORE*, 9, 4: 206-210; R.J. Rolf. 2008. "Preempting to Nothing: Neoliberalism and the Fight to De/Re-Regulate Agricultural Biotechnology." *Geoforum*, 39, 3: 1423-1438.

[32] J. Louv. 2013. *Monsanto vs. the World: The Monsanto Protection Act, GMOs and Our Genetically Modified Future*. CreateSpace Independent Publishing Platform; D. Bartlett and J. Steele. 2008. "Monsanto's Harvest of Fear." *Vanity Fair*, 4: 1—9; Gregory Plast. 1999. *Index on Censorship*, 28, 3: 5, 62; Theo Colborn, Dianne Dumanoski and John Peterson Myers. 1996. *Our Stolen Future*. New York: Penguin Books, p. 90; Peter H. Schuck. 1987. *Agent Orange on Trial: Mass Toxic Disasters in the Courts*. Cambridge, Massachusetts: Harvard University Press, pp. 86-87, 155-164; Cate Jenkins, "Criminal Investigation of Monsanto Corporation - Cover-up of Dioxin Contamination in Products - Falsification of Dioxin Health Studies", USEPA Regulatory Development Branch, November (in this study Jenkins is explicit about Monsanto's deception: "According to testimony from the trial, Monsanto misclassified exposed and non-exposed workers, arbitrarily deleted several key cancer cases, failed to verify classification of chloracne subjects by common industrial dermatitis criteria, did not provide assurance of untampered records delivered and used by consultants, and made false statements about dioxin contamination in Monsanto products"); Brian Tokar. 1998. "Monsanto: A checkered history." *The Ecologist*, 28, 5 (September-October). Tokar references Jenkins' piece above: "A subsequent review by Dr. Cate Jenkins of the EPA's Regulatory Development Branch documented an

even more systematic record of fraudulent science: 'Monsanto has in fact submitted false information to EPA which directly resulted in weakened regulations under RCRA [Resources Conservation and Recovery Act] and FIFRA [Federal Insecticide, Fungicide and Rodenticide Act] ...' reported Dr. Jenkins in a 1990 memorandum urging the agency to undertake a criminal investigation of the company. Jenkins cited internal Monsanto documents revealing that the company 'doctored' samples of herbicides that were submitted to the US Department of Agriculture, hid behind 'process chemistry' arguments to deflect attempts to regulate 2,4-D and various chlorophenols, hid evidence regarding the contamination of Lysol, and excluded several hundred of its sickest former employees from its comparative health studies: Monsanto covered up the dioxin contamination of a wide range of its products. Monsanto either failed to report contamination, substituted false information purporting to show no contamination or submitted samples to the government for analysis which had been specially prepared so that dioxin contamination did not exist." Tokar continues later on: "This is only the latest in a series of major fines and rulings against Monsanto in the United States, including a $108 million liability finding in the case of the leukaemia death of a Texas employee in 1986, a $648,000 settlement for allegedly failing to report required health data to the EPA in 1990, a $1 million fine by the state Attorney General of Massachusetts in 1991 in the case of a 200,000 gallon acid wastewater spill, a $39 million settlement in Houston, Texas in 1992 involving the deposition of hazardous chemicals into unlined pits, and numerous others. In 1995, Monsanto ranked fifth among US corporations in the EPA's Toxic Release Inventory, having discharged 37 million pounds of toxic chemicals into the air, land, water and underground."

[33] J. Smith. 2003. *Seeds of Deception: Exposing Industry and Government Lies About the Safety of the Genetically Engineered Foods You're Eating.* New York: Yes! Books.

[34] K. Hubbard and N. Hassanein. 2013. "Confronting Coexistence in the United States: Organic Agriculture, Genetic Engineering, and the Case of Roundup Ready® Alfalfa." *Agriculture and Human Values*, 30, 3: 325-35; Janet E. Carpenter. 2001. *Case Studies in Benefits and Risks of Agricultural Biotechnology: Roundup Ready Soybeans and Bt Field Corn.* Washington, DC: National Center for Food and Agricultural Policy.

[35] V. Lehmann. 1998. "Patent on Seed Sterility Threatens Seed Saving." *Biotechnology and Development Monitor*, 35: 6-8; J. Sudduth. 2001. "Where the Wild Wind Blows: Genetically Altered Seed and Neighboring Farmers." *Duke Law & Technology Review*, 1, 1: 15.

[36] J. Savich. 2007. "Monsanto v. Scruggs: The Negative Impact of Patent Exhaustion on Self-Replicating Technology." *Berkeley Technology Law Journal*, 22, 1, Annual Review of Law and Technology, pp. 115-135; M.-M. Robin. 2013. *The World According to Monsanto.* New York: The New Press.

[37] B. Verhaag (Dir.). 2003. *David vs Monsanto*; J. Sudduth. 2001. "Where the Wild Wind Blows: Genetically Altered Seed and Neighboring Farmers." *Duke Law & Technology Review*, 1: 15.

[38] *David vs Monsanto.*

[39] N. Louwars and M. Minderhoud. 2001. "When a Law is Not Enough: Biotechnology Patents in Practice." *Biotechnology and Development Monitor*, 46: 16-1; D.L. Barrett and J.B. Steele. 2008. "Monsanto's Harvest of Fear." *Vanity Fair*, 4: 1-9.

[40] M.-M. Robin (Dir.). 2008. *The World According to Monsanto.*

[41] J. Savich. 2007. "Monsanto v. Scruggs: The Negative Impact of Patent Exhaustion on Self-Replicating Technology"; C.N. Pendleton. 2004. "The Peculiar Case of 'Terminator' Technology: Agricultural Biotechnology and Intellectual Property Protection at the Crossroads of the Third Green Revolution." *Biotechnology Law Report*, 23, 1: 1-29; R. Caplan. 2006. "The Ongoing Debate over Terminator Technology." *Georgetown Environmental Law Review*, 19: 751.

[42] T. Jefferson. 1785. "Letter to John Jay, Paris, August 23, 1785." *The Avalon Project: The Letters of Thomas Jefferson*. Retrieved at http://avalon.law.yale.edu/18th_century/let32.asp.

[43] R. Kenner (Dir.) 2009. *Food, Inc.*

[44] R. Kenner (Dir.). 2009. *Food Inc.*

[45] T. Capehart. 2004. *Trends in U.S. Tobacco Farming*. TBS-257-02. Washington, D.C.: United States Department of Agriculture; Campaign for Tobacco-Free Kids. 2016. *The Shrinking Role of Tobacco Farming and Tobacco Manufacturing in Virginia's Economy*. Retrieved at www.tobaccofreekids.org/research/factsheets/pdf/0346.pdf.

[46] D. Deering (Dir.). 2014. *Under Contract.*

[47] Fusion TV. 2014. *Cockfight*. Retrieved at http://interactive.fusion.net/cock-fight/.

[48] M. van Zeller. (Dir.). 2015. *Cock Fight*; J. Shepard. (Dir.). 2010. *The Sharecroppers.*

[49] J. Shepard (Dir.). 2013. *Sharecroppers*. https://www.youtube.com/watch?v=2erLkMuVqt4

[50] S. Edwards. 2012. "Rude Awakening in America's Farmland." *The Huffington Post*. November 13. Retrieved at www.huffingtonpost.com/scott-edwards/rude-awakening-in-america_b_2116415.html; Deering. 2014. *Under Contract.*

[51] C R. Knoeber. 1989. "A Real Game of Chicken: Contracts, Tournaments, and the Production of Broilers." *Journal of Law, Economics, & Organization*, 5, 2: 271—92; D.H. Constance and R. Tuinstra. 2005. "Corporate Chickens and Community Conflict in East Texas." *Culture & Agriculture*, 27, 1: 45—60; N. Johnson and D. Carr. 2015. "Does the Chicken Industry Pluck Farmers?" *Grist*. November 16. Retrieved at http://grist.org/food/does-the-chicken-industry-pluck-farmers/.

[52] R. Bussell. 2003. "Taking on" Big Chicken" The Delmarva Poultry Justice Alliance." *Labor Studies Journal*, 28, 2: 1-24. J. Norwell. 2001. "A chicken in

every pot: at what price?" *NEW SOLUTIONS: A Journal of Environmental and Occupational Health Policy*, 10, 4: 325-38.

Chapter Six

1 G. Orwell. 1949. *1984*. London: Harvey Secker Publishing.

2 S. Blair. 2015. Quoted in "GEBN: Getting the Word Out." *YouTube*. Retrieved at www.youtube.com/watch?v=9xBV_Enlh1A.

3 S. Blair. 2015. Letter posted at GEBN.org and reprinted in M. Nestle. 2015. "Muhtar Kent, Coca-Cola's CEO, and Scientist Steven Blair Respond to Critics." *Food Politics*. Retrieved at www.foodpolitics.com/2015/08/muhtar-kent-coca-colas-ceo-and-scientist-steven-blair-respond-to-critics/.

4 M. Simon. 2006. *Appetite for Profit: How the Food Industry Undermines Our Health and How to Fight Back*. New York: Nation Books; K. Brownell and K. Battle Horgen. 2004. *Food Fight: The Inside Story of the Food Industry, America's Obesity Crisis, and What We Can Do About It*. New York: McGraw-Hill.

5 A. O'Connor. 2015. "Coca-Cola Funds Scientists Who Shift Blame for Obesity Away From Bad Diets." *New York Times*. August 9. Retrieved at http://well.blogs.nytimes.com/2015/08/09/coca-cola-funds-scientists-who-shift-blame-for-obesity-away-from-bad-diets/?_r=0.

6 J. Hills and R. Welford. 2005. "Coca-Cola and Water in India." *Corporate Social Responsibility and Environmental Management*, 12, 3: 168—77; G. Lesley. 2009. "The Limits of Solidarity: Labor and Transnational Organizing against Coca-Cola." *American Ethnologist*, 36, 4: 667—80; M. Pendergrast. 2013. *For God, Country, and Coca-Cola: The Definitive History of the Great American Soft Drink and the Company that Makes It*. New York: Basic Books.

7 M. Kent. 2015. "We'll Do Better." *The Wall Street Journal*. August 20. Retrieved at http://www.wsj.com/articles/coca-cola-well-do-better-1440024365

8 J. Hills and R. Welford. 2005. "Coca-Cola and water in India." *Corporate Social Responsibility and Environmental Management*; S. Ghoshray. 2006. "Searching for Human Rights to Water Amidst Corporate Privatization in India: Hindustan Coca-Cola Pvt. Ltd. v. Perumatty Grama Panchayat." *Georgetown International Law Review*, 19: 643.

9 Michael F. Jacobson. 2016. *Marketing Coke to Kids: Broken Pledges; Unhealthy Children*. Washington, D.C.: Center for Science in the Public Interest.

10 Sean Cook, and Stephen Petrina. 2009. "Changing tastes: Coca-Cola, water and the commercialization of higher education." *Workplace: A Journal for Academic Labor* 13:1-5; David S. Almeling. 2003. "The problems of pouring-rights contracts." *Duke Law Journal*, 53, 3: 1111-1135; Alex Molnar. 2013. *School commercialism: From democratic ideal to market commodity*. New York: Routledge. Many "pro-bottled-water" videos and materials are available at Bottled Water Matters, a website of the International Bottled Water Association: www.bottledwatermatters.org/.

11 A. Bellatti. 2013. "Coca-Cola's Assault on Tap Water." *Civil Eats*. November 13. Retrieved at http://civileats.com/2013/11/13/coca-colas-assault-on-tap-water/; G.M. Chessman. 2012. "Bottled Water Industry Launches Battle

Against Tap Water." *Triple Pundit*, August 9. Retrieved at www.triplepundit.com/2012/04/bottled-water-industry-launches-marketing-battle-against-tap-water/.

12 G.M. Chessman. 2012. "Bottled Water Industry Launches Battle Against Tap Water." *Triple Pundit*; R. Wilk. 2006. "Bottled Water: The Pure Commodity in the Age of Branding." *Journal of Consumer Culture*, 6, 3: 303-25.

13 D. Yack and S.A. Bialous. 2001. "Junking Science to Promote Tobacco." *American Journal of Public Health*, 91, 11: 1745—8; N. Oreskes and E.M. Conway. 2001. *Merchants of Doubt: How a Handful of Scientists Obscured the Truth on Issues from Tobacco Smoke to Global Warming*. New York: Bloomsbury Publishing USA.

14 N. Oreskes and E. Conway. 2011. *Merchants of Doubt: How a Handful of Scientists Obscured the Truth on Issues from Tobacco Smoke to Global Warming*. New York: Bloomsbury Books; R. Kenner (Dir.) 2015. *Merchants of Doubt*.

15 R. Grundman. 2007. "Climate Change and Knowledge Politics." *Environmental Politics*, 16, 3: 414—32; T. Noah. 2002. "Did Exxon Mobil Get Bush To Oust the Global Warming Chief?" *Slate Magazine*. April 22. Retrieved at www.slate.com/articles/news_and_politics/chatterbox/2002/04/did_exxon_mobil_get_bush_to_oust_the_global_warming_chief.html.

16 S. Shulman. 2008. *Undermining Science: Suppression and Distortion in the Bush Administration*. Berkeley, C.A.: University of California Press.

17 R. Grundman. 2007. "Climate Change and Knowledge Politics."

18 Neela Banerjee, Lisa Song and David Hasemyer. 2015. "Exxon: The Road Not Taken." *Inside Climate News*. September 16—December 22. Retrieved at https://insideclimatenews.org/news/15092015/Exxons-own-research-confirmed-fossil-fuels-role-in-global-warming; S. Coll. 2013. *Private Empire: ExxonMobil and American Power*. New York: Penguin Books.

19 C. Hamilton. 2010. *Requiem for a Species: Why We Resist the Truth About Climate Change*. New York: Routledge.

20 R. Dunlap, and A.M. McCright. 2011. "Organized Climate Change Denial." in J.S. Dryzek, R.B. Norgaard, and D. Schlosberg (Eds.) *The Oxford Handbook of Climate Change and Society*. Oxford: Oxford University Press, pp. 144-60; R. Dunlap and A.M. McCright. 2010. "14 Climate change denial: sources, actors and strategies." in C. Lever-Tracy (Ed.) *Routledge Handbook of Climate Change and Society*. New York: Routledge, p. 250; G. Monbiot. 2006. "The Denial Industry." *The Guardian*. December 19. Retrieved at https://www.theguardian.com/environment/2006/sep/19/ethicalliving.g2.

21 Oregon Institute for Science and Medicine. 1998, 2007. *Petition Project*. Retrieved at www.oism.org/project/.

22 K. Grandia. 2011. "The 30,000 Global Warming Petition Is Easily-Debunked Propaganda." *The Huffington Post*. May 25. Retrieved at http://www.huffingtonpost.com/kevin-grandia/the-30000-global-warming_b_243092.html; G. Monbiot. 2006. "The Denial Industry"; D. Morrison. 2011. "Science Denialism: Evolution and Climate Change." Reports of the National Center for Science Education, 31, 5:1-9; A. McCright and R.E.

Dunlap. 2003. "Defeating Kyoto: The Conservative Movement's Impact on US Climate Change Policy." *Social Problems*, 50, 3: 348—73.

[23] M. Morano. Quoted in R. Kenner (Dir.). 2014. *Merchants of Doubt*.

[24] J.K. Harders. 1998. "The Unconstitutionality of Iowa's Proposed Agricultural Food Products Act and Similar Veggie Libel Laws." *Drake Journal of Agricultural Law*, Spring: 251; D.J. Bederman, S.M. Christensen, and S.D. Quesenberry. 1997. "Of Banana Bills and Veggie Hate Crimes: The Constitutionality of Agricultural Disparagement Statutes." *Harvard Journal on Legislation*, 35:135; Melissa Denchak. 2016. "All About Alar: How a growth regulator sprayed on apple trees inadvertently became a major player in NRDC's fight to protect children from toxic pesticides." March 14. Retrieved at https://www.nrdc.org/stories/all-about-alar; Bradford H. Sewell, Robin M. Whyatt. 1989. "Intolerable Risk: Pesticides in our Children's Food." Washington, D.C.: Natural Resources Defense Council.

[25] Environmental Working Group. 2013. "Ten Years Later, Myth of 'Alar Scare' Persists: How Chemical Industry Rewrote History of Banned Pesticide." Retrieved at www.soc.iastate.edu/sapp/alar3.pdf; R. Wiles, K.A. Cook, T. Hettenbach, and C. Campbell. 1999. "How 'bout Them Apples: Pesticides in Children's Food Ten Years After Alar." Washington, D.C.: Environmental Working Group.

[26] D. Sarathchandra, T.T. Eyck, and A. Toby. 2013. "Tell the Truth Food." *Culture & Society*, 16, 1: 107-124; S. Rampton and J. Stauber. 2002. *Trust Us We're Experts: How Industry Manipulates Science and Gambles with Your Future*. New York: Tarcher Publishing.

[27] Elliot Negin. 1996. "The 'alar' scare" was for real: and so is that 'veggie hate-crime' movement." *Columbia Journalism Review*, 35: 3: 13-16; A. Blay-Palmer. 2008. *Food Fears: From Industrial to Sustainable Food Systems*. New York: Routledge.

[28] Negin, "The alar scare" was for real.

[29] E. Whelan. 1996. "Letter to the Editor." *Columbia Journalism Review*, 35, 4.

[30] E. Negin. 1996. "Reply to Letter to the Editor."

[31] H. Kurtz. 1996. "Dr. Whelan's Media Operation." *Columbia Journalism Review*, 35, 4.

[32] Oprah. 1998. "'No Beef with Beef': Talk Show Queen Finishes Her Testimony." *CNN*. February 5. Retrieved at www.cnn.com/US/9802/05/oprah. beef/.

[33] T. Colborn and D. Dumanowski. 1997. *Our Stolen Future: Are We Threatening Our Fertility, Intelligence, and Survival? A Scientific Detective Story.* New York: Plume Publishers; R. Musil. 2014. *Rachel Carson and Her Sisters: Extraordinary Women Who Have Shaped America's Environment*. New Brunswick, NJ: Rutgers University Press.

[34] Jerry H. Berke. 1997. "Book Review: Living Downstream: An ecologist looks at cancer and the environment." *New England Journal of Medicine*; 337:1562, November 20; *Civil Action* was directed by Steve Zaillien and released in 1998 by Touchstone Pictures; L. Orlando. 2002. "Industry Attacks on Dissent: From Rachel Carson to Oprah." *Dollars & Sense*, March/April, 240.

Retrieved at http://www.dollarsandsense.org/archives/2002/0302orlando.html.

[35] L. Orlando. 2002. "Industry Attacks on Dissent"; S. Rampton and J. Stauber. 2002. *Trust Us We're Experts: How Industry Manipulates Science and Gambles with Your Future.*

[36] S. Ewen. Quoted in L. Alper and S. Jhally (Producers). *Toxic Sludge Is Good For You: The Public Relations Industry Unspun.*

Chapter Seven

[1] S. King. 2013. *Guns.* Bangor, ME: Philtrum Press.

[2] Jack Healy, Mike McIntire and Julie Turkewitz. 2015. "Oregon Killer's Mother Wrote of Troubled Son and Gun Rights." *The New York Times.* October 5. Retrieved https://www.nytimes.com/2015/10/06/us/mother-of-oregon-gunman-wrote-of-keeping-firearms.html

[3] Data in this paragraph and the following one taken from www.gunviolencearchive.org, in which each incident is linked to at least one local report. Many of the incidents can be cross-checked with local, regional, and sometimes national media sites.

[4] R. Feldman. 2007. *Ricochet: Confessions of a Gun Lobbyist.* New York: John Wiley & Sons; P. Brown and D. Abel. 2010. *Outgunned: Up Against the NRA—The First Complete Insider Account of the Battle Over Gun Control.* New York: Free Press; S. Melzer. 2009. *Gun Crusaders: The NRA's Culture War.* New York: NYU Press.

[5] R. Cherlin. 2012. "'We Do Absolutely Anything They Ask': How the NRA's Grading System Keeps Congress on Lockdown." *GQ.* June 24. Retrieved at www.gq.com/story/nra-grades-and-congress.

[6] C. Amicon and S. Childress. 2015. "How Loaded is the Gun Lobby?" *PBS Frontline.* January 6. Retrieved at www.pbs.org/wgbh/pages/frontline/government-elections-politics/gunned-down/how-loaded-is-the-gun-lobby/; S. Stein and P. Blumenthal. 2012. "The Gun Lobby: Why the NRA is the Baddest Force in Politics." *The Huffington Post.* December 17. Retrieved at www.huffingtonpost.com/2012/12/17/gun-lobby-nra_n_2317885.html; J. Carlson. 2015. *Citizen-Protectors: The Everyday Politics of Guns in an Age of Decline.* New York: Oxford University Press.

[7] D. Herszenhorn. 2016. "Senator's 15-Hour Filibuster Gains 'Path Forward' on Gun Control Measures." *New York Times.* June 16. Retrieved at www.nytimes.com/2016/06/17/us/politics/senate-filibuster-gun-control.html; S. Siddiqui. 2016. "Senate Fails to Pass New Gun Control Restrictions in Wake of Orlando Shooting." *The Guardian.* June 20. Retrieved at https://www.theguardian.com/us-news/2016/jun/20/senate-gun-control-vote-orlando-shooting.

[8] M. Planty and J.L. Truman. 2013. Firearm Violence, 1993-2011. Bureau of Justice Statistics. Washington, D.C.: U.S. Department of Justice; D'Vera Cohn, P. Taylor, M. Hugo Lopez, C.A. Gallagher, K. Parker and K.T. Maass. 2013. "Gun Homicide Rate Down 49% Since 1993 Peak; Public

Unaware." Washington, D.C.: Pew Research Center. Retrieved at www.pewsocialtrends.org/2013/05/07/gun-homicide-rate-down-49-since-1993-peak-public-unaware/.

[9] L. Bell. 2013. "Disarming Realities: As Gun Sales Soar, Gun Crimes Plummet." *Forbes*. May 16. Retrieved at www.forbes.com/sites/larrybell/2013/05/14/disarming-realities-as-gun-sales-soar-gun-crimes-plummet/#4af93aa87de9; M. Vespa and M. Perry. 2015. "Chart of the Day: More Guns, Less Gun Violence Between 1993 and 2013." *American Enterprise Institute Ideas*. Retrieved at www.aei.org/publication/chart-of-the-day-more-guns-less-gun-violence-between-1993-and-2013.

[10] A. Blumstein and J. Wallman. 2006. *The Crime Drop in America: Revised Edition*. Cambridge: Cambridge University Press; O. Roeder, L.-B. Eisen and J. Bowling. 2015. *What Caused the Crime Decline?* New York: Brennan Center for Justice. Retrieved at www.brennancenter.org/publication/what-caused-crime-decline.

[11] Data for these statistics compiled from FBI data from annual *Crime in the United States* reports, issued by the FBI and retrieved at www.fbi.gov.

[12] A. Cooper and E.L. Smith. 2011. "Homicide Trends in the United States, 1980-2008: Annual Rates for 2009 and 2010." Washington, D.C.: Bureau of Justice Statistics. May. Retrieved at https://www.bjs.gov/content/pub/pdf/htus8008.pdf.

[13] National Center for Health Statistics. 2016. "Suicide and Self-Inflicted Injury." Washington, D.C.: Center for Disease Control. Retrieved at http://www.cdc.gov/nchs/fastats/suicide.htm; M. Miller, D. Hemenway, and D. Azrael. 2004. "Firearms and Suicide in the Northeast." *Journal of Trauma*, 57: 626—32; M. Matthew and D. Hemenway. 1999. "The Relationship between Firearms and Suicide: A Review of the Literature." *Aggression and Violent Behavior: A Review Journal*, 4: 59—75; J. Birckmayer and D. Hemenway. 2001. "Suicide and Gun Prevalence: Are Youth Disproportionately Affected?" *Suicide and Life Threatening Behavior*, 31: 303—10; R.M. Johnson, C. Barber, D. Azrael, D.E. Clark, and D. Hemenway. 2010. "Who are the Owners of Firearms Used in Adolescent Suicides?" *Suicide and Life Threatening Behavior*, 40: 609—11.

[14] R. Florida. 2011. "The Geography of Gun Deaths." *The Atlantic*. January 3. Retrieved at www.theatlantic.com/national/archive/2011/01/the-geography-of-gun-deaths/69354/.

[15] J.P. Blair, M.H. Martaindale, and T. Nichols. 2014. *A Study of Active Shooter Incidents in the United States Between 2000 and 2013*. Washington, D.C.: Department of Justice.

[16] J.R. Lott. 1998. *More Guns, Less Crime: Understanding Crime and Gun Control Laws*. Chicago: University of Chicago Press.

[17] I. Ayers and J. Donohue III. 2003. "The Latest Misfires in Support of the 'More Guns, Less Crime' Hypothesis." *Stanford Law Review*, 55, 4: 1371—98; C. Mooney. 2003. "Double Barreled; Double Standards." *Mother Jones*. October 13. Retrieved at http://www.motherjones.com/politics/2003/10/double-barreled-double-standards; J. Laurie. 2015."When the Gun Lobby

Tries to Justify Firearms Everywhere, it Turns to This Guy." *Mother Jones*, July 28. Retrieved at http://www.motherjones.com/politics/2015/07/john-lott-guns-crime-data.

18 C.F. Wellford, J.V. Pepper, and C.V. Petrie. 2004. *Firearms and Violence: A Critical Review.* Washington, D.C.: National Academies Press.

19 A. Aneja, J.J. Donohue III, and A. Zhang. 2011. "The Impact of Right-to-Carry Laws and the NRC Report: Lessons for the Empirical Evaluation of Law and Policy". *American Law and Economics Review*, 13, 2: 565—631.

20 Letter written by E. William Colglazier (Executive Officer, National Academy of Sciences and National Research Council, Washington D.C.) in 2005. Retrieved at http://scienceblogs.com/deltoid/2005/01/26/naspanel10/; A.W. Alschuler. 1997. "Two Guns, Four Guns, Six Guns, More Guns: Does Arming the Public Reduce Crime?" *Valparaiso University Law Review*, 31, 2: 365; Daniel W. Webster, Jon S. Vernick, Jens Ludwig, and Kathleen J. Lester. 1997. "Flawed Gun Policy Research Could Endanger Public Safety." *American Journal of Public Health*, 87, 6: 917-921; Franklin Zimring and Gordon Hawkins. 1997. "Concealed handguns: The counterfeit deterrent." *Responsive Community*, 7: 46-60.

21 E. DeFilippis and D. Hughes. 2014. "Shooting Down the Gun Lobby's Favorite 'Academic': A Lott of Lies." *Armed with Reason*. December 1. Retrieved at www.armedwithreason.com/shooting-down-the-gun-lobbys-favorite-academic-a-lott-of-lies; D. Hemenway. 1997. "Survey Research and Self-Defense Gun Use: An Explanation of Extreme Overestimates." *The Journal of Criminal Law & Criminology*, 87, 4: 1430-1445; Kieran Healey. 2005. "John Lott Strikes Again." *Crooked Timber*. May 10. Retrieved at http://crookedtimber.org/2005/05/10/john-lott-strikes-again/.

22 M. Alexander. 2012. *The New Jim Crow: Mass Incarceration in the Age of Colorblindness*. New York: The New Press.

23 G.L. Kelling and J.Q. Wilson. 1982. "Broken Windows: The Police and Neighborhood Safety." *Atlantlic Monthly*. March. Retrieved at http://www.theatlantic.com/magazine/archive/1982/03/broken-windows/304465/.

24 M. Alexander. 2010. *The New Jim Crow: Mass Incarceration in the Age of Colorblindness.*

25 N. Smith. 2001. "Global Social Cleansing: Postliberal Revanchism and the Export of Zero Tolerance." *Social Justice*, 28, 3: 68-74.

26 Smith. 2001. "Global Social Cleansing."

27 D. Barry. 1998. "Political Memo; The Mussolini Of Manhattan? Giuliani Grins and Bears It." *New York Times*. June 24. Retrieved at www.nytimes.com/1998/06/24/nyregion/political-memo-the-mussolini-of-manhattan-giuliani-grins-and-bears-it.html?_r=0.

28 M. Cooper. 1999. "Vote by P.B.A. Rebukes Safir and His Policy." *New York Times*, April 15. p. A1.

29 Mike Bostock & Ford Fessenden. 2014. "'Stop-and-Frisk' Is All but Gone from New York, *New York Times*. September 19. Retrieved at http://www.nytimes.com/interactive/2014/09/19/nyregion/stop-and-frisk-is-all-butgone-from-new-york.html.

[30] Statistics on unarmed black men and women killed by police are kept at http://mappingpoliceviolence.org/unarmed/; H. Giroux. 2003. "Zero Tolerance, Domestic Militarization, and the War Against Youth." *Social Justice*, 30, 2: 59-65.

[31] J. Bouie. 2014. "Broken Windows Policing Kills People." *Slate Magazine*. August 5. Retrieved at www.slate.com/articles/news_and_politics/politics/2014/08/broken_windows_policing_deaths_racism_in_chokeholds_arrests_and_convictions.html.

[32] G. Kelling. 2015. "Don't Blame My 'Broken Windows' Theory For Poor Policing" *Politico*. August 11. Retrieved at www.politico.com/magazine/story/2015/08/broken-windows-theory-poor-policing-ferguson-kelling-121268?o=0.

[33] Kelling and Wilson. 1982. "Broken Windows."

[34] R.J. Sampson and S.W. Raudenbush. 2004. "Seeing Disorder: Neighborhood Stigma and the Social Construction of 'Broken Windows.'" *Social Psychology Quarterly*, 67, 4:319-342; R. Taylor. 2001. *Breaking Away From Broken Windows: Baltimore Neighborhoods and the Nationwide Fight Against Crime, Grime, Fear, and Decline*. Boulder, C.O.: Westview Press; B.E. Harcourt. 2001. *Illusion of Order: The False Promise of Broken Windows Policing*. Cambridge, M.A.: Harvard University Press.

[35] J. Butler and G. Yancy. 2015. "What's Wrong With 'All Lives Matter'?" *New York Times*, January 12; J. Camp and C. Heatherton. 2016. *Policing the Planet: Why the Policing Crisis Led to Black Lives Matter*. London: Verso; A. Davis and F. Barat. 2016. *Freedom Is a Constant Struggle: Ferguson, Palestine, and the Foundations of a Movement*. Boston: Haymarket Books.

[36] R.D.G. Kelley. 2016. "What Does Black Lives Matter Want?" August 17. Retrieved at https://bostonreview.net/books-ideas/robin-d-g-kelley-movement-black-lives-vision; The Movement for Black Lives Matter. "A Vision for Black Lives: Policy Demands for Black Power, Freedom & Justice." Retrieved at https://policy.m4bl.org/.

[37] D. Enck-Wanzer. 2011. "Barack Obama, the Tea Party, and the Threat of Race: on Racial Neoliberalism and Born Again Racism." *Communication, Culture & Critique*, 4, 1: 23-30.

[38] S. Jaffe. 2016. *Necessary Trouble: Americans in Revolt*. New York: Nation Books.

[39] M. Tesler. 2012. "The Spillover of Racialization into Health Care: How President Obama Polarized Public Opinion by Racial Attitudes and Race." *American Journal of Political Science*, 56, 3: 690-704; E.D. Knowles, B. Lowery, and R.L. Schaumberg. 2010. "Racial Prejudice Predicts Opposition to Obama and His Health Care Reform Plan." *Journal of Experimental Social Psychology*, 46, 2: 420-423; A. Banks. 2014. "The Public's Anger: White Racial Attitudes and Opinions Toward Health Care Reform." *Political Behavior*, 36, 3:493-519.

[40] J. Lubin. 2012. "Race and the Fight Against Obamacare." *The Huffington Post*. June 26. Retrieved at http://www.huffingtonpost.com/judy-lubin/race-and-fight-against-obamacare_b_1633115.html; T. Skocpol and V.

Williams. 2013. *The Tea Party and the Remaking of Republican Conservatism.* New York: Oxford University Press.

41 A. Marcotte. 2015. "The Obamacare Fight Has Always Been About Race And Gender Anxiety." *TPM*, March 15. Retrieved at http://talkingpointsmemo.com/cafe/obamacare-fight-race-and-gender-anxiety-michael-carvin; P. Waldman. 2014. "Yes, Opposition to Obamacare is Tied Up with Race." *Washington Post*, May 23. Retrieved at https://www.washingtonpost.com/blogs/plum-line/wp/2014/05/23/yes-opposition-to-obamacare-is-tied-up-with-race/?utm_term=.4060fddda504; B. Knoll. 2015. "'Simply Un-American': Nativism and Support for Health Care Reform." *Political Behavior*, 37, 1: https://www.washingtonpost.com/blogs/plum-line/wp/2014/05/23/yes-opposition-to-obamacare-is-tied-up-with-race/?utm_term=.4060fddda504.

Part Four: Overview

1 J. Randers and D. Meadows. 2004. *The Limits to Growth: A 30-year Update.* River Junction, VT: Chelsea Green Publishing; D.A. Pennebaker, and Chris Hegedus (Dirs.) 1993. *The War Room.*

2 D.A. Pennebaker, and Chris Hegedus (Dirs.) 1993. *The War Room.*

3 W.E. Leuchtenburg. 1997. *The FDR Years: On Roosevelt and His Legacy.* New York: Columbia University Press; E. Berkowitz. 1991. *America's Welfare State: From Roosevelt to Reagan.* Baltimore, M.D.: Johns Hopkins University Press.

4 G. Kabaservice. 2013. *Rule and Ruin: The Downfall of Moderation and the Destruction of the Republican Party, From Eisenhower to the Tea Party.* New York: Oxford University Press; K. Phillips-Fein. 2009. *Invisible Hands: The Making of the Conservative Movement from the New Deal to Reagan.* New York: W.W. Norton & Co.

5 J. Quadagno. 1994. *The Color of Welfare: How Racism Undermined the War on Poverty.* New York: Oxford University Press; M. Linder. 1986. "Farm Workers and the Fair Labor Standards Act: Racial Discrimination in the New Deal." *Texas Law Review*, 65: 1335—93; G. Davies and M. Derthick. 1997. "Race and Social Welfare Policy: The Social Security Act of 1935." *Political Science Quarterly*, 112, 2: 217—35.

6 Quoted in B. Moyers. 1988. "What a Real President Was Like; To Lyndon Johnson, the Great Society Meant Hope and Dignity." *The Washington Post.* November 13. Retrieved at https://www.washingtonpost.com/archive/opinions/1988/11/13/what-a-real-president-was-like/d483c1be-d0da-43b7-bde6-04e10106ff6c/?utm_term=.12a861946c91.

7 B. Ehrenreich. 1990. *Fear of Falling: The Inner Life of the Middle Class.* New York: Harper-Collins.

8 C. Wright Mills. 1956. *The Power Elite.* New York: Oxford University Press; M. Davis. 2000. *Prisoners of the American Dream: Politics and Economy in the History of the US Working Class* (2nd Edition). London: Verso Press.

9 E. Hatton. 2010. *The Temp Economy: From Kelly Girls to Permatemps in Postwar America.* Philadelphia, P.A.: Temple University Press; V. Smith and E.B.

Neuwirth. 2008. *The Good Temp.* Ithaca, N.Y.: Cornell University Press; K. Henson. 1996. *Just a Temp.* Philadelphia, P.A.: Temple University Press.

[10] C.B. Short. 1989. *Ronald Reagan and the Public Lands: America's Conservation Debate, 1979—1984.* College Station, T.X.: Texas A&M University Press.

[11] Citizens United v. Federal Election Commission, No. 08-205, 558 U.S. 310 (2010).

[12] Nicholas Confessore, Sarah Cohen and Karen Yourish. 2015. "Buying Power." *The New York Times.* October 10. Retrieved at www.nytimes.com/interactive/2015/10/11/us/politics/2016-presidential-election-super-pac-donors.html?_r=0; L. Lessig. *Republic, Lost: Version 2.0.* New York: Twelve Books.

[13] Samantha Lachman. 2014. "Sheldon Adelson Gives $10 Million to Karl Rove Group, Just One-Fifteenth of 2012 Contributions." *The Huffington Post.* September 8. Retrieved at www.huffingtonpost.com/news/sheldon-adelson-donations/; Peter Stone. 2015. "Marco Rubio leads race for donations from casino billionaire Sheldon Adelson." *The Guardian.* Retrieved at www.theguardian.com/us-news/2015/oct/29/marco-rubio-campaign-funding-sheldon-adelson.

[14] M. Gold. 2015. "Koch-backed Network Aims to Spend Nearly $1 Billion in Run-up to 2016." *The Washington Post.* 25 January. Retrieved at https://www.washingtonpost.com/politics/koch-backed-network-aims-to-spend-nearly-1-billion-on-2016-elections/2015/01/26/77a44654-a513-11e4-a06b-9df2002b86a0_story.html.

[15] D. Kellner. 2005. *Media Spectacle and the Crisis of Democracy: Terrorism, War, and Election Battles.* New York: Routledge.

Chapter Eight

[1] Retrieved at www.rubio.senate.gov/public/index.cfm/press-releases?ID=66BD09D9-2ACC-41C0-B853-B43EE6F27AD2.

[2] M. Rubio. 2011. Floor Speech to United States Senate. December 16. Retrieved at www.rubio.senate.gov/public/index.cfm/press-releases?ID=66BD09D9-2ACC-41C0-B853-B43EE6F27AD2.

[3] T. Frank. 2012. *Pity the Billionaire: The Hard-Times Swindle and the Unlikely Comeback of the Right.* New York: Picador/Macmillan.

[4] E. Saez and T. Picketty. 2013. "Top Incomes and the Great Recession: Recent Evolutions and Policy Implications." *International Monetary Fund Economic Review,* 61, 3: 456—78.

[5] D.S. Hamermesh and E. Stancanelli. 2014. "Long Workweeks and Strange Hours." Discussion Paper No. 8423. Bonn, Switzerland: Institute for the Study of Labor.

[6] A. Kallenberg. 2012. *Good Jobs, Bad Jobs: The Rise of Polarized and Precarious Employment Systems in the United States, 1970s to 2000s.* New York: Russell Sage Foundation.

[7] P. Terrell. 1986. "Taxing the Poor." *Social Science Review,* 60, 2: 272-286; D. Baker. 2016. *Rigged: How Globalization and the Rules of the Modern Economy*

were Structured to Make the Rich Richer. Washington: Center for Economic and Policy Research.

8 E. Saez and M. Veall. 2005. "The Evolution of High Incomes in Northern America: Lessons from Canadian Evidence." *The American Economic Review*, 95, 3: 831-49; L. Bartels. 2005. "Homer Gets a Tax Cut: Inequality and Public Policy in the American Mind." *Perspectives on Politics*, 3, 1: 15-31; J. Hacker and P. Pierson. 2011. *Winner-take-all Politics*. Old Saybrook, CT: Tantor Media, Incorporated.

9 R. Reich. 2012. "Mitt Romney and the New Gilded Age." *The Nation*, July 16-23. Retrieved at https://www.thenation.com/article/mitt-romney-and-new-gilded-age/; W. Buffet. 2011. "Stop Coddling the Super-Rich." *The New York Times*. August 14. Retrieved at http://www.nytimes.com/2011/08/15/opinion/stop-coddling-the-super-rich.html?_r=0&mtrref=www.google.com&gwh=72240A6CE2CA95539046A4E0BA72A23E&gwt=pay&assetType=opinion.

10 Robert Reich. 2012. *Beyond Outrage: Expanded Edition: What has gone wrong with our economy and our democracy, and how to fix it*. New York: Vintage Books; Haynes Johnson. 2003. *Sleepwalking Through History: America in the Reagan Years*. New York: W. W. Norton. Another important trend was the series of statewide propositions for cutting taxes from 1979 through the 1990s. Hatched in 1979 by Howard Jarvis in California, limiting property tax rates was a popular, middle-class tax revolt that paralleled Reagan's tax cuts on a federal level. With similar arguments about individual wealth and freedom, Jarvis argued people knew what to do with their money better than the government—an argument not only echoed but still valorized by the "kill it to save it" crowd today. See A. O'Sullivan, T.A. Sexton, and S.M. Sheffri. 1995. *Property Taxes and Tax Revolts: The Legacy of Proposition 13*. New York: Cambridge University Press.

11 D. Baker. 2007. *The United States Since 1980*. New York: Cambridge University Press.

12 Baker. 2007. *The United States Since 1980*, pp. 202-6.

13 T. Frank. 2016. *Listen, Liberal! Or, What Ever Happened to the Party of the People?* New York: Metropolitan Books.

14 G.W. Domhoff. 2013. "The Rise and Fall of Labor Unions in the U.S. from the 1830s until 2012 (but mostly the 1930s-1980s)." Retrieved at http://www2.ucsc.edu/whorulesamerica/power/history_of_labor_unions.html.

15 Baker. 2007. *The United States Since 1980*, pp. 203-10.

16 L. Mishel, J. Bevins, E. Gould and H. Schierholz. 2012. *The State of Working America, 12th Edition*. New York: ILR Press.

17 Rubio. 2011. Floor Speech to United States Senate.

18 H. Johnson. 1991. *Sleepwalking Through History: America in the Reagan Years*. New York. W.W. Norton Company; Michael Rogin. 1988. *Ronald Reagan the movie: And other episodes in political demonology*. University of California Press; Gil Troy. 2013. *Morning in America: How Ronald Reagan Invented the 1980's*. Princeton University Press.

19 Rubio. 2011. Floor Speech to United States Senate.

[20] D.P. Szatmary. 1980. *Shays' Rebellion: The Making of an Agrarian Insurrection.* Amherst, M.A.: University of Massachusetts Press; A.T. Vaughn. 1978. "The 'Horrid and Unnatural' Rebellion of Daniel Shays." In R. Land and J.J. Turner, Jr. (Eds.). *Riot, Rout, and Tumult: Readings in American Social and Political Violence.* Westport, C.T.: Greenwood Press, pp. 56—69.

[21] C.A. Scwantes. 1985. *Coxey's Army: An American Odyssey.* Moscow, I.D.: University of Idaho Press.

[22] S. Ortiza. 2006. "Rethinking the Bonus March: Federal Bonus Policy, the Veterans of Foreign Wars, and the Origins of a Protest Movement." *Journal of Policy History*, 18, 3: 275—303.

[23] Rubio. 2011. Floor Speech to United States Senate.

[24] H. Meyerson. 2003. "Las Vegas as a Workers' Paradise." *American Prospect*, December 11:168-169. M. Rubio. 2012. *An American Son: A Memoir.* New York: Sentinel; Eugene. P. Moehring and Michael S. Green. 2005. *Las Vegas: A centennial history.* University of Nevada Press.

[25] J. Nichols. 2015. "A Billionaire, Some Millionaires, and a No-Show Senator Debate How Best to Block Wage Hikes." *The Nation.* November 11. Retrieved at https://www.thenation.com/article/a-billionaire-some-millionaires-and-a-no-show-senator-debate-how-best-to-block-wage-hikes/.

[26] W.F. Mackey and V.N. Beebe. 1977. *Bilingual Schools for a Bicultural Community: Miami's Adaptation to the Cuban Refugees.* Rowley, M.A.: Newbury House Publishers; Rubio. 2012. *An American Son.*

[27] A. DePalma. 1991. "A College Acts in Desperation and Dies Playing the Lender." *The New York Times.* April 17. Retrieved at http://www.nytimes.com/1991/04/17/education/a-college-acts-in-desperation-and-dies-playing-the-lender.html?pagewanted=all.

[28] Information taken from State of Florida education websites on June 6, 2016. Retrieved at www.floridacollegeaccess.org/wp-content/uploads/2013/08/SUS-Tuition-2013-14-Table2.pdf and www.sfa.ufl.edu/basics/cost-of-attendance/.

[29] M. Rubio. 2015. *American Dreams: Restoring Economic Opportunities for Everyone.* New York: Sentinel.

[30] University of Central Florida Department requirements. Retrieved at http://catalog.ucf.edu/content/documents/programs/Human_Communication_BA.pdf.

[31] Rubio. 2011. Floor Speech to United States Senate.

[32] P. Krugman. 2014. "Voodoo Economics: The Next Generation." *New York Times*, October 5. Retrieved at http://www.nytimes.com/2014/10/06/opinion/paul-krugman-voodoo-economics-the-next-generation.html?_r=0&mtrref=www.google.com&gwh=C85EBF3912DDCD7C5646370320384B17&gwt=pay&assetType=opinion.

[33] Rubio. 2011. Floor Speech.

Chapter Nine

1 A. Duncan. 2010. Quoted in "Education Secretary Duncan Calls Hurricane Katrina Good for New Orleans Schools." *Washington Post*, January 30.

2 G. Scott Heron. 2000. *Now and Then*. London: Canongate Publishers.

3 N. Klein. 2007. *Shock Doctrine: The Rise of Disaster Capitalism*. Toronto: Knopf Canada, p. 14.

4 N. Klein. 2007. *Shock Doctrine*, p. 11; M. Friedman. 1982. *Capitalism and Freedom*. Chicago, IL.: University of Chicago Press.

5 M. Friedman. 2005. "The Promise of Vouchers." *Wall Street Journal*. December 5. Retrieved at http://www.wsj.com/articles/SB113374845791113764.

6 R.W. Kates, C.E. Colten, S. Laska and S.P. Leatherman. 2006. "Reconstruction of New Orleans after Hurricane Katrina: a research perspective." *Proceedings of the National Academy of Sciences*, 103, 40: 14653-14660; E. Fussell, N. Sastry and M. Van Landingham. 2010. "Race, Socioeconomic Status, and Return Migration to New Orleans after Hurricane Katrina." *Population and Environment*, 31, 1-3: 20–42; K. Buras. 2011. "Race, Charter Schools, and Conscious Capitalism: On the Spatial Politics of Whiteness as Property (and the Unconscionable Assault on Black New Orleans)." *Harvard Educational Review*, 81, 2: 296-331.

7 C. Kimmett. 2015. "10 Years After Katrina, New Orleans' All-Charter School System Has Proven a Failure." *In These Times*. August 28. Retrieved at http://inthesetimes.com/article/18352/10-years-after-katrina-new-orleans-all-charter-district-has-proven-a-failur; D. Cimarusti. 2015. "Policy Brief: Should Louisiana and the Recovery School District Receive Accolades for Being Last and Nearly Last?" *The Network for Public Education*. Retrieved at http://networkforpubliceducation.org/2015/08/policy_brief_louisiana/#_edn1.

8 D. Ravitch. 2015. "John Thompson: A Sad, Sad Year for Corporate Reformers." *Diane Ravitch's Blog*. Retrieved at http://dianeravitch.net/2015/10/13/john-thompson-a-sad-sad-year-for-corporate-reformers/.

9 E. Brown. 2015. "Katrina Swept Away New Orleans' School System, Ushering in New Era." *The Washington Post*. September 3. Retrieved at https://www.washingtonpost.com/news/education/wp/2015/09/03/katrina-swept-away-new-orleans-school-system-ushering-in-new-era/; A. Dixson. 2011. "Whose Choice? A Critical Race Perspective on Charter Schools." In C. Johnson (Ed.). *The Neoliberal Deluge: Hurricane Katrina, Late Capitalism, and the Remaking of New Orleans*. Minneapolis, M.N.: University of Minnesota Press: 130-151; D. Holley-Walker. 2011. "The Accountability Cycle: The Recovery School District Act and New Orleans' Charter Schools." *Connecticut Law Review*, 40: 125-64.

10 Klein. *Shock Doctrine*, pp. 18-19.

11 A. Lowenstein. 2015. *Disaster Capitalism: Making a Killing out of Catastrophe*. London: Verso, pp. 18-19.

12 B. McLean and P. Elkind. 2013. *The Smartest Guys in the Room: The Amazing Rise and Scandalous Fall of Enron*. New York: Penguin Books; K. Eichenwold.

2005. *Conspiracy of Fools: A True Story*. New York: Broadway Books; M. Swartz. 2003. *Power Failure: The Inside Story of The Collapse of Enron*. New York: Crown Books.

[13] R. Perlstein. 2014. *The Invisible Bridge: The Fall of Nixon and the Rise of Reagan*. New York: Simon & Schuster, pp. 549-51.

[14] American Legislative Exchange Council. Retrieved at https://www.alec.org/about/.

[15] D. Ladipo. 2001. "The Rise of America's Prison Industrial Complex." *New Left Review*, 7:109-123; T. Jones and T. Newburn. 2005. "Comparative Criminal Justice Policy-Making in the United States and the United Kingdom." *British Journal of Criminology*, 45, 1: 58-80.

[16] A. Friedman. 2013. *Capitalist Punishment: Prison Privatization and Human Rights*. London: Zed Books; M. Elk and B. Sloan. 2011. "The Hidden History of ALEC and Prison Labor." *The Nation*, August. Retrieved at https://www.thenation.com/article/hidden-history-alec-and-prison-labor/.

[17] C. Mason. 2012. *Too Good to Be True: Private Prisons in America*. Washington, D.C.: The Sentencing Project. Retrieved at http://sentencingproject.org/wp-content/uploads/2016/01/Too-Good-to-be-True-Private-Prisons-in-America.pdf; P. Ashton and A. Petteruti. 2011. "Gaming the System: How the Political Strategies of Private Prison Companies Promote Ineffective Incarceration Policies." *Justice Policy Institute*, 11.

[18] L. Fang. 2013. "How Private Prisons Game the Immigration System." *The Nation*. February 27. https://www.thenation.com/article/how-private-prisons-game-immigration-system/; L Fang. 2013. "Disclosure Shows Private Prison Company Misled on Immigration Lobbying." *The Nation*. June. Retrieved at https://www.thenation.com/article/disclosure-shows-private-prison-company-misled-immigration-lobbying/.

[19] The National Immigration Forum. 2013. *The Math of Immigration Detention*. Washington, D.C. Retrieved at http://immigrationforum.org/blog/themathofimmigrationdetention/.

[20] T. Schnacke, M. Jones, and C. Brooker. 2010. *The History of Bail and Pretrial Release*. Washington, D.C.: Pretrial Justice Institute. Retrieved at https://cdpsdocs.state.co.us/ccjj/Committees/BailSub/Handouts/HistoryofBail-Pre-TrialRelease-PJI_2010.pdf.

[21] S.B. Baughman. 2016. "Costs of Pretrial Detention." *Boston University Law Review*, 2017: 1-34.

[22] Sourcewatch. "The American Bail Coalition." The Center for Media and Democracy. Retrieved at www.sourcewatch.org/index.php/American_Bail_Coalition; see also The American Bail Coalition at www.americanbailcoalition.org/About-Us/.

[23] M. Gottschalk. 2015. *Caught: The Prison State and the Lockdown of American Politics*. Princeton, N.Y.: Princeton University Press; L. Sullivan. 2010. "Bondsman Lobby Targets Pretrial Release Programs." NPR. January 22. Retrieved at http://www.npr.org/templates/story/story.php?storyId=122725849.

[24] A. Santo. 2015. "When Freedom Isn't Free." *The Marshall Project*. February 23. Retrieved at www.themarshallproject.org/2015/02/23/buying-time#.8omL08UQp.

[25] S. Maruna, D. Dabney, and V. Topalli. 2012. "Putting a Price on Prisoner Release: The History of Bail and a Possible Future of Parole." *Punishment and Society*, 14, 3: 315-337.

[26] B. Fischer. 2014. "ALEC Politicians Caught Plagiarizing ALEC Bill, Drafting Error and All." *PRWatch*. Retrieved at www.prwatch.org/news/2014/07/12526/alec-politicians-caught-plagiarizing-alec-bill-drafting-error-and-all#sthash.cSKbh7LC.dpuf; A. Sietz-Wald. 2012. "Oops: Florida Republican Forgets to Remove ALEC Mission Statement From Boilerplate Anti-Tax Bill." *ThinkProgress*. Retrieved at http://thinkprogress.org/economy/2012/02/02/417488/florida-gop-alec-forget/.

[27] The Center for Media and Democracy. "ALEC EXPOSED: Voting Rights." Retrieved at www.alecexposed.org/wiki/ALEC_%26_Voting_Rights; S. Keyes, I. Millhiser, T. Van Ostern, and A. White. 2012. "Voter Suppression 101 How Conservatives Are Conspiring to Disenfranchise Millions of Americans." *The Center for American Progress*. April 4. Retrieved at https://www.americanprogress.org/issues/democracy/reports/2012/04/04/11380/voter-suppression-101/.

[28] W.R. Weiser and L. Norden. 2011. *Voting Law Changes in 2012*. New York: Brennan Center for Justice. October. Retrieved at http://www.brennancenter.org/publication/voting-law-changes-2012; J. Levitt. 2007. *The Truth About Voter Fraud*. New York: Brennan Center for Justice. November 9. Retrieved at https://www.brennancenter.org/publication/truth-about-voter-fraud.

Chapter Ten

[1] M. Katz. 2002. *The Price of Citizenship: Redefining the American Welfare State*. New York: Holt Publishers; F.F. Piven and R. Cloward. 1985. *The New Class War: Reagan's Attack on the Welfare State and its Consequences*.

[2] K. Wing. 1985. "Medicare and President Reagan's Second Term." *American Journal of Public Health*, July, 7: 782-784; P. Pierson. 1995. *Dismantling the Welfare State? Reagan, Thatcher and the Politics of Retrenchment*; G. Ladson Billings and W. Tate. 2006. *Education Research in the Public Interest: Social Justice, Action and Policy*. New York: Teachers College Press.

[3] L. Kotlikoff. 1986. "Deficit delusion." *The Public Interest*, 84, 53-62; P. Krugman. 2003. "The Tax-cut Con." *The New York Times*, September 14, pp. 59-60; M. Prasad. 2012. "The Popular Origins of Neoliberalism in the Reagan Tax Cut of 1981." *Journal of Policy History*, 24, 3: 351-83.

[4] B. Bartlett. 2006. *Impostor: How George W. Bush Bankrupted America and Betrayed the Reagan Legacy*. New York: Doubleday; J.S. Hacker and P. Pierson. 2005. "Abandoning the Middle: the Bush Tax Cuts and the Limits of Democratic Control." *Perspectives on Politics*, 3, 1: 33-53.

[5] D. Rasor, R. Bauman, and J. Alter. 2008. *Betraying Our Troops: The Destructive Results of Privatizing War*. New York: St. Martin's Griffen; D. Briody. 2004. *The Halliburton Agenda: The Politics of Oil and Money*. New York: John Wiley & Sons, Inc.

[6] S. Dewan. 2014. "In Many Cities, Rent Is Rising Out of Reach of Middle Class." *The New York Times*. April 14; T.A.Sullivan, E. Warren, and J.L. Westbrook. 2000. *The Fragile Middle Class: Americans in Debt*. New Haven, C.T.: Yale University Press.

[7] N. Klein. 2008. *The Shock Doctrine*, pp. 357-387.

[8] N. Silver. 2009. "So Just Who Did Vote For The Bailout? Five Thirty Eight. January 27. Retrieved at http://fivethirtyeight.com/features/so-just-who-did-vote-for-bailout/; S. Goldberg. 2008. "Desperate Plea—Then Race For a Deal Before 'Sucker Goes Down.'" *The Guardian*. September 26. Retrieved at https://www.theguardian.com/business/2008/sep/27/wallstreet.useconomy1.

[9] T.B. Edsall. 2012. *The Age of Austerity: How Scarcity Will Remake American Politics*. New York: Doubleday.

[10] F. Schui. 2014. *Austerity: The Great Failure*. New Haven, C.T.: Yale University Press.

[11] M. Blythe. 2013. *Austerity: The History of a Dangerous Idea*. New York: Oxford University Press.

[12] J. Boehner. 2013. "Every Family Must Balance Its Budget, Washington Should Too." *Paul Ryan: Speaker of the House* website. Retrieved at www.speaker.gov/video/speaker-boehner-every-family-must-balance-its-budget-washington-should-too#sthash.254cxG0K.dpuf.

[13] M. Wilson. 2013. "Ryan: Democrats' Budget puts U.S. on Path 'Straight into Debt Crisis.'" *The Hill*. Retrieved at http://thehill.com/blogs/blog-briefing-room/news/288567-ryan-dem-budget-puts-us-on-path-straight-into-debt-crisis.

[14] G. Becker. 2009. *Human Capital: A Theoretical and Empirical Analysis with Special Reference to Education*. Chicago: University of Chicago Press; B.A. Weisbrod. 1962. "Investment in Human Beings." *Journal of Political Economy*, LXX, 5: 106-123.

[15] Blythe. 2013. *Austerity*, p. xi.

[16] Blythe. 2013. *Austerity*, p. xi.

[17] Blythe. 2013. *Austerity*, p. 13.

[18] Reinhart, Carmen M., and Kenneth S. Rogoff. 2010. "Growth in a time of debt (digest summary)." *American Economic Review*, 100, 2: 573-578.

[19] Herndon, Thomas, Michael Ash, and Robert Pollin. 2014. "Does high public debt consistently stifle economic growth? A critique of Reinhart and Rogoff." *Cambridge Journal of Economics*, 38, 2: 257-279; R. Pollin. 2014. "Response to Charges Concerning the Herndon/Ash/Pollin Replication of Reinhardt and Rogoff's 'Growth in a Time of Debt.'" Amherst, M.A.: PERI Institute Research Brief. Retrieved at www.peri.umass.edu/fileadmin/pdf/research_brief/Pollin--Response_to_RR_critiques---January_2014.pdf.

[20] R. Alexander. 2013. "Reinhart, Rogoff ... and Herndon: The Student Who Caught Out the Profs." *BBC Magazine*. April 20. Retrieved at http://www.bbc.com/news/magazine-22223190.

[21] A. Fatas and L. Summers. 2015. "The Permanent Effects of Fiscal Consolidations." Discussion Paper 10902. London: Centre for Economic Policy Research.

[22] P. Krugman. 2015. "Austerity's Grim Legacy." *The New York Times*. November 16. http://www.nytimes.com/2015/11/06/opinion/austeritys-grim-legacy.html?_r=0.

[23] L. Gulino. 2011. "Tennessee Fire Dept. Watches Home Burn Because Homeowner Didn't Pay Fee." *Syracuse.com*. December 7. Retrieved at www.syracuse.com/news/index.ssf/2011/12/fire_department_watches_home_b.html.

[24] K. McCoy. 2012. "USA TODAY Analysis: Water Costs Gush Higher." *USA TODAY*. September 29. Retrieved at http://www.usatoday.com/story/money/business/2012/09/27/rising-water-rates/1595651/.

[25] J. Peck. 2015. "Austerity Urbanism: The Neoliberal Crisis of American Cities." New York: The Rosa Luxemborg Siftung.

[26] Transcript of the Democratic Presidential Debate in Flint, Michigan. 2016. *The New York Times*. March 6. Retrieved at www.nytimes.com/2016/03/07/us/politics/transcript-democratic-presidential-debate.html.

[27] "Michael Moore calls for arrest of Gov. Snyder." *Detroit Free Press*. January 6 2016. Retrieved at www.detroitnews.com/story/news/politics/2016/01/06/michael-moore-calls-arrest-gov-snyder/78394712/.

[28] J. Counts. 2016. "How Government Poisoned the People of Flint." *Michigan News*. January 16. Retrieved at www.mlive.com/news/index.ssf/page/flint_water_crisis.html.

[29] J. Conyers. 2016. "Flint Is the Predicted Outcome of Michigan's Long, Dangerous History with Emergency Managers." *The Nation*. March 7. Retrieved at https://www.thenation.com/article/flint-is-the-predicted-outcome-of-michigans-long-dangerous-history-with-emergency-managers/; J. Hohman. 2012. "Public Act 101 and Public Act 72." *Policy Brief*. Midland, MI: Mackinac Center for Public Policy. October 22. Retrieved at https://www.mackinac.org/17862; J.M. Akers. 2013. "Making Markets: Think Tank Legislation and Private Property in Detroit." *Urban Geography*, 34: 1070-1095; excellent chart of the history of Michigan Governor's use of both Public Act 101 and 72 found at Wikipedia. Retrieved at https://en.wikipedia.org/wiki/Financial_emergency_in_Michigan.

[30] D.O. Kasdan. 2014. "A Tale of Two Hatchet Men Emergency Financial Management in Michigan." *Administration & Society*, 46, 9: 1092-1108; D.O. Kasdan. 2016. "Emergency Management 2.0." *Urban Affairs Review*, 52, 5, 864-82; P. Eisinger. 2014. "Is Detroit Dead?" *Journal of Urban Affairs*, 36, 1: 1-12; C.G. Loh. 2016. "The Everyday Emergency." *Urban Affairs Review*, 52, 5: 832-63.

[31] V. Collier and B.-Z. Ptashnik. 2014. "Rev. Edward Pinkney Imprisoned for Fighting the Whirlpool Corporation." *Truth-Out*. December 16. Retrieved

at www.truth-out.org/news/item/28050-whirlpool-corporation-sentences-edward-pinkney-to-prison-with-no-evidence; Tyler C. Reedy. 2013. "Democracy & despair Riots, economic development, and an emergency manager in Benton Harbor, MI." Unpublished Master's Thesis, Iowa State University. Retrieved at http://www.whatisthebigsqueeze.com/SITE_VER2/wp-content/uploads/Democracy-Despair.pdf; P. Street. 2007. "Saving a public park: Benton Harbor citizens fight to stop Whirlpool's luxury golf course." *In These Times*. November 19. Retrieved from http://www.inthesetimes.com/article/3412/saving_a_public_park/; Reverend Edward Pinkney. 2016. Prison Radio. May 25. Retrieved at http://www.prisonradio.org/media/audio/rev-pinkney/reverend-edward-pinkney-speaks-prison-407.

[32] Owen Kirkpatrick and Nate Breznau. 2016. "The (Non) Politics of Emergency Political Intervention: The Racial Geography of Urban Crisis Management in Michigan." Available at SSRN 2754128; Mike Martindale. 2015. "Owners want $30M for Silverdome." *The Detroit News*. June 12. Retrieved at http://www.detroitnews.com/story/news/local/oakland-county/2015/06/12/silverdome-sale/71111062/; Julie Bosman and Monica Davey. 2016. "Anger in Michigan Over Appointing Emergency Managers." *New York Times*. January 26. Retrieved at http://www.nytimes.com/2016/01/23/us/anger-in-michigan-over-appointing-emergency-managers.html?_r=0; Steven Yaccino. 2013. "Pontiac's Rough Road to Recovery Could Foreshadow Detroit's Path." *New York Times*. September 16. Retrieved at http://www.nytimes.com/2013/09/16/us/pontiacs-rough-road-to-recovery-could-indicate-detroits-path.html?mtrref=www.google.com&gwh=A74DA52E5326341BC3899C5178FC3F3D&gwt=pay; Kristen Longley. 2011. "Other emergency managers provide glimpse of what Flint can expect under state takeover." *Flint Journal*. November 18. Retrieved at http://www.mlive.com/news/flint/index.ssf/2011/11/other_emergency_managers_provi.html.

[33] M. Kennedy. 2016. "Lead-Laced Water in Flint: A Step-By-Step Look At The Makings Of A Crisis." National Public Radio. April 26. Retrieved at www.npr.org/sections/thetwo-way/2016/04/20/465545378/lead-laced-water-in-flint-a-step-by-step-look-at-the-makings-of-a-crisis; The National Council on Public History. 2016. "The public history of the Flint water crisis—Part 1." March 4. Retrieved at http://ncph.org/history-at-work/public-history-of-flint-water-crisis-part-1/;The Network for Public Health. 2016. "Flint Water crisis: Issue Brief." July. Retrieved at https://www.networkforphl.org/_asset/08y7g6/Flint-Water-Crisis-Issue-Brief.pdf.

[34] K.L. Burke. 2016. "Flint Water Crisis Yields Hard Lessons in Science and Ethics." *American Scientist*, 104, 3: 134-152; S. Kolowich. "The Water Next Time: Professor Who Helped Expose Crisis in Flint Says Public Science Is Broken." *The Chronicle of Higher Education*. Retrieved from www.chronicle.com/article/The-Water-Next-Time-Professor/235136; N. Zhu and S. Roy, 2015. "The Unintended Consequences of Migrating to Flint River Water."

The Flint Water Study. August 23. Retrieved at http://flintwaterstudy.org/tag/tthm/.

[35] S. Roderick. 2016. "Who Poisoned Flint, Michigan?" *Rolling Stone*. January 22. Retrieved at www.rollingstone.com/politics/news/who-poisoned-flint-michigan-20160122; L. Pulido and L. Flint. 2016. "Environmental Racism, and Racial Capitalism." *Capitalism, Nature, Socialism*, 27, 3:1-16.

[36] M. Rangenathan. 2016. "Thinking with Flint: Racial Liberalism and the Roots of an American Water Tragedy." *Capitalism, Nature, Socialism*, 27: 3, 17-33; A. Campbell and M. Hannah-Attisha. 2016. "Flint Blood Levels: Four Questions." *American Journal of Public Health*, 106: 6-7.

[37] E. Osnos. 2016. "The Crisis in Flint Goes Deeper Than the Water." *The New Yorker*. January 20. Retrieved at http://www.newyorker.com/news/news-desk/the-crisis-in-flint-goes-deeper-than-the-water; Committee on the Flint Water Emergency. 2016. "Flint Water Crisis: Report of the Joint Select Committee on the Flint Water Emergency." Lansing, MI. Retrieved at http://flintwaterstudy.org/wp-content/uploads/2016/10/FINAL-Report-of-the-Joint-Select-Committee.pdf.

[38] Mona Hanna-Attisha, Jenny LaChance, Richard Casey Sadler, and Allison Champney Schnepp. 2016. "Elevated blood lead levels in children associated with the Flint drinking water crisis: a spatial analysis of risk and public health response." *American Journal of Public Health*, 106, 2: 283-290.

[39] K. Bouffard. 2016. "Hospital ties Legionnaires' to Flint water." *Detroit News*. January 23. Retrieved at www.detroitnews.com/story/news/politics/2016/01/22/legionnaires-bacteria-found-tests-mclaren-medical-centers-water/79183428/; House Committee on Oversite and Governmental Reform. 2016. "Examining Federal Administration of the Safe Drinking Water Act in Flint, Michigan." February 3. Retrieved at https://oversight.house.gov/hearing/examining-federal-administration-of-the-safe-drinking-water-act-in-flint-michigan/; M. Kennedy. 2016. "Lead-Laced Water in Flint: A Step-By-Step Look At The Makings Of A Crisis." National Public Radio. April 26. Retrieved at www.npr.org/sections/thetwo-way/2016/04/20/465545378/lead-laced-water-in-flint-a-step-by-step-look-at-the-makings-of-a-crisis.

[40] D. Fasenfest and T. Pride 2016. "Emergency Management in Michigan: Race, Class and the Limits of Liberal Democracy." *Critical Sociology*, 42, 3: 331-34; M. Ranganathan. 2016. "Thinking with Flint: Racial Liberalism and the Roots of an American Water Tragedy." *Capitalism, Nature, Socialism*, 27, 3: 17-33.

[41] R. Newby. 2016. "The Flint Water Crisis, the Governor and the New Jim Crow." *The Morning Sun*. January 16. Retrieved at http://www.themorningsun.com/article/MS/20160123/NEWS/160129890.

Epilogue

[1] M. Twain. 1871. *Innocents Abroad*. Knoxville, TN: Wordsworth Classics edition, 2010, p. 245.

2 W. Guthrie. "This Land is Your Land." In Robert Santelli. 2010. *This Land Is Your Land: Woody Guthrie and the Journey of an American Folk Song.* Philadelphia: Running Press.

3 Y. Saloojee and E. Dagli. 2000. "Tobacco Industry Tactics for Resisting Public Policy on Health." *Bulletin of the World Health Organization*, 78, 7: 902-10; M.L. Myers. 2002. "Philip Morris Changes Its Name, But Not Its Harmful Practices." *Tobacco Control*, 11, 3: 169-70.

4 B. Horner and M. Stern. 2006. *Blowing Away the Smokescreen: The Case Against Big Tobacco*. Albany: New York Public Interest Research Group. Retrieved at www.nypirg.org/pubs/health/BlowingAwayTheSmokeScreen.pdf; C. Joffe-Walt. 2010. "Act Three. Get Rich or Die Trying." *This American Life*, July 16. Retrieved at www.thisamericanlife.org/radio-archives/episode/412/transcript.

5 A. D. Little International. 2000. "Public Finance Balance of Smoking in the Czech Republic." Retrieved at http://hspm.sph.sc.edu/courses/Econ/Classes/cbacea/czechsmokingcost.html.

6 A. D. Little International. 2000. "Public Finance Balance of Smoking in the Czech Republic."Emphasis added.

7 H. Ross. 2004. "Critique of the Philip Morris Study of the Cost of Smoking in the Czech Republic." *Nicotine & Tobacco Research*, 6, 1: 181-89; Reuters. 2001. "Philip Morris Issues Apology For Czech Study on Smoking." *New York Times*. July 27. Retrieved at www.nytimes.com/2001/07/27/business/philip-morris-issues-apology-for-czech-study-on-smoking.html?_r=0.

8 T. Friedman. 1999. *The Lexus and the Olive Tree*. New York: Bantam Books; D. Brooks. 2004. "Good News About Poverty." *New York Times.* November 27. Retrieved at www.nytimes.com/2004/11/27/opinion/good-news-about-poverty.html.

9 E.S. Herman and N. Chomsky. 1995. *Manufacturing Consent: The Political Economy of the Mass Media*. New York: Vintage Press.

10 A. Mittal. 2008. "Voices From Africa: African Farmers & Environmentalists Speak Out Against a New Green Revolution in Africa." Oakland, C.A.: Oakland Institute; M. Ludwig. 2011. "Monsanto and Gates Foundation Push GE Crops on Africa." *Truth-Out*. July 12. Retrieved at http://www.truth-out.org/article/item/2105Joel; J. Vidal. 2010. "Why is the Gates Foundation Investing in GM Giant Monsanto?" *The Guardian*. September 29. Retrieved at https://www.theguardian.com/global-development/poverty-matters/2010/sep/29/gates-foundation-gm-monsanto; Carol Thompson. 2012. "Alliance for a Green Revolution in Africa (AGRA): advancing the theft of African genetic wealth." *Review of African Political Economy*, 39, 132: 345-50.

11 B. Glaeser. 2010. *The Green Revolution Revisited: Critics and Alternatives*. New York: Routledge Press.

12 E. Holt-Gimenez, M.A. Altieri, and P. Rosset. 2006. "Food First Policy Brief No. 12: Ten Reasons Why the Rockefeller and the Bill and Melinda Gates Foundations' Alliance for Another Green Revolution Will Not Solve the Problems of Poverty and Hunger in Sub-Saharan Africa." Oakland, C.A.:

Institute of Food and Development Policy: 1-8; S.R. Gliessman. 1998. *Agroecology: Ecological Processes in Sustainable Agriculture.* Chelsea, M.I.: Ann Arbor Press.

[13] P. McMichael. 2016. *Development and Social Change: A Global Perspective.* Thousand Oaks, CA: Sage Publications.

[14] P. McMichael. 2012. "The Land Grab and Corporate Food Regime Restructuring." *The Journal of Peasant Studies*, 3, 3-4: 681-781.

[15] H. Swanby. 2013. "Africa Bullied to Grow Defective Bt Maize: The Failure of Monsanto's Mon810 Maize in South Africa." *African Center for Biodiversity.* October. Retrieved at http://acbio.org.za/monsantos-failed-sa-gm-maize-pushed-into-rest-of-africa/; Elizabeth Renter, 2013. "Failed Monsanto GMO Corn Pushed on African Countries with Help of Bill Gates." *The Natural Society*, November 16. Retrieved at http://naturalsociety.com/failed-monsanto-gmo-corn-pushed-african-countries/.

[16] C.B. Flora. 2010. "Food Security in the Context Of Energy and Resource Depletion: Sustainable Agriculture in Developing Countries." *Renewable Agriculture and Food Systems*, 25, 2: 118-128; A. Mushita and C. Thompson. 2008. "Agricultural Biodiversity: African Alternatives to a 'Green Revolution.'" *Development*, 51: 488-495; Ken E. Giller, Ernst Witter, Marc Corbeels, and Pablo Tittonell. 2009. "Conservation agriculture and smallholder farming in Africa: the heretics' view." *Field crops research*, 114, 1: 23-34.

[17] E. Lavendera. 2015. "Texas Hunter Bags his Rhino on Controversial Hunt in Namibia." CNN. May 19. Retrieved at www.cnn.com/2015/05/19/africa/namibia-rhino-hunt/index.html; U.S. Fish and Wildlife Services International Affairs Division. 2013. "USFWS Statement on Dallas Safari Club Auction: Questions and Answers." U.S. Fish and Wildlife Services website. Retrieved at www.fws.gov/international/permits/black-rhino-import-permit.html; Tom Bawden. 2015. "Cecil the lion death: White men go to Africa to prove their manhood – but at a cost." *The Independent.* July 29. Retrieved at http://www.independent.co.uk/voices/editorials/cecil-the-lion-death-white-men-go-to-africa-to-prove-their-manhood-at-a-cost-10425316.html.

[18] Jeff Flocken. 2015. "Trophy hunting: 'Killing animals to save them is not conservation.'" CNN. May 19. Retrieved at http://www.cnn.com/2015/05/19/opinions/trophy-hunting-not-conservation-flocken/; Brian Clark Howard. 2013. "Rhino Hunt Permit Auction Sets Off Conservation Debate Dallas Safari Club hopes to raise money for conservation, but critics pounce." *National Geographic.* October 29. Retrieved at http://news.nationalgeographic.com/news/2013/10/131028-dallas-safari-club-black-rhino-hunt-auction-conservation/; P.A Lindsey, P. A. Roulet, and S. S. Romanach. 2007. "Economic and conservation significance of the trophy hunting industry in sub-Saharan Africa." *Biological conservation*, 134, 4: 455-469.

[19] E. Holt-Gimenez, M.A. Altieri, and P. Rosset. 2006. "Food First Policy Brief No. 12", p. 5; F. Pearce. 2004. "Asian Farmers Sucking the Continent

Dry." *New Scientist*, 28. Retrieved at https://www.newscientist.com/article/dn6321-asian-farmers-sucking-the-continent-dry/; D. Sharma. 2000. "The Green Revolution Turns Sour." *New Scientist*, 2246, 167: 44-45; Eric Holt Giménez, and Annie Shattuck. 2011. "Food crises, food regimes and food movements: rumblings of reform or tides of transformation?" *The Journal of Peasant Studies*, 38, 1: 109-144.

[20] Govindan Parayil. 1992. "The green revolution in India: A case study of technological change." *Technology and culture*, 33, 4 (1992): 737-756; T. Philpott. 2015. "No, GMOs Didn't Create India's Farmer Suicide Problem, But ... " *Mother Jones*. September 30. Retrieved at http://www.motherjones.com/tom-philpott/2015/09/no-gmos-didnt-create-indias-farmer-suicide-problem; Mishra, Srijit. 2008. "Risks, Farmers' Suicides and Agrarian Crisis in India: Is There A Way Out?." *Indian Journal of Agricultural Economics*, 63, 1; Pierre Spitz. 2010. "The Green Revolution Re-examined in India," in B. Glaeser. 2010. *The Green Revolution Revisited: Critics and Alternatives*, Oxon: Routledge.

[21] Rohan D. Mathews. 2011. "The Plachimada Struggle against Coca Cola in Southern India." *diálogos, propuestas, historias para una Ciudadanía Mundial.* Retrieved at http://base.d-p-h.info/es/fiches/dph/fiche-dph-8891.html; Jonathan Hills and Richard Welford. 2005. "Coca-Cola and water in India." *Corporate Social Responsibility and Environmental Management*, 12, 3: 168-177; C.R. Bijoy. 2006. "Kerala's Plachimada Struggle: a narrative on water and governance rights", in *Economic and Political Weekly*, October 14: 4332–4339;

[22] Arundhati Roy. 2014. *Capitalism: A Ghost Story*. Boston: Haymarket Books.

[23] S.C.J. Cummins, L. McKay, and S. MacIntyre. 2005. "McDonald's Restaurants and Neighborhood Deprivation in Scotland and England." *American Journal of Preventive Medicine*, 29, 4: 308-310; F. Sassi, M. Devaux, M. Cecchini, and E. Rusticelli. 2009. "The Obesity Epidemic: Analysis of Past and Projected Future Trends in Selected OECD Countries." *OECD Health Working Papers*, 45. Retrieved at www.researchgate.net/profile/Marion_Devaux2/publication/46456903_The_Obesity_Epidemic_Analysis_of_Past_and_Projected_Future_Trends_in_Selected_OECD_Countries/links/0c96052a861395ba53000000.pdf.

[24] M. Lewis. 2011. *Boomerang: Travels in the New Third World*. New York: W.W. Norton. p. 153.

[25] Mark Blyth. 2015. *Austerity: The History of a Dangerous Idea*. New York: Oxford University Press. p. 37.

[26] C. Afoko and D. Vokins. 2013. "Framing the Economy: The Austerity Story." *New Economics Foundation*. September 11. Retrieved at www.neweconomics.org/publications/entry/framing-the-economy-the-austerity-story.

[27] T. Killick. 2003. *IMF Programmes in Developing Countries: Design and Impact*. Oxford: Routledge; D.W. Githua. 2013. "The impact of International Monetary Fund (IMF) and the World Bank structural adjustment programmes in developing countries, Case study of Kenya." PhD diss; J. Glassman and P. Carmody. 2001. "Structural adjustment in East and Southeast Asia: Lessons from Latin America." *Geoforum*, 32, 1: 77-90.

[28] Quoted in P. Bond. 2004. *Against Global Apartheid: South Africa Meets the World Bank, IMF and International Finance*. London: Zed Books.

[29] Network X. 1999. Interview with Dennis Brutus, recorded November 27, at Benaroya Hall in Seattle, WA. Retrieved at https://www.youtube.com/watch?v=g8TpLXrhqok; Anup Shah. 2011. "Public Protests Around the World." *Global Issues*. November 7. Retrieved at http://www.globalissues.org/article/45/public-protests-around-the-world#Globalprotestsuptoearly2000s.

[30] M. O'Hara. 2014. *Austerity Bites: A Journey to the Sharp End of Cuts in the UK*. Bristol, U.K.: Policy Press.

[31] C. Hemsherk. 2015. "Socialists and the EU Referendum." *Socialism Today*, July-August. Retrieved at socialismtoday.org/190/eu.htm; D. Byrne. 2016. "Left Parties Turning Against Bosses' Europe." Socialistworld.net. October 6. Retrieved at socialistworld.net/doc/7619.

[32] J. Yellin. 2014. "Perspectives on Inequality and Opportunity from the Survey of Consumer Finances." Speech given at the Boston Federal Reserve Bank. October 17. Retrieved at www.federalreserve.gov/newsevents/speech/yellen20141017a.htm.

[33] J. Halsted. 2016. "The Real Reason White People Say All Lives Matter." *Huffington Post*. July 28. Retrieved at http://www.huffingtonpost.com/john-halstead/dear-fellow-white-people-_b_11109842.html; G. Yancy and J. Butler. 2015. "What's Wrong With 'All Lives matter?'" *New York Times*. January 12. Retrieved at http://opinionator.blogs.nytimes.com/2015/01/12/whats-wrong-with-all-lives-matter/.

[34] B. Ransby. 2015. "The Class Politics of Black Lives Matter." *Dissent*, 62, 4: 31-34.

Index

Note: Page numbers for figures appear in italics.

D

E

F

G

H

I

T